Living with Uncertainty

The **Institute of Southeast Asian Studies (ISEAS)** was established as an autonomous organization in 1968. It is a regional centre dedicated to the study of socio-political, security and economic trends and developments in Southeast Asia and its wider geostrategic and economic environment.

The Institute's research programmes are the Regional Economic Studies (RES, including ASEAN and APEC), Regional Strategic and Political Studies (RSPS), and Regional Social and Cultural Studies (RSCS).

ISEAS Publishing, an established academic press, has issued more than 2,000 books and journals. It is the largest scholarly publisher of research about Southeast Asia from within the region. ISEAS Publications works with many other academic and trade publishers and distributors to disseminate important research and analyses from and about Southeast Asia to the rest of the world.

Living with Uncertainty

Social Change and the Vietnamese Family in the Rural Mekong Delta

SETSUKO SHIBUYA

INSTITUTE OF SOUTHEAST ASIAN STUDIES
Singapore

First published in Singapore in 2015 by
ISEAS Publishing
Institute of Southeast Asian Studies
30 Heng Mui Keng Terrace
Pasir Panjang
Singapore 119614

E-mail: publish@iseas.edu.sg
Website: bookshop.iseas.edu.sg

ISEAS Library Cataloguing-in-Publication Data

Living with Uncertainty : Social Change and the Vietnamese Family in the Rural Mekong Delta / by Setsuko Shibuya.
1. Families—Vietnam—Can Tho.
2. Families—Mekong River Delta (Vietnam and Cambodia)
3. Can Tho (Vietnam)—Social conditions.
4. Mekong River Delta (Vietnam and Cambodia) —Social conditions.
5. Can Tho (Vietnam)—Rural conditions.
6. Mekong River Delta (Vietnam and Cambodia)—Rural conditions.
I. Shibuya, Setsuko.
HQ674.5 Z9C21L78 2015

ISBN 978-981-4620-29-1 (soft cover)
ISBN 978-981-4620-27-7 (E-book PDF)

Cover photos:
(*middle right*) A Vietnamese farmer in the Mekong Delta travels by boat to sell products from her family farm.
(*bottom*) Cai Rang floating market on the Mekong River.
Both photographs were taken by Setsuko Shibuya.

Typeset by International Typesetters Pte Ltd
Printed in Singapore by Mainland Press Pte Ltd

CONTENTS

ACKNOWLEDGEMENTS

This book would not have been completed without the kind support of a number of people whom I came to know over the years since I started studying anthropology and Vietnam. Among them, Abito Ito, Takeo Funabiki, Shinji Yamashita, Michio Suenari, Moto Furuta, Mary Steedly, David Maybury-Lewis, James Watson, Hue-Tam Ho Tai, Hy Van Luong were some of the most helpful inspiring me with their comments and suggestions. Their ideas, advices and constructive critiques always guided me and helped me proceed with my project with positive perspectives.

My research in the Mekong Delta was realized with the great help of Masaki Kunieda, the former Japanese Consul-General in Ho Chi Minh City. I am grateful to Can Tho University, particularly to the former rector Tran Thuong Tuan for admitting me as their research fellow. Le Viet Dung, Dao Van Khanh, Pham Xuan Binh, and other staff members of the International Cooperation Office of the university were always helpful and tried to meet my demanding requests. Many faculty members befriended me and especially Tran Thi Phan always cared for me like a real sister.

The conduct of my research in Long Tuyen Village owed much to the provincial government of Can Tho Province and Can To City as well as Long Tuyen Village Committee. My greatest gratitude goes, however, to my host family. My host parents Nguyen Van Dau and Nguyen Thi Hon and their children and grandchildren welcomed a strange foreigner with such kindness and affections. I am always appreciative of their openness and friendliness. Besides the family members, Pham Thi Kim Lan and Dao Hiep enthusiastically assisted me to carry out my research.

My research in Vietnam was assisted by grants from a number of sources. Yamada Foundation and Nakatou Foundation, Mellon Funding from Harvard University, Matsushita International Foundation Research Scholarship and Asia Research Center Fellowship funded the first phase of the research. The second phase of the fieldwork was funded by Iwakuni Foundation Fellowship and Toyota Foundation Scholarship.

Ng Kok Kiong, the Managing Editor of ISEAS Publishing, and the editor Sheryl Sin Bing Peng, have been a supportive and patient guide, facilitating the completion of the book. Kalina Manova and Kathy Duffin proofread and edited my earlier draft very carefully and gracefully. A few friends, among whom is Fiona Miller, read pieces of my draft and gave me helpful comments. My conversations with John Kleinen, Charles MacDonald, Shaun Malarney, Ann Marie Leshkowich, Narquis Barak, Chihiro Miyazawa, Masao Kashinaga and Hiroko Furuya guided me to different issues and perspectives.

My final but deep thanks go to my parents Hisashi and Yumiko Owada, my elder sister Crown Princess Masako, and my twin sister Reiko Ikeda, whose love and support gave me the courage to continue even at the most difficult times. My husband Kenji Shibuya encouraged me to pursue my interest in people's lives in the rural Mekong Delta and always supported me with his strength and kindness.

1

INTRODUCTION
Family and Society in Vietnam

When I first travelled to Can Tho in 1997, a province about 170 km from Ho Chi Minh City in southern Vietnam, the family life of farmers in the rural Mekong Delta was still hidden from me behind a veil.[1] While I looked for a field site and waited in Can Tho City for permission from the local government to conduct research in a rural area of the province, I spoke with some college students at Can Tho University, the main educational institution of the Delta.[2] These urbanites often believed that rural life was different from theirs. When asked about family life in Vietnam, many people would give answers that reflected these assumptions. For instance, explaining family structure, the students said, "traditionally, the family is extended, but now more families are nuclear. Things are changing. In the city, families are nuclear, but in the countryside, they still are extended." Or, "in the city, people have only one or two children, but in the villages they have five to seven, or more", "in urban areas, any child may take care of the old parents; in rural areas, they follow tradition, and the youngest son is especially responsible for supporting the parents when they are old", and "in the city, women get married at twenty-four or twenty-five, but in the countryside they marry early, at around eighteen."

These statements reveal the common assumption in urban areas that life in rural areas is more "traditional" than life in an urban setting. It is a widely shared view that rural life retains traditional patterns, family structures and relations, while life in the city is changing rapidly with modernization. *Moden,* or modern, is a word often used by contemporary Vietnamese, especially urban dwellers. The urbanites think of themselves as living in a time of transition from tradition to modernization, and perceive the world around them in terms of the contrasting framework of "modern vs. traditional". Often, "modern" is associated with "western", "foreign", and "new", while "traditional" refers to what is perceived as "Vietnamese", "indigenous", and "old". The words "countryside" (*nong thon*) or "homeland" (*que huong*) are used with nostalgic feelings as a place where their old good life is still preserved. One interesting example I liked is packets of postcards sold at post offices in towns which are named "countryside" or "homeland" and have pictures of the rural life.

To some extent, this picture of rural life presented by urban dwellers is accurate. In urban areas, older parents and their children sometimes live separately, while in rural areas, one of the children usually lives with and takes care of the parents, a pattern that may create more extended families than that exist in towns and cities. In villages, many families have three or more children, but in the cities, most young parents have only one or two children, in accordance with the national family planning policy. In rural areas few people are familiar with modern technologies, such as computers, and many people live in the same house that their ancestors lived in and toil on the same land the same way that their forefathers did. People's ideas may not be as influenced by foreign and global trends as in the urban areas. Change is slower in rural areas, while urban life seems to be transforming quickly.

However, this does not mean that rural life is static. On the contrary, my research on village life has shown that the life in the rural Mekong Delta is also dynamic. Particularly, during the late 1990s and the beginning of the 2000s people were experiencing a series of uncertainties brought about by many social factors. In this book, by focusing on the family and its functions within the society, I will try to capture some crucial aspects of people's lives in the rural Mekong Delta in those years.

I focus on the family because much of village life in the Delta revolves around the family, which is not only the basic unit of society, but also the centre of people's everyday world in a special way. I examine what meaning and role the family gains, or has gained, through its relations with and interactions with society as a whole. I view the family not only in the social context of the village and the Delta region but also within national and international frameworks. This is because the family is not a unit that exists independently of the larger society, nor a closed space that rejects influence from the outside. To the contrary, my research strongly suggests that the family of the Delta exists in the midst of local, national and global influences. It is affected, both directly and indirectly, by social, economic, and political factors at the national and global levels. The family is not only affected by the larger society but also deals with it. In order to understand and portray family life in the Delta, investigating its precise structure and mechanisms in isolation is not sufficient.

This book portrays Vietnamese families in the rural Mekong Delta through their struggles against uncertainties in various aspects of their lives mainly during the end of 1990s and the beginning of the 2000s when the people were experiencing rapid social changes associated with a national economic reform. It is an attempt to capture how social factors affect the family's daily life by examining its roles and meanings in a specific cultural and social context. In many ways the characteristics of the family presented here are observed in today's rural Mekong Delta too.

DOI MOI REFORM

It is useful to look at larger social and economic situations in which the family of the rural Mekong Delta exists. Although the social and historical background of the delta is not well known and it often differs from that of the rest of Vietnam, knowing the national context is crucial.

It is generally considered that the nation of Vietnam has entered a new era since the reform was officially endorsed in 1986. It was at the Sixth Party Congress that year that the Vietnamese Communist Party declared a reform called *doi moi*, or renovation. What is *doi moi*? The reform was particularly aimed at the economic sector of the nation in order to build a new, distinctively Vietnamese socialism (Dapice 1993; Furuta 1996).[3] According to Furuta, it is an attempt to transform the society, which entails three major changes. First, it is a departure from an old socialist model, in which poverty was shared by the whole society. Second, it is a quest for a new Vietnamese model of socialism that is different from the universal model. Third, it is an attempt to build a new society for the future generation (Furuta 1996, p. 3).

Before the reform, the Vietnamese economy was facing a crisis. One reason for its failure was that the development model adopted by the re-united country after the end of Vietnam War in 1975 was mainly based on the experiences of North Vietnam.[4] This model did not function well in other parts of the country, especially in the south. Also, the failure of the socialist economy can be attributed to a lack of monetary discipline, state budget constraints, an inward-oriented development strategy, and discrimination against agriculture (de Vylder 1990). In addition to the inadequacies of state economic policies, the international environment also isolated the country. After the war, Vietnam, South and North united, experienced not only political but also economic separation from the United States. The United States-led trade embargo on Vietnam meant disconnection from one of the world's economic leaders. In 1978, Vietnam's invasion of the neighbouring country of Cambodia grew into a war with China, which had been a strong supporter of Vietnam until then. By opposing the northern communist country, Vietnam inevitably isolated itself in the international community. In 1981, to make matters worse, economic aid from the Soviet Union was suspended, leaving little international economic assistance to the country.[5]

Domestic and international economic conditions were not the only causes of economic difficulty for Vietnam. There were also natural disasters such as the nationwide drought of 1977 and the disastrous floods and climate fluctuations in 1978 that affected the national economy, especially the agricultural sector (Tsuboi 1994). By the end of the 1970s, only several years after its victory in the long war, Vietnam was facing an economic crisis in which poverty threatened the population daily.[6]

The need for economic reform became more and more apparent and movement toward it began as early as 1981. That year, a "household contract system" was sanctioned for the agricultural sector. In this system, the collective land of the cooperatives was distributed to individual households that were then in charge of a certain amount of production. When a household harvested more rice than it was under contract to give to the cooperative, it could sell the excess on its own and keep the income. Some argue that this system was originally started by the peasants, rather than the government. In the late 1970s and the early 1980s the system was developed at the village level — without reporting to or requesting permission from higher officials — in order to stimulate the farmers' labour and to enhance productivity, and peasants themselves dismantled collective farming and re-expanded family farm (Furuta 1996; Kerkvliet 2005). In 1981, after discussing the plan for two years, the central committee acknowledged this "household contract system" and decided to apply it to the whole country. At this stage, the contract system still functioned within the framework of collective farming. However, it was a significant change because it eventually led to the disintegration of collective farming, showing the effectiveness of the household as a unit of agricultural production. (Most studies on the reform of the agricultural sector come from North Vietnam and not much is written on the evolution of the process in the south. Those on the south include: Quang Trong 1987; Trung Dinh Dang 2010.)

Hence, the reform was part of the process that began in the late 1970s and stretched into the 1990s. 1986 marked the year when the authority endorsed this process (Forde and de Vylder 1996; Beresford and Dang Phong 2001; Kerkvliet 2005; Dang Phong 2009). Under *doi moi* reform, it was argued that Vietnam was in a long transition period on the way to ultimate socialism, and it was acknowledged that during this period, socialist disciplines should not and could not be achieved in haste. To ultimately achieve true socialism, free market economic disciplines could be incorporated into the system, enabling drastic reform of the economic sector. Also, besides state-run and collective organizations, private companies and household firms were welcome, bringing about a mixed economic system. Though the phrase "market mechanism" was not yet used, market and commodity economic disciplines were being employed. The Vietnamese economy also aimed at participating in the international economic system and playing a part in the international division of labour by utilizing its unique strengths, rather than trying to build a nation within which all aspects of the economic system were achieved and completed.

A big change in the agricultural sector took place in 1988, when the Politburo of the Party Central Executive Committee, with the "Renovation in Agricultural Economic Management", also called Decision Ten, acknowledged each household as the basic unit of agricultural production. This guaranteed peasants more control over their lives and the fruits of their labour (de Vylder 1990; Ngo Vinh Long 1993; Dao 1995).[7] The viewpoint of the government was that cooperatives are units of a self-controlled and self-managed economy, and a cooperative's households are units able to sign contracts with the cooperatives. However, this plan was not well received by the farmers, who wanted the cooperatives to return lands to each household, and as a consequence the cooperatives gradually lost their functions and went bankrupt leaving each household with more control over their land (Ngo 1993; Luong Hong Quang 1997).

It is important to note that while all these economic reforms were taking place, the political system remained socialist. The main objective of the *doi moi* reform has been to change and improve the economic situation of the country. From a political perspective, the ultimate goal has been to assure stability. Transformations in the political system have been attempted only gradually, and only if they will not threaten the political stability of the nation. It is a generally shared view that political stability is indispensable to the advent of the *doi moi* reform; thus unnecessary political transformations and confusions should be avoided.

Some studies suggest that the *doi moi* reform caused transformations not only in the economic sector but also in the social realm. Most of these studies come from the north, and their results may not apply directly to the Mekong Delta, but raise some interesting issues.[8] One large consequence of the reform that has often been reported is the widening gap between the rich and poor. As mentioned above, socialism was a system in which everyone was poor. Under the reform, this equality of socialism has been disappearing. Inequality and gaps in wealth have been emerging at various levels in the society: between urban settings and rural areas, among regions, between the major ethnic groups of the Kinh (or Vietnamese) and the minorities, across class, and gender. For instance, intra-village income levels and the gaps between the various household categories have been increasing since the beginning of the reform. Differentiation has grown more severe in areas close to urban centres or in regions where the market economy is more developed (Ngo Vinh Long 1993).[9]

As for gender, the period of socialism emphasized women's employment and gender equality. In the reform era, however, as Pelzer (1993) suggests, women's role and status may be changing. For instance, women's representation in political activities has been declining and their social status is diminishing. Gender relations are also changing, placing women in a more complex position between traditional roles and newly emerging demands. Leshkowich (2011), in a study of female traders at Ben Thanh market in Ho Chi Minh City, argues that both class and gender are negotiated and constantly in the making under the Vietnamese market economy generated by socialist government. Particularly in respect of gender, she states that qualities of masculinity and femininity are nurtured by the socialist regime as if they were innate, which the traders in turn enact in their everyday struggles as "petty traders" (see also Leshkowich 2000). Other studies suggest that other social relations, such as labour relations, have been changing under the economic reform, bringing about more inequality in society (Hy Van Luong and Diep Dinh Hoa 1991; Hy Van Luong 1993; Fahey 1995).

Changes in the systems of education and health have also been reported, though they have not been directly connected to the economy. The Socialist Republic of Vietnam has made notable achievements in health and education since 1975, and Kaufman and Sen noted in 1993 that "despite a per capita income of less than 200 US dollars a year, 84 percent of the female population is literate, the infant mortality rate is about 54 per thousand, and life expectancy exceeds 65" (Kaufman and Sen 1993, p. 233). One of the reasons for this achievement is that during the socialist era, the building of schools and health centres was encouraged, and as a result, 90 per cent of rural communes have health stations. Not only were schools and health facilities built throughout the country, but also the fees for education and health services were covered by the state, making them free to the public. (Same as with agricultural cooperatization it is not well known how much health and educational systems shifted toward socialism in the Mekong Delta during this period.)

However, the achievements in these social domains are being threatened under the *doi moi* reform. In the years after the reform, education and healthcare were reconsidered, and because of shortages of funds, they are no longer offered free of charge. One reason for this shortage is decentralization. Until 1988, the central government underwrote the majority of the investment for public services (75 per cent in the case of water supply and sanitation), while the provinces provided the rest plus operating costs. However, since 1988, the provinces have been expected to bear a larger share of the burden as part of a decentralization effort by the state (Kaufman and Sen 1993) Many provinces have been unable to make up for the shortfall in central investment, resulting in an increase in fees for public services.[10] This decline in the accessibility of education and health facilities has been one of the major challenges the population is now facing. These social factors combined with economic factors affect the farmers' lives in various ways and these will be examined in later chapters.

Family and Society

Family exists almost universally in any human society, and it is part of anyone's life, at least to some extent. While families in many societies share similar roles and meanings, it differs from one culture to another when looked more in detail in their everyday context. Therefore, the family offers a window for looking into different cultures and societies.

Studies in anthropology and other social sciences have investigated and captured the relationship between family life and society.[11] These studies discuss how social conditions, including economic systems and a variety of cultural norms, affect the role of family and its meaning in people's lives. At the same time, they illustrate how individuals and groups deal with and cope with outside social conditions. Although different studies take different and oftentimes mutually exclusive approaches to it and they may reflect diverse backgrounds and contexts, a number of studies from East and Southeast Asia suggest the variability of the social factors in the larger society that affect families in their everyday life.

Some studies are indicative in understanding Vietnamese family that is experiencing a shift in the economic system. Goode's (1963) classical study, though not anthropological in method, argues that with growing economic prosperity, nuclear families will increase, and households will become more focused on conjugal ties. His model, which was heavily based on data from Europe and North America in the 1960s, was tested with cases in China after 1960, and also in the post-Mao era.[12] Some of these studies focus particularly on relationships among members of families and examine the dynamics of their forms in post-socialist China. Some studies argue that, as patriarchal kinship system was dismantled under socialism, the focus of kinship is shifting from the vertical relationship between father and son to the horizontal relationship of a conjugal unit which has gained more independence in agreement with Goode's model (Chou 2010; Croll 2006; Yan 1997; 2009).[13]

In contrast, other studies on post-reform China suggest, disagreeing with Goode's model, that family and kinship are becoming more important as economic, social and political resources for people as the economy is shifting toward capitalism, and the presence of state power in everyday life is diminishing from the heyday of socialism. At the same time, however, the increasing importance of family does not mean that the family is returning to its traditional forms. On the contrary, Chinese families, seemingly rigidly structured, also show flexibility and an ability to take advantage of the new conditions. While the family structure has remained much the same as in the pre-socialist period, characteristics such as the division of labour and relationships among members are continuously being reshaped (Davis and Harrell 1993; Harrell 1993; Johnson 1993). For instance, Ikels (1993) shows that both parents and children have gained more control over their income than in the past, but at the same time, the strong sense of obligation for children to take care of their elderly parents financially persists in the society, especially in the post-socialist situation.[14]

In the late 1990s and the early 2000s Vietnam was experiencing changes in the economic sector similar to those of China, but the dynamics in the family may be somewhat different.[15] Some scholars studied the changing family in the midst of social transformation in North Vietnam, families in the Red River Delta in particular.[16] Discussing the parent-child relationship, for instance, Pham (1999) focuses on the socio-cultural meanings of reproduction, and states that this relationship still remains important and has not been replaced by a conjugal bond. Pham attributes this to both cultural and social factors.[17] Nguyen Tuan Anh (2010), also examining economic, social and cultural aspects of kinship relations in a changing society in the north, argues that the importance of kinship has not only remained but also increased in the reform era. Belanger and Barberini (2009), while acknowledging the centrality of the family in people's lives, too, further notes that the meaning of generational and gender relationships shift within the family in the reform era as it adapts to the new social and economic settings.

Not only in post-socialist societies, but the family in other societies in Southeast Asia also receive the effects of cash economy. For example, studies in Thailand focusing on caregiving for the elderly show how the traditional family support system function in a new economic situation. In rural Northern Thailand, Caffrey (1992) investigates the effects of the change from a kin-based to a cash-based economic system and concludes that the financial condition of the family, and of the children in particular, becomes a crucial factor determining the welfare of the elderly and the caregiving provided for them.[18] Another study by Siriboon and Knodel (1994) shows that the Thai elderly who, unlike tradition, do not live with their own children still live in situations in which the familial support system operates. They often maintain daily contact with their children or receive monetary support from them. Both these studies show the increased importance of financial support for the elder family members as cash economy begins to prevail.[19]

The effects of social and economic conditions on local systems are not confined to the family in the Mekong Delta. Other societies in Southeast Asia have also gone through economic changes and experienced their social effects, as shown in Grandstaff (1992)'s study in northern Thailand. There, economic uncertainty has led villagers to develop a twofold strategy of diversified agriculture and mobility in outside employment, and this strategy combines out-of-village employment with local resource utilization. Another work on Thailand by Piker (1968) illustrates how local social systems at the village level function in different ways under the influence of the outside world, national and international economic systems in particular. Traditional strategies no longer assure secure life of the villagers, as will be seen in later chapters.[20]

Effects of national and global factors are often beyond the control of most villagers in the Mekong Delta. This situation is shared in many Southeast Asian countries. Appell (1985), who investigates the experience of the highland minority community in Malaysian Borneo, illustrates the social and economic conditions that the residents have little control over. The Rungus peasants struggle to secure their present and future life, by providing schooling for children, for example. Appell states, "The Rungus believed in the 1960's that their political and economic futures lay in the hands of others. They were deeply concerned that they would lose control over their land...." (1985, p. 127). This is a very similar situation to that the peasants of the Mekong Delta are experiencing.[21]

One of the social changes that the rural residents of the Mekong Delta experience is industrialization of the area. Studies focusing on women in East and Southeast Asia during rapid industrialization are particularly informative in this regard. These studies, which examine the impacts of industrialization on relationships between family members, show varied conclusions. Focusing particularly on the workplace, some studies on Asian women working in factories show that existing social and cultural norms structure family relationships and raise tensions, particularly in terms of gender differences, in the new social conditions brought about by industrialization. For instance, in a case study of labour relations of women workers in urban Vietnam, Fahey (1995), discussing the place of working women in their family settings, shows that the existing norms are not much affected by industrialization, which results in women not being able to enter a new space, the workplace outside the family.[22] Salaff (1995) also discusses the complex family relationships of working daughters in Hong Kong under industrialization. She finds that working outside the home offers daughters opportunities for higher income, but existing cultural norms require them to use their income for the family welfare. Although Salaff observes that daughters are gradually gaining independence from their parents, she stresses that their independence remains limited.

The female urban migrants in Bangkok studied by Mills (1997) present more complex picture that they have retained their traditional roles as daughters at the same time as they have gained new functions. They are struggling to live both a "modern" way of life in the city, and at the same time, be "good daughters" who are morally committed to rural kin and community. Although these two aspects of the lives of migrants may seem contradictory and mutually exclusive, according to Mills, the migrants' "self-construction [does] not necessarily involve an explicit, self-conscious choice between clear and distinct identities" (1997, p. 37). Rather, they manage to accommodate the requirements of both city life and rural ties, a situation manifested in rural rituals. Similarly, residents of outskirts of Ho Chi Minh City presented by Harms (2011) negotiate seemingly contradictory social positions as city dwellers and "rural" residents.

Working daughters in Malaysia, also caught between a capitalist ideology on the one hand, and the local non-capitalist morality on the other, experience more significant shifts in the relationship with their parents (Ong 1987). For example, the workers have become important contributors to family income, which challenges the traditional patriarchal family system. Working in factories has led them to spend increasingly more time outside their home, and this new place has given daughters room to negotiate and challenge their underprivileged status in their families. In rural Java, according to Wolf (1992), industrialization had drastic effects on the families of working daughters, in which the relationships between members are constantly redefined and negotiated. "[D]aughters were at once caught in a web of obligations toward the corporate entity of the household while attempting to exert their own autonomy during a fairly new and unexplored life-cycle state.... Factory daughters frequently negotiated their position as they tested the limits of parental boundaries and responded to differing family needs and situations."[23]

The female workers in Japan that Kondo (1990) studied act as the point where family and outside spaces interact and intermingle with each other, not only making the boundary between the two blurred, but also contested. Here, both company and family stand as metaphors for each other, but not in a static way. Different actors, both the management and the workers, appropriate notions of "family as company" and "company as family" differently, in different contexts and for different purposes.[24] In a study on a small urban community in Java, Brenner (1998) also shows how women entrepreneurs transcend the boundary between the two spaces of home and outside society, making the boundary more flexible.[25]

In contrast, for Chinese women domestic and outside work seem completely separated, making it difficult for them to traverse the boundary between the two (Wolf 1985). According to Wolf, it is impossible for young mothers in rural China to work in the nearby factory or brigade enterprise because they have to take care of their children and housework. In China, kinship ties and hierarchy within the family continue to be so strong that young women are confined to their houses, and the boundary between domestic and outside society is perhaps not as easily contested and negotiated as in the case of Japanese and Javanese women.

One of the issues that I will explore, drawing upon some of the works introduced in this section, is intra-familial relationships, such as vertical relationships between generations and conjugal relationships. I will also examine relationships between the family and outside society. The following chapters pay special attention to the way these two types of relationship together determine family life in the rural Mekong Delta.

Methodology

The research for this book was carried out mostly in a rural village of Can Tho Province in the Mekong Delta between 1997 and 2000, with some additional research in 2001 and 2014.[26] In the beginning when I first started my research in 1997, it was not easy to obtain a permission to conduct a field research in villages since there had never existed an ethnographic research conducted by a foreigner in the province or most of the surrounding provinces before. Although I was permitted to visit rural areas on my own as I liked, I was not allowed to stay in a village.

Therefore, in the early phase of the fieldwork, I made daily visits to several villages, which I could commute from Can Tho City. Surprisingly, although my visits were unexpected and I was a stranger to them, most of the time the villagers were friendly and welcomed me. Knowing that people would appreciate formality, when I met villagers for the first time I usually started by formal interviews rather than casual conversations, but many villagers were open and seemed to enjoy talking with me that I sometimes spent the whole day with one family. Sometimes people offered us tea and fruit, and when I happened to visit at lunchtime, they offered to share their meal with me. Some villagers were excited about a visit by a stranger, and would insist that I should spend the night at their houses, an offer I always had to decline with regrets, because I did not have official permission. Eventually I was able to live with a Vietnamese family that I knew in town, after waiting for a few months to get permission from the local government. By living with them, I familiarized myself with a number of their customs closely related to the family life such as weddings, death anniversaries, and New Year celebrations.

Fortunately, I was able to get permission to stay and conduct fieldwork in a village between 1999 and 2000. I had an idea of the region I wanted to go, but I left it to the government to decide whether I should choose a village to stay in and a family to live with, or whether they should choose for me. They selected the village and family for me, not in the particular area I was thinking of, but a village I had known from my previous research.

Over the next several months, I developed a close bond with some members of my host family in the village. It took me a while before I could see that they felt comfortable with my presence. After several weeks in the village, however, Uncle Bay, the head of the family (he asked me to call him "Uncle Bay" or Seventh Uncle, using a kin term, which term I use in this book) started to disclose more of his feelings and opinions, although this may not necessarily mean that he told me everything. He often told me he cared for me like a real father using the Vietnamese word *thuong* which indicates affections of parents toward their children, and sometimes said he wanted to adopt me if I had been a Vietnamese. Of course, we did not become like a real father and daughter, but our deepening relationship helped me understand the emotional aspects of Vietnamese family relations. Although his wife Aunt Tam ("Eighth Aunt") was more shy about expressing her feelings and ideas, she took care of me affectionately, which also helped me experience the mother's affection toward her children. I also made good friends with some of the children in the family. I sometimes had tea with some of the daughters and daughters-in-law and talked to them about their families and other aspects of their lives as well as my family and my life in Japan. The sons and sons-in-law were often eager to help me understand village life better and took me around their gardens, taught me how to do some of their farm work, or explained their lives to me over a meal. One son who is a schoolteacher also helped me learn about education in the area. Some of the grandchildren also became my good friends. From our conversations, I found out about how the young see their future. One of the grandchildren took me to his school and introduced me to his teachers. Also, they introduced me to their other grandparents, and this gave me an opportunity to observe relationships between affinal relatives.

I spent most of my time in the village with my host family, and much of my knowledge about family life comes from what I observed in this family and what I learned from conversations with them. In addition, I visited their neighbours to interview them. In the beginning I was expecting that neighbours would come to the house of my host family, possibly out of curiosity, and hoped to have conversations with them informally. I thought if some neighbours were close to my host family and they visited regularly, I could get to know them quite well. However, I stayed in the village for a few weeks, and no one came to our house. I thought at that moment that maybe the villagers simply did not know about my presence in the village or in this house, or they were not interested in seeing me. After a while, however, I realized that they knew about me, and that they wanted to meet me, but instead of coming to see me, they were waiting for me to visit their houses. After some time I learned that neighbours seldom visited each other except on formal occasions such as weddings and death anniversaries unless they are relatives (and even then people do not make frequent visits). Therefore I decided to make formal visits to talk with the neighbours.

My host family did not think it was safe for me to be alone in the village and they thought it was their responsibility to introduce me to other villagers, so I always visited neighbours with a member of my host family. It was usually Uncle Bay who took me around the village and introduced me to the neighbours, but when he was busy with other things, such as farming, or attending death anniversaries of relatives, someone else from the family, often Youngest Brother or Second Brother, guided me.[27]

Because my host family considered it their responsibility to assure my safety in the village, even when I thought I was sufficiently acquainted with the villagers and their life, they took the trouble of accompanying me everywhere. When I went to visit the house of one of the children of Uncle Bay and Aunt Tam (located about 500 metres away from our house), I said I could go home by myself and started walking. But when I had walked for a couple of minutes, the daughter-in-law came running after me and walked with me back to the house. At another time, when I went to the market with Aunt Tam early in the morning, I stopped at a noodle shop to have breakfast, while the mother went shopping. As I waited for her after having had a bowl of soup noodles, I decided to walk around a little and take pictures of the morning market. When one of the daughters of the family found me strolling in the market, she looked shocked, asked me what I was doing, and hurriedly went to look for the mother.

My host family also always made sure that I observed the proper formal procedures not only when I visited other villagers, but also when I visited village institutions. When I was thinking of visiting the village school and interviewing the teachers, I learned that one of my friends in Can Tho was a friend of one teacher at the secondary school. I thought I could use this connection and talk with the teacher rather informally as friends. However, when I told my host family about my intention to visit the school, they looked concerned. They asked me why I wanted to visit the school, and said I should make an official visit with permission from the village committee. Since one of the sons of the family was a schoolteacher at another village, he said he would make the necessary contact and arrangements for me to get permission. Also, at another time, I wanted to see a pagoda in the village, which was located a short distance from the hamlet. When I mentioned I planned to go there, they wanted to know what my intention was. When I went to visit the People's Committee of the village, I forgot to take pictures, so the next day, I wanted to go back there just to do that. The family members discussed whether it was a good idea for me to take pictures of the office, particularly without asking the officers in charge. After one of the sons finally took me back there and I took pictures and came home, another son was still concerned that I did so without official permission. However, after the first visits, I had more freedom to revisit these places.

With my research organized in this way, the data collected for this book come from a number of sources. A large part comes from my host family in the village. I observed their daily activities, shared some, though certainly not all, of their everyday experiences, and had casual conversations with them. I also sometimes organized formal interviews with the family members in order to have focused conversations on certain topics. Other information was mainly gathered from interviews with their neighbours in the same hamlet and their relatives in the village or neighbouring villages. I also conducted interviews with village officers, schoolteachers, and clinicians. In addition, I visited factories in other villages and conducted some interviews with workers.

Furthermore, my two assistants, Ms Lan and Mr Hiep, also helped me understand some of the customs of the area and answer my questions about the geography and the history of the region, as well as the local traditions. They always took trouble to explain to me something I did not understand well in interviews and sometimes brought me books and articles they thought were useful for me. I also gained some knowledge from Can Tho University teachers, who often ran research and development projects in the rural areas throughout the Mekong Delta.[28] Sometimes they let me accompany them on field visits to villages for their own research.

I mainly conducted archival research in two libraries in Vietnam. One was the group of libraries at Can Tho University, the central educational institute of the Delta region. Though their collection mainly dealt with agriculture at the time of my research, I was able to get most of my information on the Mekong Delta from these university libraries.[29] In the College of Agriculture Library, I collected data and information on the socio-economy of the Mekong Delta, and in the College of Education Library, I found sources on the Vietnamese family, especially on family education. It was at the Central Library of the university that I learned about the history of the Can Tho region, the customs of the Mekong Delta as well as of Vietnam, and geography. The other library I accessed was the General Library of Ho Chi Minh City, the central library of southern Vietnam. There I collected sociological studies on the Vietnamese family, material on national agriculture and development, and economic studies on poverty and wealth.

Notes

1. Some readings such as Sakurai's (1995) and Tsuboi's (1994) introductions to Vietnam had given me a good general view of the people and life in contemporary Vietnam, but little had been known about the Mekong Delta, and about the rural area in particular.
2. There are different uses of the word "Mekong Delta". Sometimes, especially in Western literature, it covers the whole of southern Vietnam, including Ho Chi Minh City. In this book, however, the Mekong Delta does not include the city, and refers to the area that covers the provinces of Long An, Tien Giang, Dong Thap, Ben Tre, Vinh Long, Tra Vinh, An Giang, Can Tho City, Hau Giang, Soc Trang, Kien Giang, Bac Lieu and Ca Mau as it reflects a more common use in Vietnam.
3. Some studies by economists (e.g. Dapice 1993) also stress the peculiarity of Vietnam, which differs from other Asian countries that went through similar economic developments. Other studies, such as Marr (1995), interpret the reform in the context of a larger region of East and Southeast Asia.
4. See also Marr and White eds. (1988) on social and economic problems that the shift to socialism encountered in the country.
5. Although the reform is mainly concentrated in the economic sector, Williams (1992) also examines the political and international background for the reform.

6. There are a number of other studies, especially by economists and political scientists (e.g. Beresford and Fforde 1996) that discuss the background of reform in the early 1980s.
7. Tran Hoang Kim (1995) also summarizes the Vietnamese economic situation from 1945 until 1990.
8. See, for instance, Dahm and Houben eds. (1999) for discussions on the different responses to economic reform in different regions of the nation.
9. See also Ffords and de Vylder (1996) on social differentiations under the economic reform.
10. Haughton et al., eds. (1999) discusses the health status of the population in contemporary Vietnam.
11. Many anthropological studies have studied kinship and family in the last century. Fox (1967) claimed that "kinship is to anthropology what logic is to philosophy or [the] nude is to art." Kinship was studied not only to understand the structures of different societies (e.g. Levi-Strauss 1969). For example, Maybury-Lewis (1979; 1989) discusses how a kinship system shows the principle of thinking of the Central Brazilian peoples. Also, see Brettell (2001) for a brief comment on the significance of the study of kinship in contemporary anthropology.
12. Goode's linear model based on dichotomy was also argued against theoretically (e.g. Yanagisako and Collier 1987; McDonald 1994).
13. According to Yan, this does not necessarily imply that the son and daughter have become more independent as individuals, but it does mean that as a conjugal unit, they have gained more independence from their parents. However, Yan shows that this shift in generational relationships does not always take place peacefully. There are tensions and negotiations between the two parties not only about power and wealth, but also about emotional attachment and moralities. Chou also notes that it is "increasingly difficult for older Chinese to receive support from adult children", resulting in Family Support Agreement system (2010, p. 3).
14. Watson (1997) examines the effects of global culture in Hong Kong. The author argues that children enjoying American-style food have brought about changes in their relationships with the older generation.
15. Belanger (1997) investigates the transformations of the Vietnamese family, particularly in the north over a longer span of time since the 1960s, but does not focus on the contemporary changes due to the economic reform.
16. There are some studies from Northern Vietnam, which look at social changes in the area, although most of these works focus on village

structures and not on the family. These include: Malarney (1994; 2002), Miyazawa (1998; 1999), Kerkvliet and Porter, eds. (1995), Kleinen (1999). Also, Leshkowich (2000) examines social changes under *doi moi* in urban South Vietnam.

17. Culturally, children, especially sons, remain important because of their economic value, their obligation to take care of their parents, and their responsibility to continue ancestor worship. Socially, according to Pham, the state has not offered an adequate welfare system to replace family ties.
18. In Thailand, filial obligation is still a strong cultural value and continues to play a powerful role in the family, especially in decisions regarding the elderly. In this situation, the economic condition of the family, and of the children in particular, becomes a crucial factor determining the welfare of the elderly and the caregiving provided for them. Caffery concludes, "When land is limited, children leave to find employment elsewhere and will try to send money to help their parents as they are able" (1992, p. 105).
19. On the family in Thailand, especially in relation to economic situation, see also Piker (1968), Foster (1978), and Limanonda (1995). For traditional Thai family norms, see Smith (1979) and Foster (1984).
20. Piker discusses that traditionally in Thai society, strategies of dependence and independence functioned at the village level, making the villagers' life secure in times of economic crisis. However, during the historical development over the past hundred years at the national as well as international levels, this has changed. He argues, "Traditional and widely adopted strategies for both dependence and independence, beyond the confines of the normative life cycle, have all but disappeared." Koentjaraningrat (1982) compares the urban dwellers and rural residents and argues that in the former, the norm of dependency ceases to function and a more individualistic attitude becomes prevalent.
21. In a more historical context, Steedly (1993) illustrates the interactions between kin and market economy among the Karo people during the colonial period in Indonesia.
22. Fahey states that working women in Vietnam remain responsible for the domestic arrangements of shopping, cooking, cleaning, and organizing family ceremonies such as weddings and funerals, which makes it harder for them to enter the workplace. Fahey argues, "As a consequence, women, and especially married women, are leaving paid employment" (1995, p. 49).

23. Blanc-Szanton (1990) also discusses the effects on woman of employment and modernization in Thai society under industrialization. She discusses that the change in gender relation brought about by industrialization works negatively for women.
24. Not only do the Japanese female workers, by having jobs outside their home, bring a family atmosphere to the workplace, but the company is also required to accommodate such an atmosphere.
25. Another case study of the relationship between family and modernization is by Korson (1978) on Pakistan.
26. Can Tho Province was split into two administrative units — Can Tho City and Hau Giang Province in 2004. Can Tho City includes the city itself as well as the surrounding rural areas.
27. Siblings call each other by their birth order. The first born child is called Second Brother/Sister so there is no First Brother/Sister. The second born is called Third Brother/Sister and so on.
28. Being the educational centre of the Mekong Delta, the university is engaged in a variety of developmental projects, mainly in agriculture, often in cooperation with foreign governments and NGOs.
29. At the time of my research the college (department) of agriculture was the main and largest college of the university, though it also had colleges of medicine and foreign languages. It eventually opened other colleges such as economics and law later on.

2

ON THE BANK OF THE MEKONG RIVER

CAN THO CITY

In order to understand the life of farmers in the rural Mekong Delta, it would be useful to have a broad picture of the area. The village of Long Tuyen, where the research was done lies close to the city of Can Tho, which lies in the heart of the Mekong Delta in southern Vietnam.[1] The Mekong River splits into several branches in the Delta after flowing from the Tibetan uplands through the countries of mainland Southeast Asia, and the water provided by the river, its small branches and canals throughout the area, and the tropical climate characterized by alternating rainy and dry seasons make the land suitable for the production of many kinds of food resources. Rice is one of them, for which the Mekong Delta is particularly well known.

The Mekong Delta has more than four million hectares of natural land, rich with natural resources.[2] The Delta is the "rice bowl" of Vietnam, providing grain not only to its inhabitants, but also to the whole country.[3] With rice being the main agricultural product, the area also produces a variety of tropical fruit, sold in the regional markets as well as in large towns and cities throughout the country. The province of Can Tho had a population of over 1,900 thousand in 1997, and 70 per cent of them were engaged in agriculture (Chi Cuc Thong Ke Kinh Te Tinh Can Tho 1998) (Can Tho Province was split into two administrative units, Can Tho City and Hau Giang Province, in 2004).[4] The population comprises mainly of the Kinh (ethnic Vietnamese), the Khmer and the Chinese, the first being the majority.

On the bank of the Hau Giang River lies the city of Can Tho. The city serves as the political, economic, and commercial centre of the whole Mekong Delta region. It also serves as the educational centre of the Delta. In 1966, Can Tho University was founded; its most significant contributions have been to the field of agriculture. The commercial nature of the town is easily apparent at the big central market, where virtually everything is bought and sold: meat, fish, vegetables, fruits, rice, spices and other food products; kitchenware, furniture, hardware, fabrics, clothes — both new and used — shoes, hats, jewellery, and many other items. This central market, bustling with a crowd of people from early in the morning until long after sunset every day, is both wholesale and retail. Not only do people come to meet their daily needs, but merchants from smaller markets in the city as well as from other towns also come to purchase the products they will later sell.[5]

Walking through the market, especially the food area, one can begin to appreciate the richness of land in this area, which produces a large variety of agricultural products. Historical records also point to the land's fertility. According to a 1966 report, the province exported eight thousand tons of rice in one year. Besides rice, it produced and exported large volumes of oranges, tangerines and lemons, and also grew a variety of fruit such as bananas, mangoes, and sugar cane (Huynh 1966). Today, the province is still the agricultural centre of Vietnam, a characteristic I will explore in depth in a later chapter.

THE COMMUNE AND THE HAMLET

It would be helpful to portray the general picture of the hamlet where the people in this ethnography live their everyday life. The hamlet (*ap*) of Binh Thuong B (There are hamlets Binh Thuong A and Binh Thuong B), where the house of my host family stands, belongs to the commune (*xa*), or the village, of Long Tuyen.[6] It lies to the west of Can Tho City. It takes around half an hour to get to the hamlet entrance from the city centre by motorbike: about twenty minutes on the inter-provincial road which is constantly busy with buses and large trucks and another ten minutes on a small and peaceful rural road lined with palm trees where one seldom encounters any transportation. This rural road passes through several villages before arriving at the Long Tuyen Village centre where a few small shops stand. The entrance to the Binh Thuong B Hamlet lies here, but it is on the other side of a river. In 1997, when I first travelled to the hamlet, I had to ask my host family to come pick me up in their small wooden boat and row for about twenty minutes, or I would pay to someone's boat to cross the river and walk on a narrow dirt path along a canal for over forty minutes. In January 2000, however, before the Lunar New Year in early February, bridges were built over the branches of the rivers that meet at the village centre, connecting the village main road with the hamlets across the rivers. After these bridges were built, villagers could walk or ride bicycles to market and to schools in the village centre. It is also possible to ride a motorbike on the path to the hamlet, but it is a bumpy, muddy, and narrow dirt road, with a number of small and narrow wooden bridges over arroyos, canals and water paths, making it difficult to travel this way. I usually ride a motorbike to and from the hamlet, but I often had to get off the bike and push it, or ask someone to cross the bridges for me.[7]

Typical hamlets of the Mekong Delta are not concentrated in one area, and do not form clusters as in northern Vietnam. Instead, they line the waterways. As you ride a boat or walk into the hamlet, you see the houses line the small rivers, arroyos and canals. The size of the land of each household varies, as does that of the houses. On the banks stand coconut trees, water coconuts, bamboos, banana trees and other tropical plants, including some mangroves. In front of the houses run paths along the waterways. Because houses are not clustered, it is not always easy to tell where a hamlet begins and ends. Behind the houses are fruit orchards, and going through the gardens, you suddenly come upon open spaces, usually rice fields. Across from them stand the orchard trees, beyond which are more houses and waterways. Those houses may or may not belong to the same hamlet.

Many of the old houses in the hamlet have dirt floors with walls and ceilings made of woven water coconut leaves. In some houses, floors are covered with brick tiles, considered a symbol of wealth in the past. I heard from one person in a neighbouring village that the local government ran a project to lend money to people so they could cover dirt floors with tiles; however, I never encountered anyone who profitted from such a project in the hamlet of Binh Thuong B. It has become more popular to build brick and cement walls, zinc roofs, and floors covered with ceramic tiles. Many of these houses are painted white or other bright colours, and have front verandahs with pillars, which give a colonial feel. In May 2000, when I left the hamlet, a few houses were being rebuilt in this new style. There are also families who cannot rebuild their entire house, but decide to renovate only part of it, usually the front façade. So there are houses where old and new styles are mixed, too.

The hamlet of Binh Thuong B is one of six hamlets in Long Tuyen Commune. The commune has a relatively large area for a village in a general sense: according to the village census of April 1999, it occupied 13.96 square kilometres of land. The same census reports that the entire commune of Long Tuyen had 2,702 households, and a population of 12,821 (6,282 males and 6,539 females). The chairman of the People's Committee explained to me that the rate of population growth in the village is about 1.4 per cent per year, and there has been little migration into the commune after the war with America ended in 1975. The commune of Long Tuyen consists of six hamlets, divided into 92 smaller units called "groups" (*to*). The hamlet of Binh Thuong B is made up of 20 groups, and according to the 1999 report, 558 households, with a population of 2,716. As there was no detailed census data available on each group, I walked through the groups to count the number of houses. I counted 59 houses in Group A where my host family's house belonged, and 56 houses on one side of an arroyo constituting another group, though I may have missed some houses, as they are often hidden behind bushes and forests along narrow waterways.

Although no precise data are available, the majority of the population of Long Tuyen Commune is ethnic Kinh with a much smaller number of Chinese. There are few Khmer people in this commune.[8] Ninety-five per cent of the population is engaged in agriculture (*nong nghiep*), with the remaining 5 per cent engaged in other occupations such as small businesses (*thuong mai*), education (*giao duc*), and public service (*dich vu*).[9]

Communes and hamlets are more administrative units compared to neighbourhood groups of households, and most people have a sense of belonging to groups where most of their daily activities are conducted. However, people's everyday life also depends, to some extent, on the public and communal facilities as well. Public facilities in the commune of Long Tuyen include the People's Committee office (*uy ban*), a post and telecommunications office (*buu dien*), a security office (*cong an*), health centre (*y te*), and two primary schools and one secondary school (*trung hoc*).[10] Besides public offices and facilities, there are also two pagodas (*chua*) and two village markets (*cho*) that take place every morning on the main road through the village. These places serve the villagers as communal places in their daily activities as well.[11]

The Committee office, the post office and the health centre stand in the same compound, which was rebuilt in 1997, near the village centre on the main road through. There are twenty-five committee officers and twenty-two administrative staff working on the People's Committee, and the chairman, who was thirty-nine in 2000, was appointed at the beginning of the year to serve a five-year term. He comes from a farmer's family, and after graduating from high school, he worked as head of the agriculture department of the committee for ten years before he became chairman. The commune committee is a branch of the committee of Can Tho City, but according to the chairman, officers from the city committee rarely come to the commune, so most public matters in the commune are left in local hands. And the local commune committee rarely has a chance to cooperate or exchange ideas with neighbouring villages.

As a part of the People's Committee, there is a Farmers Union (*hoi nong dan*) in the commune with a long history going back to the 1930s. Three to five representatives from each hamlet constitute the village union, and one person from each household is registered as a member of a hamlet union. The People's Committee Chairman describes the union as a system of cells: "each family constitutes the smallest cell, a hamlet union is a group of family cells and is a member of the commune cell, which constitutes the district cell together with unions of other communes." In the commune of Long Tuyen, they hold several meetings a year, normally every two to three months, when the hamlet representatives get together, and exchange information and ideas mainly about agricultural activities. At each meeting, between thirty and fifty representatives attend.

The Farmers' Union chief of Binh Thuong B Hamlet at the time of my research had been serving for over five years, since he retired from the People's Committee of the commune, where he worked for twenty years. The chief's job is to encourage the farmers to join the union and attend meetings, and to share information and knowledge with the participants. However, he says with disappointment that only a few farmers from the hamlet participate actively in union activities, because it is not compulsory and people join only when they want to. Among the villagers I met, some are enthusiastic about these meetings where they can learn useful information, but many others confess that they have little interest, saying that their own experience is more reliable. As a farmers' organization, the Union can also raise problems of the villagers with the district union and officers, but, the chief confesses, not many measures are taken up by the higher offices.

There are two primary schools and one secondary school, all of which are public, in the village of Long Tuyen. The following is some basic information about the secondary school, which stands on the main road near the village centre, which I occasionally visited as I knew some teachers there. The history of the school is not well known to the teachers and villagers, but most of them think it was probably built some time after the "liberation" in 1975. In April 2000, 798 students (*hoc sinh*) from the sixth to ninth grade studied in the secondary school under thirty-six teachers (*giao vien*). There are seven classes in the 6th grade, five classes in the 7th, four in the 8th and also the 9th, but the school building has only eleven classrooms. So classes are divided into two teaching periods, one in the morning and one in the afternoon. The 6th and 9th grade students study in the morning, and 7th and 8th graders come in the afternoon, and each teacher usually teaches two grades, both in the morning and in the afternoon. About half of the thirty-six teachers come from the city centre of Can Tho, and the rest are mostly from other villages and provinces. Only a few teachers live in the commune of Long Tuyen. The school is a hard place to work for many teachers particularly from the city because it is in a remote area, and they have to spend a lot of time and money commuting every morning and afternoon.

The commune health centre stands next to the People's Committee office, and it belongs to the general hospital of Can Tho City. Both western (*tay y*) and traditional medicine (*dong y*) are offered there, and the two clinics stand next to each other. The health service at the centre used to be free of charge during the socialist period, but now the villagers have to pay for both treatment and medicine, and the cost depends on the type of illness and the prescribed treatment they receive. Medical costs can be extremely large for the living standard of many villagers, sometimes as high as several hundred US dollars. The health centres are rather simple in their services and facilities and there may not always be a doctor, but only a clinician on duty. Therefore, when villagers have serious illnesses, they are referred to a hospital in the nearby town of Binh Thuy, or sometimes to the general hospital in the city.[12] At these hospitals, people can receive more accurate examinations and the necessary treatment or surgery that may not be available at the commune health centre. In order to go to these hospitals outside of the village, villagers usually take a motorcycle taxi (a cart pulled by a motorcycle) (*xe loi*) from the village markets. Early in the morning, one can often see a group of older people and sick villagers sharing a *xe loi* to get to the hospitals.[13]

Besides the official health centre of the commune, a private traditional medical service is also available at a village pagoda. Dr Duc, a certified doctor in traditional medicine (*bac si dong y*), opened the medical clinic at the pagoda in 1973. He has been working for over fifty years, and before he was assigned to the Long Tuyen pagoda, he worked in several places in the neighbouring villages and provinces of the Delta. According to him, there is usually at least one traditional medical doctor in each village. Now Dr Duc lives in the hamlet of Binh Thuong B, and works at the pagoda every morning. Dr Duc became a doctor because he wanted to help sick people, and now works for free and gives medicine to people free of charge. In 1997, he received a complimentary award from the government, and proudly displays the certificate on the wall of his clinic. The medical service here is free, and both examinations and medical herbs are offered, but some people make donations (a few thousand dong) for the medicine they receive. Behind the desk where the doctor examines the patients, there are small drawers each of which contains herbal medicine. Most of the herbs are planted in the front yard of the pagoda and dried into medicine, but Dr Duc also buys some medicine from markets in town.[14]

Every morning, the doctor says, about thirty-seven or -eight patients come to see him. One day when I went there with a fever around half past eight in the morning, I was the twenty-first patient of the day and the place was already crowded with people waiting in line. According to Dr Duc, about 60 per cent of his patients are young women who come with stomach problems and coughs, and the clinic is more crowded when the weather is bad. However, in general, the doctor thinks that the villagers' health is getting better than in the past, possibly because of better nourishment. Once every three months, he also meets the western medical doctor or clinician of the commune public health centre to exchange information and ideas.

The pagoda, where Dr Duc practises traditional medicine, was built in 1953. After being closed for five years during the war after 1968, when it was destroyed by the Communist forces, it was rebuilt and reopened in 1973. In 1993, villagers donated money for renovations of the pagoda, which gave the temple a beautifully painted facade of yellow and red with its name in blue script. There is a list of donors to the 1993 renovation inside the pagoda, near the Buddha statue, which records that a majority of the people donated between one and ten thousand Vietnamese dong, with some contributing twenty to two hundred thousand. Today, there is no monk in the pagoda to practise religious activities, and only one family lives on the grounds of the pagoda to maintain it. According to this keeper, about one hundred people come to the pagoda to worship on the fifteenth day of every lunar month, with more people on days in January, April and October that are religiously significant for Buddhism. The whole month of July is a praying month, and many people come to pray every day. However, the number of worshippers has decreased, because, the keeper thinks, people have become more concerned with money than worship and prayers.[15]

As for the religious characteristics of the commune residents, 20 per cent of the people are officially registered as having a religion.[16] The four major religions are Buddhism, Christianity, Hoa Hao and Cao Dai. As part of East and Southeast Asia, Buddhism has had a long history in Vietnam, with Mahayana Buddhism being the most common practice, which suggests that it came from China in the north. Christianity was brought into the country during the French colonial period in the nineteenth century, and as a consequence, most Christians in this region are Catholics, though there are some other denominations as well. Catholicism flourished especially in Can Tho City and Province during the colonial period, and although many Catholics fled the country when the war ended in 1975 and Communists took over the country, there are still a large number of followers especially in the city. Some churches are still found in the city, but are far fewer in the rural areas. Hoa Hao and Cao Dai are Vietnamese folk religions and millenarian sects, which became particularly popular in the Delta region in the early twentieth century.[17] The Hoa Hao sect claims to be Buddhist, while the Cao Dai sect worships a collection of gods and saints of the East and the West. Can Tho is known to have been a stronghold of Hoa Hao during the revolutionary era.[18]

While 20 per cent of villagers have officially registered their religion, the remaining majority claims to have none. However, though not officially considered a religion, ancestor worship (*tho cung to tien*) is observed by almost all households. (Interestingly, there are different opinions among the Vietnamese on whether ancestor worship is a religion or a custom. Some people say, "people claim they have no religion but everyone practices ancestor worship!") The worshipped ancestors are in the third ascending generation: the grandfather and grandmother of the head of the household who is usually the father. Most houses have an ancestor altar (*ban tho*) in the front room, which is often used as a guestroom as well as a bedroom. The altar varies depending on the wealth of each household, but a typical one is a large wooden chest. In wealthier households people place on the chest three golden-painted objects that are made especially for the altars: one in the middle looks like a pot or a kettle, on top of which is a figure of a legendary lion; and the two on each side are plates with high legs. Placed near these objects are pictures of the ancestors. Two incense (*nhang*) burners are also placed there, and every morning and evening, the head of the house burns new incense and prays in front of the altar. Families who are doing well economically may also place a large, decorative picture behind the altar depicting Chinese religious folk characters.[19] On the fifteenth day of every month, or after the harvest, some fruit is put on the altar as an offering to the ancestors, and on the Lunar New Year and death anniversaries (organized two or three times every year), flowers and a large amount of fruit are offered.

Besides engaging in ancestor worship, most villagers also believe in and worship folk deities. Each house in the village has an altar in its front yard for the heavenly god (*ban ong thien*) and another in front of the gate for the wandering ghosts (*co hon*). Those who are engaged in commerce or small businesses, such as grocery shops, worship the god of fortune (*ong dia*), and place a special altar on the floor for the deity.

The Mekong Delta region is known to have historically maintained a relatively high standard of living compared to other parts of Vietnam, because of its rich land and seasonally abundant water resources, and in the city of Can Tho, electricity has been available for quite a long time. However, it seems to have taken some time for electrical power to reach surrounding villages. The time electricity was introduced varies across villages, some having used electricity since the 1980s, and others much later. It is widely known that the further you go from the main inter-provincial roads, the later the villages started using electricity. State-supplied power is usually not available in these villages, so the inhabitants have had to buy it from personal suppliers.[20] The hamlet of Binh Thuong B, where electricity was introduced in 1993, purchased power in this way. At that time, villagers contributed money in order to bring in electric power. However, not surprisingly, not everyone could contribute the same amount, or even participate. Therefore those who managed to contribute a certain amount of money got power while others did not. In the spring of 2000, as I walked to count the number of houses, I also counted the number with electricity in the particular group A and in the neighbouring group across the arroyo, and found that roughly two-thirds of the houses had electricity. Since power is provided by a private supplier, it is more expensive than in the city which relies on state-supplied electricity: some say it is three times as expensive, while others say it is over four times as much, but exact comparison is not possible as the cost sometimes varies even within a city. In houses with no grid power, villagers use kerosene lamps for light. (According to the 2009 Vietnam Population and Housing Census, the rate of houses with electricity has substantially increased in rural areas in the 2000s, though no accurate data is available on Long Tuyen Village.)[21]

Most households with electricity have some electric appliances. One of the things that people buy first when they get electricity, after lighting appliances, is a television set. In most houses that have electrical power, one can find televisions.[22] Many of the houses in Long Tuyen Village without electricity have radio-cassette players that run on batteries, so it is no surprise that people wish to buy a television set once they have electricity. Many televisions in Long Tuyen Village are second hand and many are black and white, which normally cost from about thirty to one hundred and fifty US dollars. For one hundred dollars, it is possible to buy a good quality set, but not many houses in the village can afford such televisions. A small electric fan is also common, because the area is very hot and humid, with temperatures rising to over 40 degrees Celsius in the hottest season of April and May. Besides television sets and fans, not many other electrical appliances are found in the village. (In 2014, when I revisited the village, refrigerators were also found in some houses.)

There is no plumbing or running water in Binh Thuong B Hamlet. Some houses have wells and water pumps, but most villagers use river water for their daily activities, which I will describe in further detail below. The abundance of river water may explain the lack of running water or water pumps in this area, since a shortage of water is never a concern, and securing water is not as serious a matter as in other parts of the country. However, there is a problem with the cleanliness of the water, and the area is not so fortunate in this sense. In the past, although the branches of the Mekong River are muddy and brown in colour, Can Tho was known for its clean water; it was even celebrated in a folk song. However, today the river suffers from pollution. Some villagers blame over-population, and complain that they cannot catch as many fish as they used to. Others attribute pollution to the use of pesticides and fertilizers for rice cultivation in recent years. I heard from one commune officer that the need for digging wells has increased these days due to the pollution of the rivers and canals in the surrounding areas.

Landline telephone facilities are seldom found in the village. When I first arrived in the village no house had a telephone, and the first one was connected later in 1999. The owner of this house has a telephone because his daughter, who fled to the US with her husband after the war, calls her parents from time to time.[23] He proudly told me there were only a few houses with telephones in the commune. In fact, this was the only house I knew in the hamlet that had a telephone at that time, and I never saw a telephone in other hamlets or other villages, either. One reason why telephone is not very widely found is that installing a line is very expensive, costing nearly one hundred US dollars (in 1999). Besides, most people do not have a regular need for telephones as their daily lives revolve around people they can meet. When people need to call, they go to the village post office to make calls.[24]

LIFE AND THE RIVER

As I described above, rivers, arroyos and canals run through every corner of the Mekong Delta, and a farmer's life depends on the river to a great extent. First of all, travelling by boat on the river is the most important and useful means of transportation. For instance, in my host family, every morning Aunt Tam goes to the market in a boat rowed by Third Sister-in-Law. Third Brother joins them to go to the school in a neighbouring village where he teaches and his son, a secondary school student, also travels in the same boat. At the market, the sister leaves the boat at the back of a store where she shops.

Although the market faces the road on one side, every shop has two entrances, the second facing the river at the back so that people can shop from their boats.

The river is also a place for shopping and shops are also found on boats. On the way to or from the market in the morning, we meet an ice seller's boat and stop our boat close to hers to buy a block of ice to keep food for the day or to make cold fruit drinks. While the daily market takes place in the morning at the commune centre, in the afternoon merchants come rowing boats loaded with fruits, vegetables and sometimes other daily necessities. If you want to buy from them, you call them from the bank in front of your house, and they come over to the wooden pier to offer their products. Some boat shops also sell daily necessities such as soap and oil or agricultural equipment.

On the way home from the morning market, one also sees people preparing food in the river: some are washing rice in saucepans, and others are washing and cutting vegetables and fish. The river is convenient because people can throw their garbage, such as vegetable skin, there as well. Its water is also used for cooking and drinking. Since not many houses in the whole commune have a well, for many the river has been the main source of cooking and drinking water. Because it is too muddy to be used for drinking as it is, river water is stored in a big jar made of clay to let the sediment sink for half a day or overnight. People then pour off the top clear part and boil it to use for drinking or cooking. Villagers never drink non-boiled water.

The river accommodates a number of other daily activities, too. Every morning, as we go to the market, we see many women washing their clothes in the river in front of their houses. They pour river water into plastic or metal tubs, put clothes and soap or detergent in them, and rub the clothes for some twenty minutes before rinsing them. Later in the afternoon, people bathe in the river. Also, they use the river as a toilet.

People use water not only for their everyday needs, but also for their agricultural activities, the main source of their income. Most water for farming is taken from the river. Farmers take water from the river in plastic buckets to water fruit trees in the orchards at the back of their houses — usually early in the morning and late in the day. Sometimes, they use a handmade tool, such as a bowl or plastic helmet tied to a bamboo pole, to fetch water and pour it. This is a particularly important part of their daily activities in the dry season, when there is not a single drop of rain for several months, and the land is hard and dry. Besides being used for fruit cultivation, the river water is also used in rice fields. Each family digs a narrow ditch for the water to run into their rice field from the river or canal, using the tide to water their fields (rivers of the Mekong Delta are tidal). The rich rice crop of the area is owed not only to the climate and soil, but also to the abundant water that helps grow the crop. Some people also catch river fish with nets, while others raise flocks of ducklings. Late in the afternoon, I often used to see a flock of ducklings floating on the river followed by a boat guiding them home.

Another example of the importance of rivers for farmers is the floating markets found in several places on the main rivers in surrounding areas. I mentioned earlier the big land market at the centre of Can Tho City; most farmers go to floating markets as large as the Can Tho Central Market to sell their agricultural products. When fruits are picked and ready to be sold, they are put into woven bamboo baskets, placed in a wooden boat and taken to floating markets on larger rivers, about 5-6 kilometres away from the village. When travelling far, farmers who can afford it use a motor to power their boat, while others row. There are dozens of larger wooden boats of buyers floating at the markets, and farmers negotiate the prices at which they sell their products.

HISTORY OF CAN THO

The Mekong Delta in known to be a migrant society, which is reflected in many aspects of the village life. History shows how people came to live in the area. Legend has it that the village of Long Tuyen originated in the later Le Dynasty (1428–1788). However, at that time, the area was a deserted wasteland with only a scattered population and little cultivation. The land was covered with water and arroyos that suffered terrible storms and floods.

Although I did not find any historical record of Long Tuyen Village, some historical data (Huynh Minh 1966; Canh Bang 1966; Nguyen

Dinh Dau 1999) are available on the Mekong Delta and also on Can Tho City. The Vietnamese people have lived in the Delta and cultivated the wasteland for a long time, but documents indicate that it was in the seventeenth and eighteenth centuries that the area was first extensively exploited, mainly by Chinese mandarins in exile from the Ming Dynasty in China. Towards the end of the seventeenth century the area was officially inspected for the first time. In 1698, Lord Nguyen in northern Vietnam, then the centre of the country, dispatched General Nguyen Huu Can to the south for an inspection, and established the Gia Dinh Palace in today's Ho Chi Minh City. At that time, the Mekong Delta was still listed as a frontier without any direct control from the centre. In the first half of the eighteenth century, the Delta came under the control of the Nguyen Dynasty of South Vietnam.[25] In 1732, Lord Nguyen established Long Ho Palace in today's Vinh Long Province, north of Can Tho Province. It was in 1739 that Can Tho Province, then called Tran Giang, was established along with three other provinces (parts of An Giang, Kien Giang, and Ca Mau) in the Mekong Delta. This symbolized the completion of the exploitation of the Delta and the beginning of the existence of the Can Tho of today. Around that time, Can Tho, or Tran Giang, was still a place of mixed indigo and mangrove forests inhabited by a variety of wild animals (Huynh Minh 1966).

Around the mid-eighteenth century, the southward march of the Vietnamese was encouraged by the state king of South Vietnam (residing in Hue in central Vietnam, then known as Annam) and as a result, the exploitation of the fertile land was accelerated in the south. In 1756 and 1757, other provinces and districts were established, and from then on the whole Mekong Delta region officially belonged to Vietnam. In the later half of the eighteenth century, Can Tho became a strategically important place, particularly for supporting Ha Tien, a coastal town facing the Siamese Bay. In 1772, when the Siamese army attacked Ha Tien, Can Tho was where the army retreated to prepare for a counter-attack. Can Tho was also known for its civilization and culture, and both economy and commerce flourished in the area. Throughout the latter half of the century, social development was a priority, such as an official examination system for public services, which promoted education. Not only were the economy and commerce further developed, but the agriculture sector of the region also grew. The fertile land to the south of Can Tho was exploited and the Delta became "the rice bowl" of the whole country, with Can Tho as its centre. From that time on, Can Tho became an important focus of agricultural production in the west.[26] The legend of Long Tuyen Village also shows that it was during the nineteenth century under the Nguyen dynasty that the region was transformed into a cultivated and populated area. In particular, it was Mac Thien Tu, a son of a Chinese mandarin in exile, who mainly contributed to the development of Can Tho as a strategic as well as economic and cultural centre. Today, he is considered the founder of Can Tho (ibid).[27]

In 1802, Nguyen Anh crowned himself Emperor Gia-Long in Hue, then the capital city in central Vietnam, and the country was united under the Nguyen Dynasty (Woodside 1988). Nguyen, who was in conflict with the Trinh of the north based in Hanoi, was active in the "Southward March" in order to widen his territory against the Chin and secure a centre of international trade in the south. The emperor and his followers paid much attention to the development of the south, especially that of Can Tho (then called Vinh Dinh), and the local government widened roads and built new markets in the region. In the first years of the nineteenth century, Can Tho became the centre not only of rice production in the Delta, but also of the rice trade.[28] Commerce was developed as Emperor Gia Long urged the people to widen roads and build new markets. Waterways were also developed and expanded that form the basic network for the region today. [29] Until then, there had been no adequate transportation system and in the transition season between winter and spring, boats could not pass because of the low tide. Also, areas near the river had been deserted and full of mosquitoes and leeches that made passing the river fearsome. Can Tho City, the provincial capital of Can Tho Province, was now regarded as the capital of the west.

During the reign of Emperor Minh Mang of the Nguyen Dynasty, Can Tho became a prosperous area with a high population density and several commercial markets. Commercial activities became more and more prosperous, establishing the basis for the region's present-day commercial importance. People from other parts of the country also migrated to the area to start businesses. Can Tho was "famous for fertility, good land and no flood" (Son Nam 1994, p. 77). In a common saying, "Can Tho has limpid water and white rice. Therefore, those who come say goodbye reluctantly." During the Nguyen Dynasty, the waterways were further developed. The waterways of the Can Tho River and some major canals were developed in parallel with roads, which contributed to the progress of the economy of the Mekong Delta (Son Nam 1994; Huynh Minh 1966).

However, the wave of colonialism was approaching Vietnam in the middle of the nineteenth century. In June 1862, a treaty was signed and the southern region came under French control. This was the beginning of colonialism in the Mekong Delta. People of the Delta fought against foreign rule, and in 1867, they attacked the bastions of the French in Can Tho. The ruler fought back and suppressed the people's movement, and the area was "stuffed with smoke and fire". However, the whole Delta was gradually conquered, and on 1 January 1868, the Bonard Decree was signed, placing the region under direct French rule. On 23 February 1876, the Marshal of Saigon proclaimed a decree by which Can Tho became a province under its present name. The French government created a new administrative system for the province, dividing it into five districts, eight cantons and seventy-two communes, including the commune of Long Tuyen. The French invested in the development of the Delta region (Biggs 2012)[30], especially Can Tho City, as they moved the provincial capital to the city. The Can Tho market became an important commercial centre connecting other places of the Delta and Saigon (present-day Ho Chi Minh City) (Son Nam 1994).

The French also developed the social system, opening primary and secondary schools (the first elementary school for girls opened in 1903). In 1906, an association for the encouragement of learning (Hoi Khuyen hoc Can Tho; Societe d'Enseignement Mutuel des Annamites de Can Tho) was founded in the city. In 1921, the French founded a college (today's high school) in the town, along with similar schools in Saigon and My Tho. Roads, temples, and markets in the area continued to develop during the early twentieth century, with the years 1907 and 1909 seeing the most significant transformations. Public health centres were also developed: in 1948, a general hospital was built in the city centre, which served soldiers during the war as well as people from the surrounding villages. The first newspapers in the western region were also published in Can Tho (Son Nam 1994; Huynh Minh 1966).[31]

About the same time, independence movements grew throughout the country (Marr 1981; Tai 1992; Duiker 1995*a*).[32] It was during and after World War II that the people of the Mekong Delta began to actively participate in independence movements. In June 1940, as the French surrendered to the Germans, Japanese troops started to occupy North Vietnam. In July 1941, Japan proceeded to the south, including Can Tho, and the area became a battlefield between the French and the Japanese. After August 1945, when Japan was defeated in the world war and the French regained control of Vietnam, struggles for independence by the Viet Minh (League for the Independence of Vietnam) and the Hoa Hao Buddhist sects frequently broke out in the area. In most cases, the French-British allied forces attacked the resisters, and the people's struggles were not successful in the region. According to historical records, the Communists attacked Cai Rang, a place where the present floating market lies, several kilometeres from Binh Thuong B Hamlet, but French troops arrived by warship from Can Tho, coordinating both infantry and air force, and suppressed the rebels (Huynh Minh 1966; Furuta 1995; Tap Chi Xua va Nay 1999).

In 1954, the French were defeated at Dien Bien Phu in North Vietnam, and the struggle for independence from the French ended. Under the Geneva Agreement, the whole country was divided into two military zones, north and south, and a general election was going to be held in 1956 to unify the country (Gettleman 1965). However, no election was held in 1956 and the country entered a phase of civil war between the two zones, each with a government and military. This conflict led to the war between the United States on the side of southern government and the Communist forces of the north (Duiker 1995*b*; Furuta 1995). Not much has been written about what happened in the Mekong Delta and Can Tho during these years of war, and how people lived. However, the villagers of Long Tuyen still tell stories of their war experiences, some of which I will introduce in the next chapter.

The war ended in 1975 when Saigon, the capital of South Vietnam, fell to the Communist forces of the north. In 1976, the Socialist Republic of Vietnam was founded and the country was reunited. Some sources suggest that the southern part of the country had developed some industrial production in addition to its large agricultural output prior to that year (Beresford 1991). It is also known that the region was already familiar with a capitalist-oriented economy through direct and indirect connections with the rest of the world, although this may have taken a different form from the free-market system since the reform. South Vietnam, especially its commercial sector and centres, had adopted the French and then American modes of capitalism (Nguyen Hoang Ngoc 1991).

The new communist government pushed the nation toward socialism. However, the shift to socialism in the Mekong Delta did not start with the communist victory in 1975. It took a few years before the project was launched in the area in 1978, and collectivization intensified in the early 1980s. According to Ngo, "After the Third Plenum of the Fifth Party Congress declared in early December 1982 that the cooperativization of the southern region should be 'basically completed' by the end of 1985, almost every newspaper and magazine article which deals in any way with the south repeated this refrain" (Ngo 1988, p. 164).[33] The cooperativization of the south had a number of goals: getting individual peasants to exchange labour, help each other with production, begin to produce according to central government plans, and achieve economic connections with the central government.

In the southern part of the country, the arrival of socialism meant a departure from the capitalist system that had been functioning in the region during the French occupation and American presence.[34] As will be seen in a later chapter, this was not an easy process. Ngo and some other scholars argue that cooperativization was not successful in the Mekong Delta region. Some reasons were the administrative and practical failures of the government in implementing the policy. Especially in the agricultural sector, it met resistance from the peasants, and collectivization never fully penetrated the agricultural activities of the area, nor did it adequately function as an economic system in this part of the nation. One reason for the peasants' resistance was that they had little incentive to participate in the cooperatives. In the Mekong Delta, 70 per cent of the rural population were "middle class peasants" who owned 80 per cent of the cultivated surface, 60 per cent of the total farm equipment, and over 90 per cent of the draft animals. Thus, unlike those in the northern part of the country where agriculture remained at a subsistence level, they could already produce more than enough for their own consumption by the time the government decided to run the collectivization programme (ibid.). From the peasants' perspective, members of cooperatives could enjoy only a small percentage of the final products, while the peasants could already use all of their own production (Vo Nhan Tri 1988; Beresford 1991; White 1988; and Duiker 1995*a*).[35]

Although a complete picture of the shift to socialism in Can Tho Province is not available, there is historical information on a commune in Tien Giang, another province in the Mekong Delta. According to this record, land reform was carried out in the Delta to collectivize farming. From 1976 to 1978 the rural areas of the region implemented a process of land adjustment to redistribute farmers' lands in order to collectivize the means of production. However, the cooperatives did not work effectively. Six thousand cooperatives worked moderately well, but four thousand others went bankrupt partly due to natural disasters that occurred between 1976 and 1979. During the eighties, a number of cooperatives in the Delta broke down (Luong Hong Quang 1997). This record shows the limitations and weaknesses of cooperatives in the region and points to their poor functioning.[36]

As the market-oriented economy took agricultural production away from the authority of the cooperatives after the *doi moi* reform, households regained their position as primary production units in the rural Mekong Delta. Agriculture in the Delta returned to its previous form of production, in which each family was the basic economic unit and the middle peasant class served as the main force of production. The nineties were the most progressive period for agriculture in the Delta including Can Tho, which saw a large increase in total production (Luong Hong Quang 1997).

THE LEGEND OF LONG TUYEN VILLAGE

I have found no historical record for the origin of Long Tuyen Village nor heard any story about its founding from villagers. However, an historical book about Can Tho published in 1966 has a brief introduction to a legend, which does not seem to be known to most villagers, about the origin of the village and the nearby town of Binh Thuy. According to this legend, Long Tuyen commune originated in the later Le Dynasty (1427-1789). At that time, the area was deserted, with a scattered population and pure water running throughout. Faced with many natural obstacles, its inhabitants fled to other areas, leaving the place a wasteland. At that time, a man named Le Thanh Hieu took his family and settled in a hamlet near Can Tho. He began to widen the roads and cultivate the land. In the meantime, another man named Vo Van Tuu came to the area and settled in another hamlet. He also reclaimed the land. The two men became related to each other by the marriage of their children, who are the ancestors of today's villagers.

The region continued to suffer from storms and floods, and people had to live "in the open air" for a long time. During the reign of Tu Duc (1852–), a province chief called Huynh Man Dat, who patrolled the Cong Linh Valley, faced a wild wind. His servant, observing the difficulty, suggested that the chief proceed to a calm arroyo not far away. The chief learned from the local people that strong wind and waves were rare there. The chief said, "thanks to this quiet current, I can come here safely. I would like to name this place 'Calm Water'." This is how the town of Binh Thuy (several kilometres away from Long Tuyen Village) received its name. At that time, Binh Thuy was a village that also encompassed the area of today's Long Tuyen Village.

Later, around the turn of the century, district chief Nguyen Duc Nhuan and canton chief Le Van Noan (both natives of Binh Thuy) cared for the villagers and worked hard to build roads, temples and markets for the people. They gathered the village notables and discussed with them what to rename the village. The district chief asked the villagers, "Now our society is getting more and more civilized, so in order to express our gratitude to this homeland, and to mark a new historical period, I want to rename it. What do you think?" The arroyos of the village had the shape of a lying dragon, forming two legs, a tail and a mouth with pearls, so Long Tuyen (meaning "dragon waterfall") Village was named after this shape.

When the village was renamed, the canton chief said, "We should keep the name Calm Water, too. We will use this name for the market, and Long Tuyen for the entire village." Thus, the small market town of Binh Thuy and the village of Long Tuyen got their present names. All those at the discussion supported this idea, and the district chief informed all villagers of the re-establishing and renaming of their beloved village. After that, the temple of Binh Thuy (which still stands at the centre of the town and is famous for a special annual religious festival in April of the lunar calendar) was built with contributions from local noble families (Huynh 1966).

MEKONG DELTA AS A MIGRANT SOCIETY

The Mekong Delta has always been a region of immigrants. Originally, Khmer people lived in this forest and wetland area. At the end of the seventeenth century, the Nguyen, oppressing the remaining force of the Khmer Empire of Champa, captured the lowland area of Central Vietnam and proceeded further to the Khmer-inhabited south, taking advantage of the weakening empire, which was under pressure from Siam. In 1698, the dynasty gained control over Saigon, and in the eighteenth century, proceeded to the Mekong Delta. After exiles from the Ming Dynasty in China migrated to the south, the Nguyen widened its territory, and within one century had the whole Mekong Delta region under its control (Furuta 1995). Reflecting this history of invasion and migration, the Mekong Delta today still has three main ethnic groups (the Kinh, the Khmer and the Chinese) and there are also a small number of the Cham.

The Mekong Delta was known from the beginning of its history for its rich resources, which attracted migrants. The area was abundant in fish, beehives, firewood, crocodiles and snake poisons (used by physicians). Also rich in water, the land was suitable for rice cultivation. Although cultivating the land and preparing rice fields was difficult for migrants from central Vietnam, it was often easier than farming in their place of origin. In the beginning, according to a historical record, farmers worked only three to four months a year on rice cultivation and spent the rest of the time fishing, engaged in leisure and entertainment activities, or worked as labourers (Son Nam 1974; 1985).

This record shows how mobile people's lives were in the Mekong Delta in the period before French colonialism:

> People in the upper stream used their free time before or after their own harvest to work as laborers in the Hau Giang area to help with harvesting.... Tens of small and big boats with laborers followed one another, traveling between Can Tho, Long Xuyen, Sa Dec, Rach Gia, Bac Lieu, and Soc Trang. Many people spent the New Year in strange places. Nga Nam and Nga Bay areas were very busy with cafes selling *banh tet* and *banh dua* (sticky rice cake wrapped with banana or coconut leaves). Rice noodle cafes sold noodles all day and night, and small boats rowed up and down selling sweet soup and rice soup (Son Nam 1985, p. 105) (translation by the author).

This was a time of migration and pioneering in the new area. Newcomers were welcome, regardless of their origin. Landowners accepted them not only to harvest their cultivated land, but also to convert new land into rice fields and fruit gardens. Many Chinese who came to the area were in the rice trade. They also lent money to the Vietnamese. There were also mobile casinos that the Chinese organized with several kinds of Chinese gambling. Intermarriages between the Vietnamese and the Chinese were common, with their children considered Vietnamese.

However, it was particularly during French colonialism that the agriculture of Can Tho Province largely developed. In 1819, the area devoted to rice cultivation in the year was less than 20,000 *mau* (1 *mau* equalled 6,225 square metres in mid-nineteenth century according to Son Nam 1994). During the colonial period, in one year, from 1886 to 1887 for instance, 17,000 *mau* were newly cultivated. There was still abundant land (110,000 *mau*) to be cultivated in the province, and "people saw a bright future in agriculture" (Son Nam 1994, p. 269). In 1910, the Association of Rizicole Indochinoise was established as a research institute for rice cultivation.

Population grew even more rapidly than the cultivated area. In 1819, the number of taxpayers of the Mekong Delta was only 72,000 (Nguyen The Anh 1968). (The court kept only records of number of taxpayers and not of the whole population.) According to a statistic from the French colonial period, in 1908, the population of Can Tho Province was nearly 200,000. In 1907–08 the colonial government established a system of immigration which drew people from the north to the area, and the population of the Delta grew rapidly. By 1930, it had reached 350,000, almost 80 per cent more than twenty years earlier. However, the rice-growing area was 180,000 hectares, only ten thousand hectares larger than in 1908, which meant a significant per capita reduction in rice area. In 1970, the population of the whole Mekong Delta was 6,350,000, three times as large as in 1908. The rice planting area was 1,800,000 hectares which represented an increase of 30 per cent since 1908. These figures show how rapidly the population of the Mekong Delta, including Can Tho, grew in the twentieth century (Son Nam 1994; Tap Chi Xua va Nay 1999).

There is no data on the population and rice area of Can Tho Province during the war. One reason is that after the Geneva Agreement, between 1955 and 1975, the Saigon government rearranged the Mekong Delta's administrative units, and Can Tho no longer existed as a single province. There are statistics for the whole Delta during those years, but no available data for the province until after the war. According to 1994 reports, the population of the province was 1,800,000, with a rice-planting area of 350,000 hectares. In the same year, the population of the whole Delta was almost 16,000,000, and the rice-planting area was 3,003,000 hectares. The population of the Delta represented 21.8 per cent of the country's entire population (15,850,600 out of 72,509,500), but rice output amounted to 51.52 per cent (12,120,900 out of 23,528,200 tons), supporting the area's reputation as the nation's rice bowl (Tap Chi Xua va Nay 1999).

TRADITIONS

Before the French colonized the area, a variety of customs and rituals seem to have existed in many parts of the Mekong Delta. For instance, the Chanh Chung festival on July 14 (Lunar calendar) kept people of the provinces busy. Officials decorated their carts with flowers and paraded through the streets. Carts bedecked with flowers meant the performance of lively scenes from legends by people dressed as fairies. Servants wearing their best clothes pulled a car carrying their sightseeing lord, surrounded by a band and singers. On the market wharf, flower-covered boats also passed by on the water. Two or three boats were connected together to make a larger platform, and the roof was covered with special leaves to imitate the house of an ancient king. The boats were decorated in a special and luxurious way, and some carried musicians performing traditional Vietnamese music.[37]

During the French colonial period, the Vietnamese tried to retain their traditions. One custom that survived the entire duration of foreign rule was ancestor worship. The ancestor altar was set up in each house, and all ceremonies were observed. On the New Year, if people did not burn incense and decorate the ancestor altar, they were considered negligent. Wealthier families also bought cupboards for worship. There were a variety of such cupboards, some of them very luxurious. Worship pictures also became popular. Around the beginning of the twentieth century, worship pictures were called *son thuy* (literally meaning "mountain water"), indicating that the labour and loyalty of parents is like the highest mountain and source of springs (Son Nam 1985).

How local traditions and customs were performed during the war years and the socialist era in Can Tho Province is not well known.[38] A study of Tien Giang, another province in the Mekong Delta, shows that a variety of customs were performed after the war during the 1980s and 1990s. According to Luong Hong Quang, a number of rituals related to weddings, funerals, and religious occasions were followed. For instance, for a wedding, three ceremonies were conducted: *le giap loi* (ritual of word exchange), *le hoi* (ritual of inquiry), and *le cuoi* (ritual of marriage). There were also rituals related to agriculture, such as worship of the God of agriculture (*cung than nong*) and worship of the earth (*cung dat*). The scholar argues that after 1975, in the socialist period, the procedures and meanings of the ritual changed slightly. First, the rituals became simplified. In the case of wedding ceremonies, traditionally there were six rituals to be performed, but these were reduced to the three mentioned above. Second, the meanings of the rituals became less religious and more secularized. After the war, Luong Hong Quang argues, people's main interest became more related to money and acquiring wealth, and the rituals were transformed accordingly (Luong Hong Quang 1997).[39]

In contrast to the situation in Tien Giang, in Long Tuyen Commune, not many rituals are preserved and few religious rituals are observed today. According to Uncle Bay, some villagers still perform agricultural rituals, but it depends on each household, and there are few people who continue the custom. The rituals and ceremonies that are still commonly performed relate to weddings, funerals, death anniversaries and the

Lunar New Year. Others do not seem to have survived much. Why the rituals have disappeared is not clear. They might have vanished gradually during the war as many of the villagers either fled the area, were busy supporting the soldiers, or joined the armies; or during the socialist era when religious performances were not encouraged. Considering how severe fighting was in the area, and that the Socialist control was not very tight in the vicinity of this village, it seems reasonable to think that many of the rituals did not survive the years of the intense war.

THE VILLAGE AS HOME

Villagers associate the village with their notion of "home". As we will see in a later chapter, many people's comments suggest that they consider rural life harder than life in urban areas. However, although they may think that life is generally better in the city, they do not necessarily prefer to live there.

Many villagers like living here simply because it is their homeland where their families are. One woman says, "I like living here, because it is my homeland where my father and mother lived. No other place is like that." Another woman who used to live in Ho Chi Minh City did not like living there, because, she says, "the village is her home." After she returned to the village, she has never gone back to the city. A thirty-six-year-old woman lives in Ho Chi Minh City with her husband and son, and was returning home when I visited her mother's house. She thinks that there are both advantages and disadvantages to urban life, but she prefers life in the rural area. The best thing about it is that she can live close to her parents and the neighbourhood is good. In the city, it is hot, everything is expensive and fruit is not fresh. Also, she has no family members (except for her husband) or friends in Ho Chi Minh City, so she feels lonely there. Although the woman acknowledges that facilities are better in the city and the standard of living is higher, she thinks it is better for her to live in the village, close to her family.

Fourth Sister also explained to me that she prefers to live in the village because it is where she grew up, spent most of her life, and her parents and siblings live. She thinks that it is better to live in the city if you have a good education, but if not, it is better to live as a farmer. She tells me that Father Bay and Aunt Tam once tried to arrange a marriage for her with someone from the city. However, she declined the offer, because she did not want to live in the city. She says she grew up in the village with little education, and she does not see how she could live in the city. She has lived as a farmer all her life and she thinks it is better for her that way.

Some people feel attached to their land. An old couple says they prefer to live in the village where they have a small piece of land (one thousand square metres), although their two children, a son and a daughter, live in the city of Can Tho. Other villagers like living in the village because they think the environment is better in the rural area. Some of the considerations commonly mentioned are the fresh air, clean water, and quiet atmosphere. In Long Tuyen Village, the water is still clean, and people still use it for their daily needs, including cooking and bathing. Another popular reason for preferring to live in a rural area is the low cost of living. Farmers can eat rice from their field and vegetables from their garden and do not have to buy all their food like urban dwellers. Also, they can gather firewood in their garden and do not have to pay for wood or gas for cooking. Some people also think that farmers have more freedom to be on their own. "If you work in a factory, you have to listen to your boss and you have no freedom. In farming, I can work independently and be free", says one farmer.

Notes

1. Long Tuyen Village belonged to Can Tho Province until 2004, but is now part of Can Tho City after the province was divided into two.
2. This figure is based on a 1995 Can Tho University brochure.
3. According to the national census of 2001, Can Tho Province had 254,000 hectares of rice fields in that year (*Vietnam Statistical Yearbook 2001*). However, there is some discrepancy in the size of agricultural land in the province. Nguyen Dinh Dau's (1999) data shows that it had 347,000 hectors or rice fields in 1994.
4. In 2009, the population of Can Tho City (which includes the urban area and surrounding rural areas) was nearly 1.19 million and that of Hau Giang Province was 757 thousands (General Statistics Office of Vietnam 2011*a*).

5. The market has since been moved from the centre of the city to a newly developed area in the city's outskirt.
6. *Xa* in Vietnamese translate into both commune and village. I use the word "commune" in a more administrative sense compared to the word "village" in a more general sense.
7. The road in the village is now paved with concrete and motorbikes can enter more easily.
8. Although Khmer people are not often seen in the commune of Long Tuyen, some provinces in the Mekong Delta are known for their presence. They were the original inhabitants of the area before the Kinh and the Chinese migrated there. One can also find Khmer pagodas in the city of Can Tho, indicating their (former) presence in the city.
9. From the 1999 Commune report
10. These facilities serve the villagers in Socialist Vietnam today. On the public role of the village in the national bureaucracy in traditional Vietnam, see Jamieson (1984, 1986*a*).
11. It is known that Vietnamese villages have communal pagoda called *dinh*. However, I was told by the villagers that there is no *dinh* in Long Tuyen now. Whether it existed in the past is not known.
12. Another hospital, Phuong Chau International Hospital, has opened later.
13. *Xe loi* has since been banned. Since then, people without means of transportation pay and ride on the back of motorbikes from the centre of the village.
14. For more on traditional medicine and medical practices in Vietnam, see Craig (2002), although the ethnography is from Red River Delta in the north.
15. In an ethnographic study of a village in the Mekong Delta in the 1950s, Hickey (1964) introduces a village temple (he calls it *dinh* and not *chua*) as a communal space, where village affairs and rituals took place. In Long Tuyen Village I did not obtain any information on such communal activities at the temple. Villagers gather at the People's Committee compounds when there are meetings such as those of the farmers union.
16. This percentage is taken from the census report of the commune in 1999. The percentage shows those who have officially registered their religion. It should be noted here that the accurate number of people who profess a religion is difficult to determine, partly for political reasons. My research did not closely look into the issue of religion, also partly for political reasons.
17. Tai (1983) offers an extensive analysis of the history, ideology, and political activities of the two folk religions, especially in the context of the Vietnamese revolution in the twentieth century.

18. Tai (1983) describes the followers in Can Tho as "people of little education, interested in action rather than in doctrinal or political questions" (1983, p. 121), whose activities caused tensions with the local authorities in the 1940s. According to Fall (1955), there were 1,500,000 adherents in the Mekong Delta in the early 1950s.
19. I heard some foreigners say those who have such pictures are Chinese since the images have Chinese characters, but I have seen the pictures displayed by Vietnamese families as well, and they may not understand what the character says, but they think it is highly religious and precious.
20. Officially there is no private electricity supplier in Vietnam and all electrical power is state-owned. However, in rural villages, those who buy electricity from the state connect electrical lines to village houses and sell electricity to them. That is the reason why it is more expensive than the publicly supplied energy.
21. According to the census, the percentage of the households with electricity network in rural areas increased from 72.1 in 1999 to 94.6 in 2009 (*The 2009 Vietnam Population and Housing Census*).
22. In 1999, 46.5 per cent of rural households in the whole country used TV. By 2009 the percentage was 84.9 (The 2009 Vietnam Population and Housing Survey).
23. He seldom calls his daughter in the United States, since making international calls from Vietnam is extremely expensive.
24. Landline telephone has become more widespread in rural Vietnam during the 2000s, with 38.6 per cent of households owning a line in 2009 (The 2009 Vietnam Population and Housing Survey). Some rural residents also own mobile phones.
25. At that time from the beginning of the seventeenth century, Vietnam was divided into two opposing dynasties: the Chin of the north and the Nguyen of the south.
26. The Mekong Delta region is called the "western provinces", as it lies at the southwest of the country. Can Tho City eventually became known as *Tay Do*, which means the capital of the west (exactly when the name became used is not known from the historical data I have obtained).
27. Mac Thien Tu is also well-known as a literatus of the south (Son Nam 1974).
28. According to Son Nam (1974), fruit production was introduced to some parts of the Delta during the Nguyen Dynasty, although rice was the main crop.
29. Also see Steinberg (1987) and Woodside (1988) on the reign of the Nguyen Dynasty.

30. Though not focusing on Can Tho, Biggs examines extensively the development of the Mekong Delta under French colonialism, including its waterways, agriculture, laws, etc., and how peasant society expanded as a result.
31. Although not dealing with the Mekong Delta, Ngo's (1973) work is a detailed study of peasants' life under French colonialism. See also Duiker (1995*a*) on the colonial experience of the country as a whole.
32. Hy Van Luong (1992) introduces a resistance movement at the village level in North Vietnam.
33. Also see Shiraishi (1993) on the socialism of South Vietnam after 1975.
34. Elliott (1985) also investigates the cultural and social effects of the Communist revolution on the agricultural sector.
35. See Tran Thi Van Anh and Nguyen Manh Huan (1995) for general and national views on agricultural collectivization and its disintegration before and after the economic reform.
36. Beresford (1985) examines how households were collectivized during the socialist era in North Vietnam.
37. Huynh Quoc Thanh (1999) introduces some peculiar traditional and religious rituals in South Vietnam, contrasting them with rituals in North Vietnam. He states that many of the rituals in the south were influenced by the folk ceremonies of ethnic minorities.
38. From the Communist point of view, Tran Anh Tuan (1982) criticizes social studies on the Mekong Delta conducted by the old regime during the war. From a similar viewpoint, Ho Le and Nguyen Lieu (1982) examine cultural and social backgrounds of the Mekong Delta, such as education, literacy, and hygiene, in the context of the shift to socialism.
39. Goodkind's (1996) survey shows that more traditional wedding rituals were performed in South Vietnam than in the north in the early 1990s. Hy Van Luong (1993*b*) suggests that in North Vietnam, rituals have been intensified during the reform era.

3

FAMILY AS THE SOCIAL UNIT

FAMILY LIFE

Much of the life of the residents of Binh Thuong B Hamlet revolves around the family. With the aim of illustrating how family members spend their everyday life together and interact with each other in daily activities, I follow a day in the life of my host family. Of course, every day is different, but the day introduced here is a typical one. In this family the father and mother are over seventy and the children are in their late twenties to early forties. The oldest grandchild is over twenty and the youngest are infants and babies. The head of the family is Uncle Bay, and he lives with his wife Aunt Tam and Youngest Brother, their youngest son who is single. The other six children live separately. Most of them are married except for Second Brother who is divorced, and four of them (Second Brother, Third Brother, Fourth Sister and Fifth Sister) live in the same hamlet.[1]

Morning in the village starts early, when it is still dark outside and stars are sparkling in the sky around the disc of the moon. When cocks start crowing, shortly after four, Aunt Tam gets up before anyone else in the house is awake and makes a wood fire in the kitchen hearth. Some mornings when the electricity is off, as in other houses in the village that have no electricity, the mother lights a kerosene lamp, which gives the small house a dim yellow glow. While waiting for the wood to start crackling quietly and steadily, she pumps water from the well for the kettle which she then places over the fire, which is producing red flames by now. In most other houses where they cannot afford water pumps, they boil the water they fetched from the river days before so the mud would settle. When the water boils, Aunt Tam makes a pot of tea, the first of many in the upcoming day.

Around five, other members of the family, Uncle Bay, Youngest Brother, and a grandchild (son of Second Brother) who stays in the house every night, get up, and the day's activity begins. After washing their faces in the river, the family members clean the pig hut, and sweep the house and the front garden. At six, when it is still dim outside, Youngest Brother leaves home to go to work in town, walking to the village market and then riding a motorbike. Around the same time, Third Sister-in-Law, who lives some several hundred metres up the arroyo in front of their house, comes rowing a small wooden boat. In it are Third Brother who is a teacher at a primary school in the neighbouring village, and his son, a secondary school student. Aunt Tam gets on the boat and together they travel along the arroyo for twenty minutes to the village market (*cho*).[2] The market opens every morning on the road near the village centre leading to the nearest town of Binh Thuy. As the boat approaches the market, we meet many other boats similar in shape and size, all carrying a few family members, some going to work in the village centre, some going to the market, and some going to school.

At the market, Third Brother and his son get off and the brother goes to work on a bicycle, while his son walks to school nearby. Aunt Tam and Third Sister-in-Law park the boat at one of the shops. At the market a variety of vegetables are sold such as cucumbers, beans, green leaves, cabbage, onions, most of them grown locally, as well as shrimp, river fish, pork, chicken, and duck. Market sellers and farmers from the village put their products into bamboo baskets, or sometimes plastic or steel bowls, and sell them on the street. Some villagers have a breakfast of noodle soup or cooked sticky rice at small shops or stalls along the road before they go to work or school. Shops along the street also sell a variety of daily necessities and groceries, such as soap, fish sauce, and cookies. Once or twice a week, instead of going to the village market to shop, Aunt Tam, Fourth Sister, and Third Sister-in-Law go to sell products from their gardens at a floating market. They load the boat with several baskets of fruit, place a motor on the boat, and go to a floating market at Cai Rang. The floating market is a wholesale market, where farmers come to sell their products and market sellers come to buy.

On a usual day, Aunt Tam and Third Sister-in-Law return home from the village market around seven o'clock. When they get home, they start washing the vegetables and fish they have bought in the river in front of their houses in order to prepare their first meal, which is usually ready by ten. In the meantime, Uncle Bay, who stayed in the house to watch it while his wife went to the market, now starts working in the fruit garden or the rice field. This includes a variety of tasks, such as watering trees, plowing the earth, cutting branches, spreading pesticides, harvesting fruit and other activities.

Uncle Bay and Aunt Tam have the meal around ten. After lunch, the aunt also works in the garden, picking fruits to be sold, while the uncle stays home and makes tools for gardening and rice planting, such as fruit catchers, using bamboo trees and other natural products found around the house. Since it is extremely hot in the afternoon, people often stay at home to work or take a short nap. In the off-season when they are not busy with agricultural work, the couple sometimes go to visit their children in their own village, or in other villages. However, since one of them always stays to watch the house, they always go separately. More often it is the uncle who goes to other villages to visit his children. The aunt usually walks to the houses of children who live in the same hamlet.

At three, Aunt Tam returns home from the fields or her children's houses and starts cooking supper, the second meal of the day. Farmers' meals consists mostly of vegetables, often those they grow in their own garden, and fish they catch in the river or mice they catch in the rice fields. They also eat pork and duckling and sometimes chicken that they buy in the market. Sometimes beef may also be added, but they rarely eat shrimp, saying that it is too expensive. Family members do not always eat together. Instead, they eat in turn, but the aunt usually eats after everyone else, or sometimes eats in the kitchen. Some days, a single son and grandchildren may visit the parents around supper time and share the evening meal, resulting in a joyful domestic atmosphere, but married children seldom come to share a meal.

After supper, around five, when it is a little cooler, people bathe in the river and wash the pig hut. Youngest Brother who works in town comes home around six and has supper. Uncle Bay, after burning incense on the ancestral altar and kowtowing in front of it, turns on the TV to watch dramas, news and music programmes. Some of the children and grandchildren who came to eat supper may stay and join their father, and after seven, other children in the same hamlet, or sometimes from the neighbouring villages, come to visit the parents with their own children. The family members chat with Aunt Tam and their siblings in the kitchen and watch TV in the front guest room with Uncle Bay. Also, a grandson whose house does not have electricity comes here to study at night. The children go home after eight, and the aunt goes to bed. Uncle Bay and Youngest Brother watch TV until nine or ten and go to bed, after which the grandson may continue studying until around eleven. At that time, the village is quiet and dark, with the occasional sound of barking dogs.

THE FAMILY AS THE BASIC SOCIAL UNIT

In the lives of the Vietnamese of the rural Mekong Delta, the family is known to have always had particular significance. As Jamieson states, the family has always played a role as the basis of society and the central unit of everyday life. It is not only a sphere where people's social and economic activities take place, but also a psychological world where people are tied together by emotional attachment. The family is "a living entity," and "a small world unto itself" (Jamieson 1986*b*). As a unit of everyday life, it is a primary source of people's identity.[3]

However, the characteristics of the Vietnamese family in the Mekong Delta and its relation to the society are not easily captured. Existing studies on Vietnamese society and family suggest that the family in the Delta has two seemingly contradictory aspects: Confucian and individualistic. On the one hand, some studies suggest that the family in the north, where today's southerners originated, constitutes part of the Confucian culture of East Asia, where social and political stabilities are based on family harmony. The family is a relational world where each member exists in relation to others. As these studies argue, this is especially true of the generational relationship between parents and children where the crucial element is filial piety. The relational aspect has been observed in kinship terms and the way people address each other (Hickey 1964; Hy Van Luong 1989; Tran Dinh Huou 1996).[4] On the other hand, other studies suggest that the family in the Mekong Delta also has its own peculiar characteristics that differ somewhat from the stereotypes of Confucian society. They argue that the family in the Delta are more "individualistic". Though it is not always clear what these studies mean by "individualistic", but they often mention that each family show more independent characteristics and are less community-based than in northern and central villages (Hickey 1964; Tran Anh Tuan 1982; Do Thai Dong 1991; Jamieson 1993; Brocheux 1995; Tran Dinh Huou 1996; Vo Tuan Huy 1996; Son Nam 1999).[5] Others also point to the relatively high status of women compared to other Confucian societies in East Asia. According to historians, this feature can be traced back to the seventeenth century (Yu 1990).

Moreover, there are reports and studies from other parts of the country suggesting that two contrasting phenomena are taking place at the same time: on the one hand, the family is regaining its importance; and on the other hand, the family is deteriorating. For instance, reports from major cities outside the Mekong Delta region show how family ties are disappearing with rapid economic development. One journalist in Hanoi states that "many urban middle- and upper- class parents are worried about [a new] social phenomenon: the rebellion of their children", which has taken the form of high-speed, nocturnal motorcycle races. Some attribute this phenomenon to the shortage of jobs and the city's lack of recreational facilities, while others say it is a by-product of sudden wealth after decades of war and socialism (Hierbert 1996).[6] In contrast to these reports from big cities, others argue that the household is once again regaining its position as the centre of people's lives in post-socialist Vietnam with the reform in which the household has become the primary unit of economic activities (Hy Van Luong 1993*b*; Dao The Tuan 1995).[7]

Putting aside the question of which argument is correct, one can say that these two contradictory sets of reports and studies both seem to demonstrate increasing interest in the family and stress its importance in contemporary Vietnamese society. For example, in the mid-1990s, a decade after the launch of *doi moi*, when the roles of social systems based on socialism were vanishing and diminishing, not only the significance of the family as a basic social unit but its social responsibilities in the development of nation were recognized and emphasized (Werner 2009).[8] Under the situation where the social educational system founded on socialism is declining, the family has resumed its role as an educator of citizens. The basis of a good society, these studies say, is good families, and children must be socialized in good family relationships, which will lead to the development of the whole nation (Dang Thanh Le 1996; Hong Ha 1994; Le Ngoc Lan 1994; Le Thi 1995; Le Ngoc Van 1996; Luong Thi Thuan 1998; Nguyen Khanh 1995; Nguyen Thi Khoa 1994; Tran Tuan Lo 1998; Vo Thi Cuc 1997).[9]

However, as Le Ngoc Van argues, the recognition of the family does not necessarily mean that it is resuming its "traditional" form (Le Ngoc Van 1996). Rather, it is seeking a different form with new functions and responsibility in society.[10]

THE FAMILY IN THE RURAL MEKONG DELTA

It is not easy to give a general picture of the family in the rural Mekong Delta. It tends to adjust very flexibly to situations, and changes quite fluidly. However, there are some common characteristics that most families share. In this section, I introduce the basic family structures and forms, and discuss how they are organized in reality.

The word "family" (*gia dinh*) in Vietnamese is not strict. While it usually refers to a household consisting of a father, a mother, and their children, in some cases, it may also encompass a larger group of parents, children, children-in-law and grandchildren, even if they do not live together. Therefore, "household" and "family" do not always mean the same group of people.[11] Most households in the Long Tuyen

Village are nuclear, consisting of parents (*cha me*) and their unmarried children (*con*), which concurs with some quantitative sociological studies conducted in the area (e.g. Hirschman and Vu Manh Loi 1996).[12] Children, usually upon marriage, start living independently from their parents, although some stay with them up to three years after marriage. The youngest son (*con uc*) is an exception and he is supposed to bring his wife to his natal home, live with his parents, and take care of them when they are old, constituting an extended household.[13]

The number of children varies from family to family. One big determinant is the age of the parents suggesting changes over time: those over sixty often have ten or more children; many younger generations in their thirties or forties have four to five children. The Vietnamese government runs a family planning programme, and encourages each family to have only two children, but the programme has not really penetrated the lives of the farmers in rural areas of the Delta. (A new law on marriage and family was adopted in 2000, and the policy on family planning and large families has become more permissive since 2003 (Scornet 2009).) However, the government still encourages two-child families (see, for instance, *Viet Nam News*, 30 July 2013), and there are reports of women being forced to abandon their children by their bosses in state-run organizations (Leshkowich 2012). According to some residents, there are only a few couples in the hamlet of Binh Thuong B who follow the policy and have received medical treatment for birth control.[14] The exact number of villagers who actually adhere to the birth control programme is not known. However, only one woman out of those with whom I discussed the matter declared that she and her husband used the programme. Fourth Sister explained to me that a health worker has come to the village and explained the programme to each family, but not many people have followed it.[15]

The age of marriage (*ket hon*) also varies. I often heard city-dwellers say "people marry early in the rural area, around fifteen for women and eighteen for men, while in the city, the average age is twenty-four for women and twenty-seven for men." However, in the villages where I visited, people do not marry as early as people in the city believe. Most of the men and women marry after they turn twenty, and it is common for women to marry between twenty-one and twenty-five, and for men between twenty-four and twenty-eight, though there are many cases in which people marry later. Today, most marriages are "love marriages", in which the couple met at school, at the market, or at wedding parties of friends or relatives. The couple get permission from the man's and the woman's parents, who then arrange the engagement and wedding ceremonies. There are also many cases where the parents of the couple knew each other and arranged the marriage of their children. Although much less often than in the past, arranged marriages by matchmakers are still practised. Some of the matchmakers are "professionals" who live in the village or in surrounding areas, and others are relatives or acquaintances familiar with people of the area. In the past, according to elderly villagers, marriages arranged by matchmakers were more common, or marriages were decided by parents, and the couple themselves had little say. One woman born in the 1930s recalls that she did not even meet her future husband until the day of their wedding. Nowadays, even in arranged marriages, young couples can participate in the decision-making process, and spend some time together before the day of the marriage in order to get to know each other. However, some single young women, like one twenty-two-year-old woman working in a textile company, confess that they would prefer to have their parents choose their future husband, saying that "the parents have more experience".[16]

Contrary to a study by Luong Hong Quang (1997) on a village in another province in the Delta where a series of rituals was performed for marriages during the 1980s and the 1990s, in the region of Long Tuyen Village, auspicious consultation, engagement and the wedding itself were the only marriage ceremonies. (It is not clear if other ceremonies and rituals were performed in this village in the past, and if they were, when and how they were abolished.) Upon marriage, the family of the bridegroom pays a bride price to the bride's family. The bride price is usually paid in cash or in some cases, gold. Brides customarily do not take dowries with them, but in cases where they do not receive land from their parents because they are leaving their natal village to live in their husbands' villages, brides may be given jewellery or gold by their parents to take with them. The amount of the bride price and dowry vary greatly, depending mostly on the economic condition of the families. The two families discuss these amounts before the rituals.

People often say, "it is a Vietnamese tradition that husbands stay in their natal villages and receive wives who follow their husbands to live in their home village." However, this seems to be only an ideal, and in practice, the decision about residence is quite flexible. Although the majority follows the "traditional way" (*truyen thong*), there are also many cases in which the husband lives in the wife's village, near her parents. One of the major considerations for the couple is the availability of land for agriculture as well as for living. Sometimes, a couple lives in the wife's natal village, because the size of the land she received from her parents is larger than the land the husband received from his parents. Another common factor that determines where the couple lives after marriage is relationships with in-laws. One couple, for some time after their marriage, lived with the husband's parents, but since the relationship between the wife and the mother-in-law (*me chong*) was not good, they decided to move to the wife's village, where they could get some land and live independently.

Upon marriage, children receive land (*dat*) from their father (and mother). "Traditionally", as many farmers explain, in the Mekong Delta region, parents divide their land equally among their children, both sons (*con trai*) and daughters (*con gai*).[17] In practice, however, there are many variations in how land is inherited from one generation to the next. For example, in my host family, Second Brother owns three thousand square meters of land that he got from Uncle Bay and Aunt Tam, while Third Brother has only one thousand. The reason for the difference is not clearly explained by the brothers or the parents, but the piece of land to be inherited often depends on the situation at the time of marriage, such as how much land the parents have at that time. It is not necessarily birth order that determines the relative land distribution. Older children may not receive the largest piece of land. In reality people sometimes sell and buy land after marriage, and not everybody remembers exactly how much land they got from their parents upon marriage. This makes it difficult to compare the size of inherited parcels of land.[18]

It seems slightly more common for men to inherit land from their parents than for women. However, this is not a strict rule, and whether daughters inherit land or not also depends on the family and also on each marriage. For example, while Fourth Sister did not inherit any land from Uncle Bay and Aunt Tam, Fifth Sister did. This happened because Fifth Sister stayed in her native village and her husband came to live with her from another place. Fourth Sister now lives in the same hamlet as her parents, but the land she and her husband toil was not inherited from the parents. She lived in her husband's native village for four years after marriage, but because the land her husband received from his parents was not sufficient, they bought new land in this hamlet and came back. The couple still retains the land in the husband's village, about 5 kilometres away. This rule of land distribution applies to men as well: if a man goes to live in his wife's village, he may not receive any land from his parents.

As in the case of Fourth Sister, if a woman leaves her native village upon marriage and does not receive land from her parents, it is unlikely that she will get any land from them later on. In one family in a nearby village, I met a divorced woman who ran a small grocery shop in front of her parents' house. There she sold instant noodles, oil, soap, snacks and other daily goods to earn her living. She opened the shop since she did not receive any land from her father because, she first explains, she was a daughter and in her family, only sons got land. It became clear through our conversation that when she was married, she lived in her ex-husband's village so she did not inherit any land, while her brothers, who stayed in the village, did. After she got divorced, she came back, but since she did not have any land here, she decided to run the shop. Her shop is small, and she finds it difficult to make enough money to live on, but it remains her only source of income.

However, some daughters get land from the parents even if they leave their natal village upon marriage. A male farmer in another village says that although he will divide his land among his sons, he will keep some for his daughters in case they will need it even after they marry and leave their native village. Although it remains to be seen how he will actually divide his land among his children, at least he intends to give part of it to his daughters even if she leaves the village. If both the husband and wife receive land from their respective parents, they work both areas if they are not too far away from each other.

Since married children receive land from their parents, they usually reside in the parental village of either the husband or the wife. It is quite common for both families to live close to each other and for the children to live in the same hamlet or village as both sets of parents. It is also common for them to live in neighbouring villages. In relatively rare cases, people marry someone from other provinces in the Mekong Delta, and there are also people who move to cities upon marriage. In Binh Thuong B Hamlet, there are not many people whose children or siblings lived in Can Tho City or Ho Chi Minh City. However, in other villages in the surrounding area, I met a few people whose children went to live in Ho Chi Minh City after marriage. Those who live in the city often have relatives there with whom they can live and who can help them get jobs. People seldom move to the city in search of jobs or opportunities unless they have connections there, especially family and kin relations.

Married couples, except for the youngest son and his wife who stay with his parents, usually build their own houses (*nha*) with their own money on land they receive from their parents. Since young couples may not have enough money to build a house at first, some couples choose to live in their parent's house for the first few years. During this period, they cultivate the land that they received and live on a separate income from the parents. After having saved enough money, they build their own house and start an independent life, not only financially but also physically. Some people, especially women, confess that the first few years when they lived with their parents-in-law (*cha me chong*) were difficult, and life became easier after they started a separate life. Although a couple may build a house close to the parents' house, there seems to be a big difference between living with the parents and living independently nearby. Many couples prefer having an independent life.

Married children who reside in the same village or hamlet as their parents visit them very frequently. In the family of Uncle Bay and Aunt Tam, some children come every day during the day or in the evening, after they have had supper and finished work and before they go to bed. However, they seldom come to share a meal except on special occasions. Each household usually takes meals separately. People list a variety of reasons for visiting their parents, but some of the major reasons for everyday visits are "to help parents when they need help", "to see how parents are doing, and to make sure that they are all right", "to deliver some of the fruit we picked for our parents to eat", "to talk about and consult on agriculture and get opinions from the parents", and "to meet and talk with siblings (*anh chi em*)". For children who live in neighbouring villages, visits to their parents' home are much less frequent. Commonly they come once every week or two weeks. These children sometimes visit at night or on Sundays, especially if they have work outside of the agricultural sector. However, the frequency of visits varies greatly depending on each person's situation and relationship with the family. Third Sister-in-Law explained to me that she goes only once in several months to visit her parents in a neighbouring village about one hour's walk from her house because she is too busy with farm work and she wants to make the most of her time. In her case, since her husband works as a teacher, she bears the responsibility for most agricultural activities at home and finds it hard to spare any time for visiting her parents. Although there may be other reasons such as the nature of the relationship with her parents, distance and time are the reasons she gave for not visiting them very often. Moreover, she often visits her parents-in-law, who live close by, in order to help them, so visiting her own parents in addition is rather difficult for her. A few people, who live in other provinces or in Ho Chi Minh City, only return home to their parents a few times a year, on the Lunar New Year (*Tet*) and a major death anniversary (*dam gio*), or on special occasions such as weddings of their siblings. These people often think that returning home takes too much time, and it is too expensive to take the bus, so they only visit the village on special occasions. The New Year is when, in most families, many children return home from far away places, and the largest number of family members get together.[19]

Uncle Bay tells me that he feels very happy when his grown-up children gather at home, despite the difficult lives some of them have. When children return home, common conversations concern agriculture and everyday life, especially the quality of agricultural products, their selling prices, or the price of needed fertilizer or equipment. They often talk about money, living conditions and agricultural expenses, which I will discuss more extensively in a later chapter. Other topics include the education of grandchildren, the sickness of relatives or neighbours, or sometimes the government's agricultural development plans and policies in general. Although people say they seldom talk about politics, these political issues are also raised in their daily conversations.

While children often visit their parents' home, parents, too, visit their children's homes, though less frequently. Aunt Tam sometimes brings food to one of the daughters' homes after lunch. In the afternoons, when there is little work to do in the garden or field, Uncle Bay gets dressed up to go out and visit his sons who lives in neighbouring villages. While there are frequent visits between parents and married children who live nearby, visits between siblings occur much less frequently. They usually visit each other only when they have some business to conduct, such as working together in the parents' rice field; going to the market together to sell products; or borrowing some agricultural equipment. However, this does not mean that they do not interact as frequently, since they usually meet each other at their parents' house. In other words, the parents' home, or the children's natal home, is the gathering place for all members of the family, even after they get married and live separately.

KINSHIP

In a study on kinship in a village in North Vietnam, Miyazawa (1999) introduces the patrilineal descent group called *dong ho* (also called *toc*), and a group of affinals called *ngoai toc*. The author argues that although there are different forms of these groups in different villages, for most people *dong ho* is an especially important notion, and everyone except infants and babies knows which *dong ho* they belong to. According to Miyazawa, *dong ho* is a group that includes ancestors, and most people in the village can trace their roots back somewhere between the third and fifth generations. While most genealogies were lost during the historical upheavals from 1945 onward, especially after the land reform in 1955, in the village that he studied, some families retain a complete genealogy of their *dong ho*. Whether people preserve a complete genealogy today or not, Miyazawa suggests that genealogy existed in each family in North Vietnam until quite recently.[20]

In contrast, in an ethnographic work on the Mekong Delta published in 1964, Hickey introduces a different view of kinship. He recognizes the existence of a patrilineal descent line (he uses the word *toc* instead of *dong ho*). However, unlike the descent lines in northern and central Vietnam, where the male ancestor is often in the fifth ascending generation, the common ancestor is in the third generation in the rural Delta. While the patrilineal head is traditionally selected according to age priority in the north, the head in the south is "selected by a council of adult male and female members of the family" (1964, p. 82). According to Hickey, the head "maintains family tombs, and should the family keep a genealogy book, the [head] is charged with making the proper entries. Well-to-do families attempt to conform to these prescriptions, but for most village families they represent only the ideal" (ibid.). Only a few genealogy books are found in the village according to Hickey, and most Delta families do not keep, and have not kept, their genealogies.[21]

In Long Tuyen Village, kinship is recognized, both on the father's and the mother's side. Structurally, it is a patrilineal descent system, in which the family line is traced through the father, and most formal rituals take place on the father's side. Upon marriage, a woman is considered to marry into the man's family, and their children belong to the father's family. However, as in the case of the Kinh in other regions of Vietnam, as well as many other patrilineal societies in the world, women do not change their last name when they married, and only children get the husband's last name. For most of the families in this village, ancestors (*to tien*) are the third ascending generation, that is, the parents of one's father. Few families can trace generations higher than the third. Ancestors beyond grandparents are usually not remembered or recognized by the villagers, who say, "we worship as our ancestors only those whom we have met. Beyond our grandparents, we have never met, so they are forgotten." Both men (father's father) and women (father's mother) are recognized as ancestors. Few families have a written genealogy (*gia pha*), and when asked about it, villagers often do not have any idea what it looks like and what it is about. As one person from Can Tho City explained to me, "in the north, people have written genealogies, but very few in the south keep them."[22]

In the family of Uncle Bay and Aunt Tam, kinship (here, I use the word "kinship" to refer to a larger group of relatives, including affinals, and not only the extended family of the father and the mother, their children and children-in-law, and their grandchildren) does not seem to play a big role in their everyday life.[23] However, I observed that kinship entails some formal and ritual responsibilities. Kin people (*ba con*) get together for the New Year, death anniversaries, funerals, and weddings. On most of these occasions, one can see villagers getting dressed up and visiting their relatives' houses. In rituals, both agnates and affinals play roles, and there is not much distinction between the two. For instance, on death anniversaries, both groups of relatives burn incense, kowtow and pray in front of the ancestral alter, and have a banquet together afterward.[24]

Apart from these rituals and formal occasions, relationships between relatives are quite weak in the family of Uncle Bay and Aunt Tam. For instance, if Aunt Tam meets her sister-in-law or her niece on the street on the way to the market in the morning, she might stop and greet them and chat briefly, but would rarely talk for a long time. Nor do they usually visit each other's houses informally. Even when Aunt Tam was sick in bed, all the children gathered at home, but few relatives paid visits. However, when Aunt Tam's sister was hospitalized with a serious illness she and other relatives visited her to inquire after the health of the sick and offer something, usually food like skim milk and sugar. This shows that the seriousness of the illness plays a part, too. Many adults say that they visit their relatives, such as uncles and aunts, cousins, or affinals, only about twice a year. People have a close relationship with their grandparents (*ong ba*), visiting them quite regularly in childhood.

THE *TET* CELEBRATION

The Lunar New Year is the time of year when family ties are most visible. In this festive season, the ties are recognized and played out in a ritualistic manner that differs in many ways from the everyday interactions.

The Lunar New Year, or *Tet*, generally falls between mid-January and mid-February. The preparation for *Tet* starts about a week before the date, when people start to clean and decorate their houses in order to welcome the New Year. For instance, they take off the old short lace curtains on top of wooden windows and put new ones that are often bright yellow or pink. People decorate their houses with flowers. Around *Tet*, yellow plum flowers blossom in the front gardens of the village houses, usually close to the altars for the God of Heaven (*ong thien*).[25]

The most ornate decoration is found on the ancestor altar, where family members of each house prepare offerings. *Tet* is a time of year when the ancestors return to the house, and preparing offerings for them is an important component of the celebration. One could say that *Tet* is an occasion when both the living and the dead celebrate together, and the living prepare to receive their ancestors. Walking in the village a few days before *Tet*, one can see many villagers polishing gold-painted plates and ornaments especially designed for making offerings in their front yards. The offerings on *Tet* are special, consisting of oranges, a watermelon, bananas and other fruit as well as some cakes or cookies. Watermelon is a fruit for *Tet* and before the New Year, large watermelons are often seen piled up to be sold in the market as well as on the street. A special red piece of paper is pasted on the watermelon which is placed in the middle of the altar. However, the less wealthy, who do not own these items, only place pictures of the deceased on the altar.

A few days before *Tet*, people stop their farm work and start to enjoy the holiday with their family, and two days before *Tet*, people are already in a celebratory mood. Married children gather at their parents' house and start having a feast. Men drink beer and wives cook special food, such as duck and potato curry, steamed pork, roast chicken and vegetable and sausage salad. The family eats on the front porch, instead of in the back room next to the kitchen, where they take their everyday meals. Uncle Bay and Aunt Tam look very happy surrounded by their children, who now live in separate houses. Grandchildren, including those working or studying in the city, also visit the house of their grandparents. In my host family's house, a granddaughter who is a student at the teacher's college in Can Tho comes to help Aunt Tam with the cooking. The atmosphere becomes cheerful and festive.

The day before *Tet* people seem busy making final preparations for the New Year, such as shopping for food. Brothers get together at someone's house and go out with one another to run errands. In the evening, after supper, the sisters of Uncle Bay and their children visit him and Aunt Tam. They are welcomed in the front guest room (which is also used as a bedroom), where the ancestor altar is placed and where there are a table and chairs for guests. The guests are offered tea and sweets and they chat with the couple for over an hour. After the aunts and cousins leave, the family members watch TV and chat until midnight. Since they usually go to bed around nine or ten in the evening, staying up until midnight is a special event. At midnight, they can hear the fireworks in Can Tho City, which they can watch on TV as well. After the fireworks is over and it is quiet again, the family members go to bed.

On the morning of *Tet,* family members get up around six, about one hour later than usual. Since the *Tet* is the first day of a new beginning, many people, especially women, wear new clothes, such as newly tailored blouses. In the morning, they eat thin crackers (*banh trang*), sweet rice cake (*banh nep*) and dried fruit (*muc*), which are special foods for the New Year, and drink tea. On *Tet,* the village market is closed, so women do not go there. Instead, men go to the village centre where they gather at the small open cafes near the market and drink coffee and tea. However, women are not excluded from the scene and a few of them have coffee with the men or by themselves. I also went to one of the coffee shops with Fifth Sister who took me there to have breakfast noodles. One reason why few village women are found in these morning cafes is that most are busy cooking at home on the morning of *Tet*. For most men, however, *Tet* is a time of enjoyment. As one walks in the village in the morning, one encounters groups of men watching cockfights. Although cockfighting is not exclusively a game for *Tet,* it is a particularly popular type of entertainment on the New Year. Around ten to twenty men gather at the corners of the village path and watch the birds fight. The only participants are men; there are no women to be seen. Fifth Sister and I passed by quickly and did not stop to watch.

The first day of *Tet* is a day for the whole family. At the house of Uncle Bay and Aunt Tam, sons and daughters and grandchildren visit throughout the day, spending between one to two hours. Because of the many visitors, houses are filled with the chatter of voices and laughter. Adults eat and talk, while children who are cousins play in the house and outside in the yard. Men also drink beer and rice wine. Children receive money from their grandparents and uncles and aunts. Although the amount they get varies, each adult usually gives about ten thousand dongs to each child. (In the city, a special small red envelope is often used to give money to children, but I never saw such an envelope in Binh Thuong B Hamlet. Usually, adults gather the grandchildren, nephews and nieces at the back of the house and give them money there.) After visiting the parents' house, married siblings visit each other's houses. In particular, they visit the houses of siblings who live outside of the village, because they can rarely visit them at other times. This is a special visit for *Tet*.

In general, the men eat and drink, while the women cook and eat. Daughters-in-law also help Aunt Tam cook and entertain the men. It is generally considered to be the daughter-in-law's (*con dau*) responsibility to help her mother-in-law with cooking. Often women and men eat separately: men have a feast in the front guest room, while women drink tea and eat sweets in the back room near the kitchen. The front guest room is a social and formal sphere, and the back room is more intimate and casual. During *Tet*, the division of labour between genders is especially visible: women do a lot of cooking together, while men spend much time eating and drinking together, and exchanging information. There is a slight difference between men and women in what they talk about when they get together. Men are more engaged in conversations about local politics and the year's economic conditions, while women mostly talk about market prices of commodities and daily foods they purchase.

However, this rule is not strict, and in some cases, women and men eat together in the same room, though often at different tables. Sometimes women also join the men's conversations in the front room casually, sitting on the wooden beds beside the table where the men are eating and drinking. The main table is usually considered the most formal place to greet guests, and the beds beside it are a more casual and informal place. For instance, when family members gather in the front room to watch TV, they sit on the beds instead of at the table. If a guest sits on the bed, he/she is often urged to sit at the table. Some men also sit on the bed instead of at the table. In some families like Seventh Brother's, women are not the only people who cook; men also help out. This seems especially common among young couples in their twenties and thirties.

The meal for *Tet* is not only shared by the family members, but is also offered to the ancestors as during the time of *Tet* they are considered to return to the house. At each meal, before the family members eat, all of the food, each dish along with some rice, is placed on the table in front of the ancestor altar. Along with the food, four sets of empty rice bowls and pairs of chopsticks are placed as if people were about to sit and eat. Uncle Bay burns incense sticks and kowtows in front of the altar. Only after this ritual, do people share the meal.

On the second day of *Tet*, men and women do laundry in the river as they do on ordinary mornings. However people still refrain from farm work. The second day is spent visiting relatives. Brothers gather at the house of Uncle Bay and Aunt Tam around eight in the morning, and then go together to visit the houses of their uncles and aunts. Nephews and nieces come to greet Uncle Bay and Aunt Tam. On this day affinal relatives also visit each other's houses. For example, Eighth Brother comes with his wife and her parents. Siblings of Uncle Bay and Aunt Tam who live in the same village visit, bringing their own children and grandchildren, too. Relatives share a meal and inquire about each other's health, about their family members and also talk about agriculture and the market. Since relatives do not get together very often, *Tet* is an opportunity for them to meet formally, and the holiday plays a ritualistic role of strengthening the ties among them. By cooking and drinking together, the relatives re-recognize and re-affirm their ties with one another.

The second day of *Tet* is a particularly good time to observe and experience the hierarchies that exist between family members as many members of the family and relatives get together. For instance, a teenage grandson of Uncle Bay and Aunt Tam talks a lot when he is alone with me, but when his uncle (*chu*) Youngest Brother is with us, he rarely speaks. Youngest Brother, who usually makes tea for me, orders the grandson to bring tea for me or to clean the table, and the teenage boy obeys.

The third day of *Tet* is reserved for friends. Friends of Uncle Bay and Aunt Tam, and also of the Brothers and Sisters, come to greet the family, arriving from the same or neighbouring villages or from Can Tho City. These visits by friends are rather brief, about one hour, compared to the visits of family members and relatives who spend a couple of hours or more together. Also, not as much food is offered to friends. The family sometimes provides the friends with beer and snacks or tea and sweets but not the chicken curry and other special meals for *Tet*. Friends often inquire about each other's health, since they meet rarely, often for the first time since last year's *Tet*. Conversations are similar to those between family members or between relatives, but may not be as intimate. When the friends are from the city, rather than talking about the local economy or politics, they sometimes engage in conversations about urban life, such as motorbikes and other technologies. Also, the third day of *Tet* is a day to visit teachers who receive special respect in Vietnamese society. Some Brothers and Sisters go to visit their former teachers who live in the village.

On the third day, which is quieter than the first two days of *Tet*, the pace of everyday life begins to resume. For example, in the morning, the grandson who is a high school student waters the fruit orchard, as he always does. Women do not spend as much time cooking special meals, and men do not drink as much alcohol. No cockfighting is seen in the village. When there are no visitors, Uncle Bay starts working on the farm or taking care of his agricultural tools.

The fourth day of *Tet* is the last. More precisely, *Tet* ends on the morning of that day. In the early morning hours, Youngest Brother and the son of Second Brother, the high school student staying at Father Khan's house at night, begin preparing a duck for meal. After it is plucked, cleaned and boiled, Uncle Bay places a small table in the front yard of the house. He puts the whole boiled duck on the table, and slices of watermelon, some sweet cake, empty rice bowls and chopsticks besides it. Then he burns incense sticks and stands them on the table. Next to the table, Uncle Bay places a small boat made of wood and paper. After burning incense and praying, he puts the duck, sweet cake and watermelon into the small boat. He takes the boat to the narrow arroyo in front of the house, wades into the water and floats the boat, then pushes it until it floats away. Thus, the spirits of the ancestors are sent back to heaven with food offerings.

In the afternoon, some relatives and friends still pay brief visits, the final *Tet* guests of this year. Fourth Sister comes to the house in the afternoon, and tells me, "*Tet* is over now."

THE DEATH ANNIVERSARY

A death anniversary (*dam gio*) is another occasion when ties between family members and relatives are played out ritually. Same as ancestor worship, death anniversaries are celebrated for up to the third generation: in other words, for deceased parents and grandparents. There is one death anniversary a year for each deceased person. The anniversaries are often celebrated at the house of the youngest son of the family who has inherited the land and house from the parents. However, not all anniversaries are held there. Rather, the responsibility for holding the ritual is shared among the children and grandchildren. For instance, at the house of Uncle Bay, one or two anniversaries are held each year, and other anniversaries are held at the houses of his siblings.

There are differences between the death anniversary held one year after the death of the person and those celebrated in subsequent years. Until one year after the death, the soul of the person is thought to still exist in the real world. Therefore, the anniversary held at the end of the year is a highly religious ritual to send the soul off to heaven, and Buddhist monks are usually called to perform it. I never had a chance to attend a one-year death anniversary in the village, but had a chance to observe it in Can Tho City. There several monks are called from a family temple, and they recite sutras. The sons of the deceased wear white long headbands and the daughters wear white scarves on their heads, as white symbolizes mourning. After the recitation of sutras, each child has his or her headbands or scarves removed by a monk, which enable them to part from the soul of the deceased. After this ritual, a new ancestor altar is placed in the house, a picture of the deceased is put on top of it, and incense is burnt. Those attending the ritual, mostly relatives, then share a vegetarian meal specially prepared for the occasion.

For anniversaries held two years after the death and beyond, the religious aspect is diminished. In death anniversaries I observed at Uncle Bay's house, no monk was called and there was no recitation of sutras. The anniversary starts in the morning, around eight o'clock, when the relatives attending the ritual start to gather. Those who attend are mostly elderly people: siblings of Uncle Bay and Aunt Tam, and also affinal relatives such as parents of a daughter-in-law or a son-in-law of the father and the mother. The attendants are dressed formally, women wearing traditional blouses and men wearing traditional suits. Nephews and nieces do not attend, so it is the generation of Uncle Bay and Aunt Tam that gathers for the occasion. Sons and daughters of the father and the mother also attend, but more as organizers rather than attendees. The anniversary starts with the ritual burning of incense. Uncle Bay fills a glass with uncooked rice, and puts an incense stick in it. He places the glass on a table at the front porch, on which food dishes are placed. He then burns the incense, prays and kowtows with his hands together, moving them up and down in front of him. Then other attendees repeat the prayer and kowtows, one by one.

After this ritual, all attendees share a meal. The dishes are somewhat similar to those shared on the occasion of *Tet*, such as duck stew, chicken curry and radish salad. Also, some special sweet cakes, called *banh tet*, *banh nep* and other *banh* (cake in general), are offered. Men and women eat at separate tables as on *Tet*: men eat on the front porch and women eat in the guest room. Brothers and Sisters do not join the tables. Instead, they help Aunt Tam prepare the dishes in the kitchen and entertain the guests by, for example, offering them drinks. After the meal, some people come to the back room, and continue the conversations more casually. There, Brothers and Sisters eat the food after the guests are finished with the feast. Since a lot of food is prepared and not all of it is consumed, some women take the leftovers home in plastic bags. The anniversary ends around eleven in the morning. While the anniversary held one year after a death has a highly religious connotation and is held particularly for the dead, subsequent anniversaries are more of a custom, and are held for the relatives to get together and share the occasion.

FAMILY PROBLEMS

While celebrations such as *Tet* and death anniversaries reveal the strengthening of family ties, some families experience problems, too. Divorce is not uncommon in the village of Long Tuyen. For example, Second Brother was divorced after an arranged marriage to a woman from the same village, but a different hamlet. They got divorced because they had financial problems and different ideas about money. After they came into conflict, Second Brother's wife left him to raise their three children on his own. He remarried once, but that marriage also failed, and he has since stayed single.[26] Seventh Brother was also divorced in the past. He used to work as a police officer in Can Tho City, and was married to another officer. According to Uncle Bay, Seventh Brother worked in the export-import department, and many people, including women, offered him special invitations and treats probably to get his favours because he worked in an influential department. His wife became jealous of the special treatment he received from other women, and they got divorced.[27] Seventh Brother later remarried his current wife, but then was dismissed from the police force, because, Uncle Bay claims, they found his history of divorce and remarriage unacceptable. Seventh Brother earns his living as a farmer and his wife is a schoolteacher.

Reasons for divorce vary but most commonly heard is that the couple do not get along with each other. One woman says, "I got divorced. There was no particular reason, but the relationship was just not suitable." Divorced people often say their marriage did not work because they were not compatible. Many, though not all, of these people had arranged marriages, and did not know each other before marrying.[28] However, love marriages do not always work, either. Another common reason for divorce is that the newly married couple does not get along with their families-in-law. A twenty-two-year-old woman got married three years ago when she was nineteen. She and her ex-husband had met and decided to marry, but the husband's parents did not agree to their marriage. So they married without permission from his parents, but then went to live with them. The woman thinks the marriage did not work because it was opposed by the parents-in-law whom they lived with.[29]

We can see from such a story that marriage is not only a matter of the couple who are marrying, but also of the two families who are involved. A divorce that results from a bad relationship between husband and wife can also cause serious conflicts between families. Here is a story of one woman as told by her mother. A matchmaker had arranged the marriage for the daughter. The father had died, and the mother was worried about her daughter's future, so she asked the matchmaker to arrange a marriage for her. However, the daughter could not stand her ex-husband and his family. The mother blames the ex-husband for not loving his wife, and abusing her. Now, after her divorce, the daughter has been working in Ho Chi Minh City as a maid. She went there in order to avoid the husband and his family because she is angry with them and afraid of remarrying. The mother complains that the ex-husband accuses her daughter, saying "she stole gold in order to ran away", which the mother says is not true. The mother and the ex-husband's family still quarrel with each other.

Especially when the cause of divorce is the relationship between the new daughter-in-law and the family-in-law, more serious conflicts can develop between the two families. For example, in one case, a newly married wife ran away three months after the marriage. She and her ex-husband had known each other before getting married, and lived with the husband's family in another village after marriage.[30] However, she says, the husband and his family treated her badly. She even tried to commit suicide because living with the in-laws was so difficult. Finally she ran away and has returned to her natal family and lives there. The two families are still in conflict and quarrel with each other and they have brought the case to the People's Committee of the village. If the village committee cannot solve the conflict, they are prepared to bring it to the court in town.

In most divorces, children stay with their mother. As one woman says, "Vietnamese woman always take their children." The case of Second Brother is a rare one because his ex-wife left him to raise the children. After a divorce, some men help their ex-wives raise the children by sending money to their families. Fathers are expected to contribute to the family, especially for raising children, even after divorce. However, many women complain that their ex-husbands do not support them at all after divorce. They blame their ex-husbands for being irresponsible fathers who do not fulfill their obligations toward their own children. I met about twelve divorced women, but know of only one case of an ex-husband continuing to take care of the children, by regularly sending some money, especially for education.

There are gender differences with respect to remarriage after divorce. It is more common for men to remarry than women.[31] It is not unusual for men to remain single after their wives die, but after divorce, most men remarry some years later. One divorced woman told me that her ex-husband remarried five years after they divorced. Because they live in the same village and their parents know each other, it was not hard to learn about her ex-husband's new marriage due to news and gossip. In fact, many divorced women know that their ex-husbands have remarried. Second Brother is one of the few men to remain single after divorce. However, he remarried once after parting with his first wife, too.

There are mainly two reasons why divorced women rarely remarry. One is that it is more difficult for women to get remarried. Women who have already been married are considered undesirable because they are commonly thought of as "second-hand" or "used", and therefore not suitable as new wives. In addition, divorced women are not thought to make good wives. Because of such ideas, a divorced woman faces more obstacles to remarriage. Even if she finds someone eager to marry her, she is more likely to be opposed by the relatives of the prospective husband, who may not welcome a previously married woman.

Another reason is that many divorced women have had such bad experiences in marriage that they do not wish to marry again. For example, the woman who went to Ho Chi Minh City to avoid her ex-husband has become so afraid of marriage that she does not plan to marry again. Also, a thirty-eight-year-old woman stayed single for fourteen years after her divorce and lived with her own mother. She says, "I did not want to get married again. I wanted to live with my mother." Since in many marriages, wives leave their natal home and follow the husband to his village, marriage often means a woman must part with her native village where she has spent all of her life, and with the family she has always lived with. Also, because many couples live with the parents of the husband for some time after their marriage, even if the husband is not the youngest son, for many wives, marriage means entering a totally new environment. Many women comment that they felt very lonely after getting married and going to unknown villages and living with strangers. When a woman has had bad experiences in this new environment, it seems natural that she would want to return to her natal home and not enter another strange family again.

Since most divorced women do not remarry, and it is relatively rare that their ex-husbands support the family and help raise the children, most divorced women raise their children by themselves. The thirty-eight-year-old woman had one son when she was divorced, whom she took back to the village. Her family asked the ex-husband to contribute money to help raise his son, but he has never helped in fourteen years. So the woman raised the son by herself. She has four thousand square metres of land, which she received from her mother. She says, "My mother and I work on the farm and do not hire other people to work for us. It is rather difficult with only women working on our farm, but we can manage somehow. When there is heavy work that requires men's labor, we ask for help. My brother lives in the same hamlet, so he can help us when needed."

Staying single and raising children on their own often means a difficult life for many women. Failed marriages put women in a position where they cannot expect much more from life. However, many women have chosen to live this way rather than endure difficult marriages. It is better, they think, to return to their native homes and live on their own than to live in conflict with husbands and families-in-law. Despite the difficulties, these women have managed to live by themselves and raise their children alone. They have chosen to be on their own rather than to depend on someone else and endure an unhappy life.

WAR AND THE FAMILY

In the last section of this chapter, I describe some of the war stories and experiences villagers shared with me, because the war has had a significant impact on the lives of many families in the village of Long

Tuyen as well as other villages. The experiences and memories of the war vary greatly depending on the individual, but many saw their family life affected in one way or another.[32]

When talking about their lives, farmers of Long Tuyen Village often refer to life in the past. One part of the past that some villagers, especially older generations, often like to talk about is the war period. In the villagers' perception, the war started in the area in 1954. As one villager says, "There might have been a war in the country before 1954, but we did not know. It was after 1954 that the war started in this area." The area around Can Tho City saw severe battles between the Communist forces and the US, and the villagers of Long Tuyen experienced the war in a variety of ways. Some supported the old regime (supported by the US), while others fought for the Communists, or the new regime.

Some villagers recall the time of war with nostalgia. Uncle Bay proudly says,

> During the war, I always carried weapons, and walked around the area in the bushes to support the soldiers of the new regime. When I was young, before I got married, I did not work in my parents' farm very much, because I was busy supporting the soldiers. At that time, most of the villagers here contributed to the war in some ways. Many people contributed by giving something, such as food, to the soldiers, who fought in the area.

He likes to relate how he dug shelters in the village, how he hid behind the bushes and attacked the enemies, and how he always walked around carrying weapons on his shoulders. In fact, his memory of his young adulthood seems to be full of exciting wartime experiences. Uncle Bay also recalls with pride that many high ranking officials, such as Le Duan, came to this area during the war. When talking about the war, Uncle Bay seldom mentions his family, which shows a striking contrast with his wife.

In fact, there are some gender differences in how the war is perceived, mainly stemming from the different experiences men and women had during that time. While Uncle Bay's memories of the war are filled with courage and bravery, Aunt Tam remembers it as a time of hardships.[33] For her, life before the end of the war in 1975 was difficult, and she does not seem to like to recall that time or talk much about it. When I interviewed her about her life history, I tried to get her to tell her story during the war period, but she simply replied, "It was hard, but now I forgot all the past." This brief comment of hers contrasts vividly with Uncle Bay's stories about his experiences in the war that he liked to tell me all the time.

For Aunt Tam it was a struggle to protect her family. She recalls that war intensified in the village during 1968, when many people died in battles and from starvation because no one was able to work on the farm. One or two years after 1968, as the war became even more intense in the area, she took her six children and went to a town near the Can Rang floating market to escape the severe fighting. She did not have any relatives or acquaintances in the town, so she went there by herself. According to her description, it was chaotic in the village at that time, and many people left. Many men, including Uncle Bay, stayed behind in order to contribute to the war effort, so most women and children left on their own. In Cai Rang, Aunt Tam and the children worked as hired labourers in a variety of places to make a living. Mother and children stayed in Cai Rang for several years by themselves, and then the father joined them there. When the war ended, they returned to the village to find that their farm had become a wasteland, because it was neglected for many years. Then they started re-cultivating the land.

It is often argued that during the war in Vietnam, most men left their native villages and families in order to join the fighting. The women are thought to have stayed in the village to sustain life, engaging in all economic activities including agriculture, and raising and protecting their families. The contrasting stories of Uncle Bay and Aunt Tam seem to corroborate this widely accepted image of family life during the national struggle for independence and unification: women protecting the family while men fought for the nation. However, in the case of Long Tuyen Village, because fighting was intense in the area, instead of the women staying to work the family land, many families had to abandon their fields. The women always took their children with them. It was considered a mother's responsibility to ensure children's safety during the war, when their lives were threatened.

Like Aunt Tam, for many women, the war is remembered as a time when they struggled to live. A woman in her early thirties still vividly remembers how her father died during the war. At that time, she lived with her parents and two younger sisters in the village. While working in the fields her father was hit by a bomb dropped by the Americans and was killed. The mother and the sisters buried his body and after that the four women had to toil in the fields by themselves to survive. Her mother has since passed away, and the woman, who is still single, lives with one of her sisters. She says she was too busy working on the family farm and maintaining it to get married. She was not only concerned with the family farm that she had to maintain, but, after her mother died, she was also worried about her two younger sisters. She says "I wanted to stay here and take care of the farm and my sisters, so I did not want to marry." Although it is not common to meet women who live so independently without depending on their husbands to take care of the families, her case is another example of the war's effects on the family and women in particular.

Some other women who live independently are those who lost their husbands during the war. I met several widows in Binh Thuong B Hamlet who had lost their husbands this way. A sixty-seven-year-old woman lives with her sister, who is fifty-eight years old. Her husband died in 1968, the year when the fighting was particularly severe in the area. She remembers, "At that time we lived in Long Hoa Commune, a neighboring village. My husband was a soldier of the Communist force. When he returned home from the battlefield, soldiers of the old regime came and killed him. It was terrible." After her husband died, she returned to Long Tuyen Village and lived with her parents. She did not receive any compensation from the government for her husband's death. Although she filed a petition, the government did not respond.[34] After that, she earned a living by farming her parents' land. Her younger sister had also been married, but her husband left her about twenty years ago. So when their parents died about fifteen years earlier, the two sisters started to live together and work the land. They now have one thousand square metres of land and grow oranges, tangerines and mangoes, but they do not have a rice field and have to buy rice to eat. They blame the low productivity of their farm on the absence of a man's labour.

In the memory of this woman, joining the war was not always an action to be proud of. She says, "At that time, people were afraid of joining either the new or the old governments. We just wanted to live as normal people, and did not want to join the war." Unlike Uncle Bay, who proudly assisted the new regime, some people joined the war effort not necessarily because they supported a particular party. Often they had no choice but to join one force or another. Sometimes, people say soldiers came to their houses and forced them to take part in battles. To many women it was by mere chance that their husbands joined the war and ended up supporting one of the two opposing parties. A sixty-one-year-old woman also recalls,

> The old government forced him to join the army, and he went to the city of Hue (in Central Vietnam). At that time, many other people from the village had escaped the area, but he was still here, so he had to join. He escaped the army three times, but was captured and returned. In the end, he probably died on the battlefield. But the old government did not inform me of his death, so until now, I do not know the truth. I do not even know if he died or not."

In other cases, husbands were killed even if they did not support either of the warring parties. I met a woman in Binh Thuong B Hamlet who lives in a small house with her mother. Her husband was killed in the fields during the war. He did not particularly support either regime, and did not take part in any battles. He did not die fighting, but was killed while he was working in the fields, so the family did not receive any compensation for his death. Now the woman owns only a small portion of land, so she makes a living by working as a hired labourer for her neighbours. She finds that her life has become very difficult since her husband died. Not only does she have to toil on the land and earn her living all by herself, but now that her mother is old and cannot work, she has to support her as well. Because she has no children, she cannot depend on children's labour or salaries, either.

While it is not unusual to encounter women who lost their husbands during the war, it is not common to find men whose wives were killed during that time. Since many women did not join the forces or participate in actual fighting, it is not surprising that more men were killed in the battles. As we saw above, many women took their children and fled to safer places. However, considering that a number of men were also killed as they were working in the fields, it is probable that some women also died accidentally during the war. One of the reasons for the invisibility of women's deaths during the war may be men's tendency to remarry after their wives died. Most women who lost their husbands remained widows. Thus, the war had different consequences for the genders in this sense, too. Many women who lost their husbands during the war experienced hardships after the war, enduring them independently without remarrying, while men could remarry more easily.

The war did not always have negative effects on the families of Long Tuyen Village. For some couples, it was their chance to meet. One such couple met in Ho Chi Minh City while they were both in the army there during the war. After the war, they came back to Long Tuyen Village, the husband's native village. They do not remember the war as a time of suffering or hardship, and have not experienced its negative effects on family life. Instead the war was responsible, however accidentally, for the beginning of their family. Though this is a relatively rare case, it shows how differently people experienced the war and the variety of effect it still have on the family.

It has been known in Vietnam that due to wartime male mortality, women being unable to find suitable husbands asked men to get them pregnant without marriage in order to secure children who would take care of them in old age (Phinney 2005). I did not encounter such women in Long Tuyen Village.[35]

CONCLUSION

The family of the rural Mekong Delta forms the basic unit of society. While each household consists of a nuclear family of a married couple and their single children, the members of the extended family consisting of a father and a mother, their children, their children-in law and their grandchildren share many daily activities. It is in the house of the parents that their children and grandchildren get together and share their work. Outside of the extended family, kinship seems to play a much smaller role. It is usually only on formal occasions that kin relatives visit each other and share the rituals.

One reason why the family occupies such an important place in people's daily lives is that there is relatively little sense of community in the hamlets and villages of the rural Mekong Delta. Although he entitles his ethnography *Village in Vietnam*, Hickey (1964) also claims that a strong communal sense at the village level is not found in the

Delta, although most villagers there share the same values, lifestyles and behaviour patterns:

> Cultural values and social behavioral patters are shared because the inhabitants have a common tradition, which in this case is the Vietnamese tradition as it exists in southern Vietnam. It does not necessarily follow that members of village society have strong social bonds or a sense of social solidarity. These qualities are found within the village but cannot be attributed to the village (Hickey 1964, p. 278).

Although Hickey also spends some pages on the village cult committee and the rituals they perform, he explicitly states that attendance at these rituals is limited to a few village notables and all members do not share the rituals. He does not mention cooperation between families except some examples of village-wide cooperation such as field irrigation or canal digging.

In Binh Thuong B Hamlet, too, as will be seen in the following chapters, field irrigation is not cooperative and in fact, only a few daily activities are cooperative. People mainly cooperate with and depend upon members of their nuclear and extended families.

Notes

1. I used terms such as Uncle Bay, Aunt Tam, Second Brother and so forth, instead of individual names. These terms illustrate the relational world of the family sphere, although the terms change depending on the relation in real life.
2. After bridges were built at the village centre to connect hamlets across rivers and arroyos in 1998, Aunt Tam would walk to the market alone or with Third Sister-in-Law.
3. *Family Dictionary* published in 2009 also defines family as a "cell" of the society. This view is widely shared in post-reform Vietnam where the collectives of socialist era have disintegrated and household is officially recognized as the basic social and economic unit.
4. Haines (1984) and Van Ta Tai (1981) maintain that the Confucian heritage was weaker in the Le Dynasty (1428–1788), suggesting that it was introduced and put into practice under the Nguyen Dynasty. Whitmore (1984) also states that it was in the nineteenth century that Confucian thought became dominant in Vietnamese society. Keyes (1995) maintains that in the Gia Long code of 1812, Vietnamese kinship terms were constructed with reference to Chinese prototypes.

5. Scholars attribute the "individualistic" tendency of families in southern villages to different reasons. For instance, while Do Thai Dong (1991) stresses the natural environment and the historical process of village formation, other scholars and researchers point to the influence of Western values during French colonialism (Jamieson 1993; Tran Dinh Huou 1996), or to the industrialization and urbanization that took place throughout the twentieth century (Vu Tuan Huy 1996). Some also argue that the war affected family characteristics in the south (Son Nam 1999). It should also be noted that since South Vietnamese society has a different history from the north, what is meant to be "traditional" also differs in the south. Not much is known about how the family of the area functioned during the war and socialist era because data is scarce.
6. Hierbert's reports originally appeared in *Far Eastern Economic Review* (1995, 1996).
7. Others also note that in the Mekong Delta, socialism and collectivization never functioned adequately, and the household has always remained the major economic unit (Ngo Vinh Long 1988).
8. Werner explores gendered aspect of the reform and how women's roles in production and reproduction shifted and gained new significance. On gender under economic reform and national development, see also Truong Thi Nga (1995) and Werner and Belanger (2006).
9. The National Center for Social Sciences and Humanities published a book in 1995 on the responsibility of the Vietnamese family for national development programmes (Trung Tam Khoa Hoc Xa Hoi Va Nhanh Van Quoc Gia 1995).
10. In Vietnam, the "traditional family" is often contrasted with the modern family (e.g. Nguyen The Long 1998). See also Haughton, Truong Thi Kim Chuyen et al. (1999) on quantitative studies on various issues associated with the Vietnamese family.
11. Hirschman and Vu (1996) argue that we should not conclude hastily that extended family ties are weak in Vietnamese society, even if more independent living arrangements and nuclear families are commonly found. They state, "it is quite possible for extended families to live separately, but to be engaged in a wide variety of mutual support activities, including the sharing of labor and resources" (Hirschman and Vu 1996, p. 242). The following chapters will illustrate these aspects as well.
12. Hirschman and Vu (1996) points out regional differences. See also Liljestrom and Tuong Lai eds. (1991) for surveys on Vietnamese families.
13. In North Vietnam, it is known that the oldest son, instead of the youngest son, takes care of the land and the parents. Truong Si Anh et al (1997) also

show a big difference between the north and the south (in the north, the share of parents living with a son is much higher). This living arrangement is rather a "traditional ideal". In reality, there are variations to it in Long Tuyen Village.

14. Pham (1996) studies the birth control policy and its effectiveness in different regions of the country including the Mekong Delta.
15. The reason why few people follow the programme is not clear from this research. My friends in town believe that because women in rural areas are poorly educated, they are afraid that contraception may negatively affect their body. Also, some think that few people want the government to make decisions about their personal lives.
16. Belanger and Khuat Thu Hong (1996) introduces "traditional" marriage in the urban and rural areas in the Red River Delta in the north.
17. Historical documents from the period of French colonialism suggest that both sons and daughters customarily shared the family land unless the father explicitly excluded the daughters from his will (Gentile-Duquesne 1925; Pasquier 1907; Robequain 1929). The division of land among the children in the village contrasts with land maintenance by agnatic kinship groups in South Taiwan, where land is rotated, instead of divided, among parties and descendants (Cohen 1969).
18. In the village Hickey (1964) studied, some wealthy families retained patrimony (*huong hoa*). However, they were a minority in the village (see also Luro 1878; Gaevffier 1928 on patrimony and wealth). Of around fifty families of Binh Thuong B Hamlet that I met regularly in my research, none keeps patrimony.
19. Hirschman and Vu's survey (including Can Tho) (1996) shows that how often children visit their parents' house mainly depends on distance. It also suggests that there is a gender difference in that men tend to have closer contact with their parents, although the difference is not as big in the south as in the north.
20. Hy Van Luong (1989), in a structural study of kinship in North Vietnam, also emphasizes the existence of patrilineal and non-patrilineal kinship models, which continued to exist in socialist Vietnam. However, he (in his personal comment) disagrees with Miyazawa's suggestion and argues that "genealogies are being updated or rewritten all over North Vietnam nowadays".
21. The contrast between kinship systems in the north and the south may not be as distinct in reality as it seems. Miyazawa also claims that there is a great variety of systems in the northern villages, and that they do not always conform to so-called traditions or theories. However, according to

these studies, the notion, structure, and function of kinship seem somewhat weaker in the south.

22. In urban areas, where the literacy rate is higher, it is more likely that genealogy exists for some wealthy families. Also related to literacy is the issue of class: those from a higher social class may retain their written genealogy. One fact that may explain the lack of genealogy in the village is the low literacy of the villagers. In the generation of Uncle Bay and Aunt Tam in particular, it is hard to find someone who can read and write which probably made it difficult for them to keep record of the family.
23. It is not easy to say exactly when the extended family of parents, children, and grandchildren disappears and grown-up siblings begin to be more distant. One common case is that the father and the mother are the forces that tie the whole family together, and when they die, the ties between children become weaker. As illustrated earlier, siblings often meet each other at the parents' house, but do not visit each other very often. Another possible case has to do with the development cycle of each family. When children are still too young to help their parents with farm work and other income-earning activities, the parents and their siblings seem to cooperate a lot. For instance, grown-up nephews help uncles and aunts whose children are too small to help them with their farming, or siblings cooperate in market sales activities. However, once children start to help their parents, the role of the siblings of parents seems to weaken, and each nuclear household begins to function on its own. In the case of the family of Uncle Bay and Aunt Tam, since they are already old and all of their children are grown up and help them daily, the father and the mother's siblings do not play much role in their everyday life.
24. A larger distinction is observed between genders, as men and women have banquets separately, often in different spaces. In the case of a death anniversary that took place in Uncle Bay and Aunt Tam's family, men ate in the front balcony, while women gathered in the guest room.
25. In the city, people go to the flower market before the New Year and buy plum trees as well as other decorative plants, but in the village, plum trees blossoming in the garden are the main floral decorations for the occasion.
26. Marriage is ritually established when a wedding ceremony is performed, and officially when the pair register at the village People's Committee as a married couple. For divorce, no ritual takes place, but it has to be reported to the committee to be official. However, many people in the rural area do not register their marriage at the office, making divorce easier as it does not require any paperwork.

27. There was no way for me to attest the reliability of this story, but it shows how people experience and perceive problems in their marriages. Though in a different context, Phinney (2008) argues that opportunities for men in Hanoi to have extra-marital sexual relationships have increased in the reform era as the society shifts from socialist economy to market economy.
28. Arranged marriage is less common than in the past. Most people who got married through arranged marriages were born before the 1950s.
29. Though not focusing on divorce, Le Thi (1996) studies women's position in the family in particular.
30. The conflict between the mother-in-law and the daughter-in-law seems most serious when they live in the same house, but conflicts may occur when they live in separate households, too. While I heard several stories of difficult relationships between the mother-in-law and the daughter-in-law, I did not encounter any story of a conflict between the father-in-law and the son-in-law, although the son-in-law is also often considered a member of the extended family. On the mother-in-law/daughter-in-law relationship in Taiwan, see Cohen (1976), who discusses it in light of family resources management, and Wolf (1972), who analyses it from a perspective of women's "uterine family".
31. In a study in Ho Chi Minh City, Thai Thi Ngoc Du (1996) suggests that the number of divorced women is three times that of men, indicating that men can generally get remarried more easily. Goodkind (1997) also discusses the imbalance between the numbers of unmarried men and women.
32. Although not focusing on the family, Hicky (1982; 1985) illustrates how villagers in rural Vietnam experienced the war.
33. Eisen (1985) argues that the Communist revolution liberated women in Vietnam, which may be contrasted to the stories I gathered from women in the village.
34. When people fought for the Communists and died or were injured during the war, they received compensation after the war. There are a number of people in Long Tuyen village and other surrounding communes who lived on these compensations and pensions from the government.
35. See also Schlecker (2013) on the ongoing negotiations between war experiences and social support in late-socialist Vietnam.

4

FARMING TOGETHER

FAMILY FARMING

It is mid-February 2000 and the rice of Uncle Bay's farm is ready for harvest. One morning the father's children gather to harvest rice on his farm, the first crop of the year. Around six in the morning, Second Brother, Fourth Brother-in-Law, Fifth Brother-in-Law, and Youngest Brother meet in front of Second Brother's thatched house. They take a muddy path through Second Brother's orchards (*vuon*) and other people's rice fields (*ruong*) to the field of Uncle Bay and Aunt Tam.[1] There, the four brothers begin to reap the rice rhythmically, holding a bunch of rice in their left hands and a crescent-shaped sickle in their right. A couple of hours later, about a fourth of the whole rice field has been cut in this manner. The sun is already intense by mid-morning and the brothers climb onto the dike and drink a few cups of water brought from home while sitting under lemon trees to avoid the sun. When the brothers resume working, Fifth Sister-in-Law, who just returned from the market, joins them. Because of the heat in the open rice fields, the brothers wear Western-style caps and long-sleeved shirts, while the sister wears a Vietnamese conical hat and a long-sleeved blouse. In the afternoon, after the brothers and sister return home for lunch, Uncle Bay joins them to supervise the field. Aunt Tam also puts on her conical hat and comes out to the rice field to help for a few hours. This is a job the whole family takes part in. Around four o'clock in the afternoon, after a day's work all the rice from Uncle Bay's four thousand square metre rice field has been reaped.[2]

The reaped rice is left in the field for two or three days to dry. When the rice is dried, the same family members spend another morning collecting it. A few bundles of rice are first gathered into larger bundles, which the brothers and sisters then carry on their shoulders to the centre of the rice field. When all the rice has been gathered there, they wrap it in plastic sheets and take each wrapping to the gardens in front of their homes, again on their shoulders. Upon reaching their respective houses, they open the sheets, shake the rice to remove the stems, and then place it onto vinyl sheets spread on the ground in their front yards. The husked rice is left there to dry further for about a week. On the hot afternoons of the next few days, one of Uncle Bay's grandchildren is often seen walking through the rice spread outside Fourth Brother's (his uncle's) house, mixing it to make it dry faster. Those who travel to the Mekong Delta in the rice harvest season often encounter farmers spreading rice on the road, along the edges if it is a main inter-provincial one, but sometimes all over if it is a small inter-village one. Bicycles, motorbikes and occasionally cars and trucks passing through the villages drive over the rice and pound it down. However, in the hamlet of Binh Thuong B such scenes are not common because there is no road for motorbikes and cars to pass, and the process of drying and pounding husked rice is done manually by family members.

When the rice is thoroughly dried, the brothers put it into plastic bags that can hold as much as twenty kilogrammes each. Most of the rice from Uncle Bay's four thousand square metre rice field is kept for his family's own consumption. Some of the bags are also sold at mills (*nha may xay gao*). For selling rice, the brothers load the bags into a wooden small boat and carry them to a small rice mill in the hamlet of Binh Thuong B near the village centre. Sometimes they take rice to a larger mill near Cai Rang floating market a few kilometres away. At the mill, husks are removed and the rice is cleaned. Sometimes, when the harvest is good and there is no urgent need for income, some of the rice is kept at home before taking to the mills. It is stored so that it can be sold later on, when most farmers have already sold their rice and the selling price is higher.

The reaping of Uncle Bay and Aunt Tam's rice field took place in the usual way: children working together to help their parents. During the harvest season in particular, when there is a lot of work to be done in a short time, children offer their labour to their parents. Third Sister-in-Law explained to me as we worked together in the field,

> All children including the sons-in-law and daughters-in-law work on the parents' land. The youngest son is expected to take most of the responsibility for taking care of his parents' land, but it is also responsibility of all the children. The income from the field goes to the parents, and the children do not receive any money for the work. This is because it is the children's duty to work in the parents' field, and we do not work for money on our parents' farm. It is our obligation.

Most of the children have their own rice fields, too, which they usually work themselves. This means that the husband, wife, and adult (both married and unmarried) children are the main labour force of each household. Siblings seldom assist each other regularly in their rice fields, but irregular and informal help is observed, such as renting necessary equipment or carrying each other's rice bags by boat to a mill.

Agriculture is where family cooperation is most visible and agricultural activities and family life are closely intertwined. For this reason, the family is required to — and often forced to — cope with a variety of problems associated with agriculture. In this chapter, I will introduce the agricultural activities of the Long Tuyen villagers and the uncertainties of the work that they encounter to investigate what role family plays in farming, the main occupation in the village.

RICE, FRUIT, AND OTHER PRODUCTS

In a study on the family in a northern Thai village, Potter introduces rice cultivation as the centre of people's lives:

> Just as rice land is the most important kind of land, rice growing is the most important kind of work in the village. People feel that nothing is more comfortable than eating rice, and nothing more satisfying than a full granary, which is the only real security a village family can have. The cycle of the year revolves around the seasons of the rice crop (Potter 1977, p. 54).

In the Mekong Delta, too, rice has also played a central role in farmers' lives for a long time. It is known that during the French colonial period, rice was practically the only crop produced in this area. Brocheux mentions that rice land rapidly expanded after 1880 during the colonial period with the advent of free trade, and "the arable land of Mien Tay (the former name for the Mekong Delta region of Vietnam) was almost entirely devoted to rice cultivation" (Brocheux 1995, p. 51)[3]. As in Northern Thailand, rice provided security for Delta farmers during the colonial era.[4]

To give an example of the typical rice farming process in rural Can Tho Province, if not the whole Mekong Delta, here is how Second Brother cultivates his field.[5] He has a rice field of one thousand square metres at the back of his house, and harvests three crops every year. In Long Tuyen Village, many farmers have been cultivating three crops per year for the past five years. (Before that, only one or two crops were harvested annually.) Second Brother, like many other farmers in the village, grows a different variety of rice each harvest, suitable for the climate of the spring, summer or winter season. (Although the Mekong Delta has a tropical climate and it is hot throughout the year, each rice harvest is named after the season in which it grows.) The brother learned about these varieties from a development programme run by Can Tho University, when a project team came to the village to instruct the farmers. He says he also learns a lot about farming and new technology from TV, and he seldom needs to go to farmers' union meetings. In a good season, he can harvest between twelve and twenty bags of rice weighing twenty kilogrammes each. The amount of crop varies depending on the season and the variety. One season lasts three months, and after each harvest, Second Brother burns the land, waits for the remaining rice stems and roots to die, and then sows rice seeds for the next season. Sometimes, rice falls prey to natural disasters, such as floods, droughts, and insects. The twenty-first and forty-fifth day of the rice season are particularly difficult: that is when harmful insects often strike, and Brother has to watch out for them with great diligence. If he finds insects damaging his crop, he picks them off his crop one by one by hand. Although he sometimes uses pesticide, he rarely uses much, because he thinks the chemical is very expensive, and he can do the job with his hands.

Small dikes divide rice fields into sections that belong to different families. When you look at an entire rice field, you notice that different plots of land are at different stages of rice growth. Second Brother explains: "Decisions on when to start planting and when to harvest depend on each family. Some families wait for more water or for better climate." Also the first crop sometimes fails and people have to replant later. In fact, when rice from almost all of the fields was already cut, I met one family harvesting its three thousand square metre rice field more than a month and a half later than most of other fields. Their original crop died from an insect infestation, and they had to quickly replant, so they were harvesting later than everyone else. Now they had to harvest in a rush so that they could catch up next season. Each family also owns and takes care of its own irrigation canal. Families who own fields closest to the river dig irrigation canals to their fields, and from there, owners of the adjacent fields draw water for their land. Each family chooses to irrigate when it is suitable for its own crop, so owners of adjacent plots of land do not always cooperate in irrigation. Of course, it does require some kind of cooperation or negotiations between families in order for every family to finish irrigation in a certain period of time, but it does not take a form such as in a Japanese village in which every villager gets together and work together to irrigate the whole system.

Rice has been a major product for farmers in Long Tuyen Village, and was the only product they grew for a long time. Today, however, most farmers have orchards at the back of their houses, and grow a variety of fruit. This is a major agricultural change in the village as well as in the surrounding areas. Uncle Bay and Aunt Tam grow mostly oranges, tangerines, lemons, and pomelos in their orchards. They also grow smaller amounts of water apples, mangoes, papayas, bananas, tamarinds, jackfruits, sapos, durians, custard apples, milk apples, rambutans, and other kinds of tropical fruit. There are a number of varieties of each fruit. For example, over thirty-five varieties of mangoes are known. Farmers recognize each fruit they grow by the variety. When I inquired about the names of the fruit the brothers and sisters grew in their orchards, I was often given the name of the variety as well as the name of the fruit, such as Honey Orange. In fact, they are quite familiar with the particularities and approximate prices of each variety. I could rarely remember these names of all these varieties, as there were so many of them, and my host family liked to tease me by quizzing me on the correct names.

Different kinds of fruit are grown in different seasons, so farmers have fruit to pick all year around. For example, oranges and tangerines are winter fruits, typical of the Lunar New Year season in January or February. Water apples grow after that, decorating the village in red and pink. In the hottest season of April, mangoes are ripe and sweet, and their deliciousness made me forget the unbearable heat and humidity. Lemon is an exception: its varieties grow throughout the whole year, making it a popular product because it ensures some continuous income. Another reason why lemon is very popular in this area is because in the past it used to sell for a high price. Usually fruit trees are planted in orchards separate from the rice fields, but I saw lemon trees on rice field dikes. Second Brother explained to me that lemons used to bring a lot of money, and farmers planted lemon trees even on the dikes, although fallen lemon tree leaves are not good for rice cultivation.

When ripe, fruit is plucked from the trees with a handmade catcher. It is a long pole of bamboo with one end divided into strips and then tied together at the very end to make a basket to catch the fruit. In the hot afternoons when Uncle Bay does not go to the fields to farm, he is often seen making these bamboo catchers. When I saw the catcher for the first time, he asked me to guess what it was used for. When I guessed it was for catching fish, he told me to follow him. He took me to his orchards and showed me how to use the tool to catch fruit. I often saw a grandson of Uncle Bay, a high school student, climbing up milk fruit and mango trees and catching fruit in his grandfather's orchards. Naturally, the amount of fruit grown and harvested depends on the size of orchards, kind of fruit, and the season, but to give an example, Second Brother plucked two hundred kilogrammes of mangoes in one season.

Fruit production in Long Tuyen Village does not have a long history. Some farmers have had their orchards since the end of the war between Vietnam and America in 1975, while others started them only three years earlier. Uncle Bay and Aunt Tam planted their fruit orchard ten years ago and started growing lemons. Although the timing of the start of fruit production varies, there are few people in Binh Thuong B Hamlet who do not own fruit gardens. It is typical of farmers to convert their rice fields into fruit orchards, rather than acquire new land for fruit production. One farmer explains, "We converted our rice field into a fruit garden in 1986, because selling fruit brought more money than rice at that time. And besides, it is easier than growing rice."

Like this farmer, the most common reason for starting to grow fruit is the low income that rice brings to households. If the rice crop was bad for a few years, farmers may turn all their fields into gardens, and live mainly on fruit production. There are other reasons as well. If a neighbouring rice field is converted into an orchard, a farmer will not be able to irrigate his own rice field because he cannot draw water directly from the river. Therefore, he must give up growing rice in that particular field.

The rising popularity of fruit growing suggests a big change in farming in Long Tuyen Village. As mentioned earlier, rice production used to be the only type of farming in the area, and it ensured the lives of the villagers. However, farmers cannot live only by rice farming and fruit production has become one of their major agricultural activities. In fact, many farmers' orchards are larger than their rice fields. As we will see, a big part of the farmers' income for daily life now depends on fruit production.

While rice and fruit are the two major products that the farmers of Long Tuyen Village produce and sell for money, many farmers pursue other agricultural sources of income, too. A popular one is raising pigs. Uncle Bay and Aunt Tam usually raised two pigs at a time. One morning, as I was sitting on the porch in front of the house, I saw Second Brother and Youngest Brother preparing their boat on the river. As I watched them wondering what was going to happen, two strangers came with a bamboo pole, and took one pig from the pig cage at the back of their house. They hung the pig upside down, tying its four legs around the pole. Then the two men carried the pig to the boat, and the brothers took it to sell to a buyer in the village. Although I was not able to accompany them due to the lack of space on their boat, I found out later that day that the price was eleven thousand Vietnamese dongs (about 80 cents) for one kilogramme, and the pig weighed one hundred and sixty kilogrammes, so they made about one million and eight hundred thousand Vietnamese dongs.[6] Youngest Brother complained to me that the price of pigs has been low in the past few years, so farmers could not make as much money from pigs as they used to.

Many, though not all, people in the village have tried raising pigs at least once in the past several years, when this business became popular among the farmers. They buy piglets from venders within or outside the village, and after raising them for about four months they sell the grown-up pigs. Sellers of piglets and buyers of grown pigs are usually different. Buyers come to the houses of farmers who want to sell their pigs, examine the pigs and negotiate prices with the raisers. Commonly, one family raises between two and four pigs, but there was one family in the hamlet of Binh Thuong B that owned eighteen pigs when I met them for the first time. Although this is rather an unusual case, I describe their business here to give a picture of pig raising. In this family, the mother is mainly responsible for pig raising. She has been raising pigs for over ten years; only a few people used to raise pigs when she started and she claims she was the first to begin this business in the hamlet. She started with a few pigs but her business grew. She buys a piglet for six hundred thousand Vietnamese dongs, and after several months, she sells it for two million dongs, so it still brings the family a good income, although the profit has been decreasing in the past few years. Right now her pigs are healthy and have no disease and the business is running smoothly, but she recalls that it was difficult in the beginning because she did not know anything about raising pigs. Once, when she was still inexperienced, her pigs fell ill and died. She had to ask someone in another village for advice, and sometimes she consulted veterinarians and applied their methods. She even tried giving pigs injections of medicine. Now she is familiar with the business, and knows enough about pig diseases to treat the animals properly. Some people, especially her family members, come to her for advice when they have problems with pig raising.

As this woman's story shows, pig raising is a relatively new business in Long Tuyen Village, developing around the end of 1980s. Many farmers have been in the business for only a few years. For most, it is a new experience, and often an experiment. There are also people who cannot afford to raise pigs because of the initial outlay it requires. One has to have enough resources to buy piglets and build a cage, usually of bricks. Some families are too poor to make such an investment. Even if people make the investment, pigs often fall ill partly because owners lack the knowledge to care for them, and the business may fail. Farmers who earn just enough to survive, or sometimes less, cannot take such a risk. There are quite a few poor families who tried pig raising in the past, but gave up after one failure, because it cost their households too much money.

Although much less common than pig raising, raising ducklings is another agricultural activity of farmers in Long Tuyen Village. Farmers also catch fish in the river and sell it in the local market. Fishing is usually a simple process of placing a small net in the river and leaving it there until some fish are caught. However, larger-scale farmers use big nets, sometimes with electrical wires.[7] Some farmers grow watercress in the river to be sold in the market, too. Others also cultivate vegetables, such as spring beans and green leaves, in their gardens, but mostly for their own consumption, and rarely for the market.[8]

AGRICULTURE AND SOCIALISM

To understand how farmers live, since the *doi moi* reform in particular, it is useful to learn how they lived before the reform, during the socialist period after the end of the war in 1975. Interestingly, the socialist period is generally not remembered by Long Tuyen villagers as drastic or dramatic.[9]

In fact, stories told by Long Tuyen villagers suggest that cooperativization did not have much effect on their lives. First of all, when talking about their lives in the past, they seldom refer to the collectivization of agriculture, or the era of socialism in general. This does not necessarily mean that farmers did not experience any of the effects of cooperativization, but it shows that they do not especially associate their past experiences with socialism when considering the changes they have lived through. One reason may be that the actual collectivization of agriculture in the area was carried out for a relatively short time. It started in the early 1980s, but by 1986 the new reform policy *doi moi* was already launched. By 1988, the land was returned to individual households. Therefore, even if farmers experienced some impact of socialist policies, the effects were too brief to be deeply felt. Farmers often remember those years simply as "years after the war".

Some farmers, however, recall the time of collectivization. For instance, Uncle Bay remembers that "after the war, in the early 80's, people could not eat what they harvested, because farmers had to give their products to the cooperatives. That is why people were very poor." Like Uncle Bay, these people remember the time of cooperativization as a difficult period of poverty, while others associate it with unsuccessful agriculture. Fourth Brother-in-Law's memory of the time also suggest unsuccessful collectivization in the village. He thinks, "Some years ago, people tried to cooperate in farming. But when there was a problem with agriculture, other people's way was different from mine, so I did not follow them." Another farmer comments, "Farmers have their own ideas and their own ways of doing agriculture, so when the government tried to gather the farmers and have them work together, people were not satisfied, and many did not join."

Collectivization of agriculture in post-war Vietnam also meant the redistribution of land. This process aimed at pooling land and using it for collective production.[10] Was that the case in Long Tuyen Village, too? Judging from the stories I gathered, collectivization differed depending on the situation. Uncle Bay explains, "Before 1975, there were some landlords who had a lot of land, but they were not very rich and were good to the farmers. So they did not lose their land after 75." By contrast, "Where the community office stands today in the village, that land belonged to a landlord. Because he was a very bad landlord, the government took the land after liberation." Now, "most of the former landlords live here, and they have sufficient money to live on, but they are not very rich." Thus, there was some variation in the situations of landlords, but the villagers do not think, or do not remember, that collectivization affected many Long Tuyen Village landlords, in terms of land ownership.

Long Tuyen Villagers' memories of the time suggest that the family never stopped functioning as a basic production unit in the Mekong Delta, even during the era of socialism.[11] Although the farmers do remember that their land was taken by the government for a few years after the war, the same land was returned to them a few years later.[12] At that time, each household declared how much land they had owned previously, and regained the same amount. A farmer explains that since the land was taken only for a few years, farmers could remember how much land they had before, so there was not much confusion. However, some villagers complain that the government actually gave them back less land, while claiming it was returning the same amount. They think the government kept a portion of their land. Besides such relatively minor complaints, there are no big conflicts or disputes over land that stem from the effects of collectivization.

Today in Vietnam, land is officially still state property, and each household only has a "right" to use and cultivate it. However, in southern Vietnam people consider land as privately owned, and farmers are free to rent or sell it when they need or want to (although they are aware that the government may take their land at anytime for its own purposes such as development projects). Farmers think their land has always belonged to their family, and was inherited from one generation to the next, unless it was purchased sometime in the near past. Most farmers are not aware how long their land has been in the family; they just know it has been theirs for a long time, often for many generations. The history of migration is not clear in Long Tuyen Village but not much recent migration has been recorded, and many farmers think their ancestors lived in the area. Most families have lived here at least for two or three generations on the land they own.

UNCERTAINTIES — NATURAL, SOCIAL AND ECONOMIC

The Mekong Delta is blessed with rich land and a climate suitable for tropical agriculture. The area has generally been known as fertile in comparison to the northern part of the country, where land is poorer, and the climate is harsher with much colder winters. For example, in the Red River Delta in the north, rice is cultivated only once or twice a year, whereas farmers in the Mekong Delta harvest three crops every year. However, this does not mean that agriculture in Long Tuyen Village is free of problems and the farmers live in security. The villagers experience many difficulties associated with the uncertainty of their occupation. Some of these problems, such as natural events, are inherent to agriculture and perhaps perturb farmers all over the world. However, many other problems are specific to the life in Long Tuyen and the surrounding villages. Although the people of Long Tuyen Village did not experience an extended and profound period of cooperativization that affected their agricultural activities, and the free-market system is not totally new to them, the changing economic situation and the social context have caused difficulties for many.

Weather is one of the factors many farmers find most troublesome. For example, one farmer comments, "life is more difficult now because the weather has been very changeable for these three years. It rains all year around, even during the dry season, [and] that is not good for fruit." This farmer had seven thousand square metres of rice fields in the past, but in 1993 he turned three thousand square metres of that land into a fruit garden, and planted lemons because other people seemed to be getting good fruit harvests and doing great business. But up until now, he has had only bad harvests. It took three years for the lemon trees to bear fruit, and when they were finally sufficiently mature, the weather started to change and there was too much rain, so the lemon trees were not productive. Floods are also related to the weather. As mentioned earlier, the area has been known for floods for a long time, and farmers still see severe floods in rainy seasons. Many villagers think that farmers' lives are difficult because agricultural success depends on the weather, which they cannot control, so they just have to accept what happens. This causes them to feel resigned.

Another natural phenomenon, and an even bigger problem for farmers, is disease of their products. One farmer showed me some red rice, and explained that "rice harvest is bad this year, because of disease. The rice turned red like this. We do not know the reason for the disease. We used pesticides, but we could not buy enough for the whole field, so that may be the reason." Every year the villagers encounter some problematic crop. In the past two years, orange and tangerine trees were plagued by a disease widespread in the Mekong Delta, and a scientist at Can Tho University explains that no cure has been found. Uncle Bay and many other farmers are now thinking of switching from orange and tangerine trees to pomelo trees in order to secure their income, because the oranges and tangerines that constitute the major part of their orchards are damaged and they cannot make enough money from fruit production. However, Father Khan admits there is another problem: it will take around three years for new pomelo trees to bear fruit. For three years farmers will have to depend on other crops and fruit, so they would need to secure other sources of income during this period. Not only are plant products damaged by disease, but the pigs that villagers raise are often victims of sickness, too.

In addition to these natural causes that may have troubled farmers all over the world for generations, the farmers of Long Tuyen Village are also facing problems caused by other factors such as local and national economic conditions. One of the biggest concerns is price fluctuations of products sold in the market. Farmers experience rapid and severe fluctuations in the selling price of their products.[13] One day, I was practising rowing a boat with Youngest Brother on a river a couple of kilometres from our house. (One needs some practice before being able to commute by boat by oneself.)[14] It was a hot but breezy Sunday afternoon, and Youngest Brother did not have to go to work in town, so he kindly offered to teach me how to row. As we went out to a slightly larger river from the arroyo that ran in front of our house, we came across Second Brother who had just returned from the floating market where he went to sell red water apples that morning. Since Second Brother was usually cheerful and liked to entertain me with conversation, I thought he would be amused to see me learning to row a boat like a Vietnamese. However, though he stopped his boat for a moment and smiled at me, he went away smoking his cigarette with a sad expression on his face. I could see that he was probably disappointed with his sales that morning. A few days later, I had the chance to see him, and asked him how his sales had been that morning. He replied, "It was not good. Price of fruit is very bad this year. Many farmers grow the same sorts and there are too many fruits in the market. Price has been going down and down over the past several years."

A few months later, I spoke with Second Brother again after he went to sell mangoes. The harvest was good that year, and he sold two hundred kilogrammes, but he complained that the price was much lower than in other years. What determine farmers' income is not only the productivity and the quality of the fruit they grow, but also the price at which they can sell their products. Unlike oranges that suffer from disease and whose productivity has declined in the past few years, mangoes enjoy a good harvest, and the kind of mangoes that Second Brother grows are generally well-priced because they are large and sweet, and have a special flavour. However, a good harvest does not necessarily bring a good income. As a matter of fact, if a good harvest does not bring a good income, it does not mean much to the producers.

The selling price of a product is determined through negotiations between sellers and buyers. So these negotiations are where farmers encounter big fluctuations in the prices of their products.[15] I sometimes accompanied Third Sister-in-Law and Fourth Sister to a floating market where they would sell their fruit. Market activities are usually a woman's job, and it is usually female members of the family who go to sell their products.[16] On some days, the sisters sell fruit from Uncle Bay's garden or Second Brother's orchards, too.

One Sunday morning, on our way to a floating market to sell several baskets of lemons, we met a buyer in a boat on the river. Third Sister-in-Law, who was running our boat's motor (when going to the floating market, the sister usually mounted a motor on the boat), pulled next to the buyer's boat and started bargaining. The first negotiations took some five minutes, but broke down because the parties could not come to an agreement, and Third Sister-in-Law started the motor again. Then when we were at some distance from the buyer, the two sisters discussed the offered price, decided upon their target price, and rowed back to the buyer. They resumed negotiations, and after some discussion, came to an agreement. Lemons are usually sorted into several baskets, depending on kind, size and quality, with different prices for each basket. On this morning, one kilogramme of lemons sold for two thousand to three thousand Vietnamese dongs, and in total the sisters made between fifty to sixty thousand dongs. Later that day, I asked Third Sister-in-Law if the price was a good one or not, and she told me that fruits were selling very low that year, almost a third to a fourth of what they used to sell for. She felt it had been very difficult to negotiate a good price with buyers, but she did not know why. Since she and her husband do not own a rice field and live off the fruits they produce, this has been a very difficult year for them.

Another economic difficulty of agriculture that bothers many farmers is the growing use of fertilizer and its cost. It is not clear when fertilizers became common in the local agriculture, but it is not very recent as many farmers remember using them when they started farming when young.[17] However, farmers think that because they now have to produce more and better products to compete in the market, they are pressed to use more fertilizers than before. For instance, Second Brother sold the water plums from his garden for two million dongs, but had to spend one million on fertilizers for the fruit trees' next harvest. Another farmer, asked about farming in the past, commented, "In the past, like during the war, the soil was rich, but now it is barren. Trees were young then, but now they are old. In the past, orange trees lived for ten years, but now they die after five or six years. Today, we have to buy fertilizers in order to harvest enough produce." The cost of fertilizer is a big burden for this farmer, and he often does not have enough money.

The problem is also the rising price of fertilizers. In fact, the growing cost of fertilizer is often at the centre of villagers' daily conversations, demonstrating that it is one of their constant concerns. When I was talking with Second Brother about farming, he explained to me how the price of fertilizer has increased since a few years ago. If he bought a certain amount for fifty dongs a few years earlier, now it would cost seventy, making it difficult for him to buy the same quantity. He thinks that because he can only afford less fertilizer now, rice productivity of his field has fallen. He needs more fertilizer after he started to harvest three annual rice crops five years ago, because the soil has become barren, but it cost too much. Uncle Bay and his affinal relative habitually complain whenever they meet that fertilizer prices have gone up recently. The father targets the sellers when he says "Those at the shop cheat us. They say twenty kilograms, but they only give us about eighteen, and keep the two kilograms for themselves, and we pay for twenty. So the price is much higher now. They know that we farmers are not knowledgeable and they cheat us."

As the conversation between Uncle Bay and his relative shows, when it comes to fertilizer, lack of information is also a problem. When I accompanied Youngest Brother to buy fertilizer, he explained to me that it is hard for farmers to know what to buy because they do not have much knowledge about fertilizers, and often end up buying whatever salespeople suggest, at the price they offer. Farmers as buyers have not gained much space to take their own initiative and negotiate about the kind of product or price. Many farmers just try different fertilizers and learn through trial and error, which is time and money consuming and leaves them at the mercy of luck. When they are ill-informed, they feel unsure about what will happen in the next few years and cannot prepare for the future.

Farmers also admit the lack of information and knowledge about diseases that afflict farm produce is another source of anxiety in their lives. The farmer who showed me the rice that turned red has no idea what caused the problem and how to solve it. In fact, many farmers have no clear idea about what has spoiled their crop and fruit trees, so they are not able to remedy the problem. The farmer describes the situation this way: "We cannot ask other people about pesticides, because not many people have the knowledge. In fact, we do not know much. For instance, when we buy pesticides, the salesperson at the shop tells us what to use, and we just have to believe them. But sometimes the chemicals we buy may not help. So that is one of the reasons for the problem we have." He is disturbed that there are some people who have the knowledge, but keep it to themselves. So the following year, the farmer thinks he may face the same problem unless he finds a solution. This feeling of helplessness about crop and tree diseases because of a lack of information is widespread. Another farmer says, "My orange trees have some disease that explain the yellow spots, but I do not know what I can do and there is nothing I can do now. I just let it be."

Lack of information causes a more serious problem in newer agricultural activities such as pig raising. As we have seen, many farmers who tried raising pigs in the past gave up after their pigs died of disease. When their stock sickened, these farmers had no one to turn to for information and help, so they tried to solve the problem on their own, but lack of experience made it difficult. The woman who has consulted veterinarians in the past seems a rare case, and most farmers depend on their own limited knowledge. One farmer who just started pig raising this year explains, "We are trying to raise two pigs this year. This is the first time we try with pigs. We bought the piglets for four hundred thousand Vietnamese dong each." However, he continues, "We do not have much knowledge or experience, so we do not know if we will succeed and how much the pigs will sell for. It depends on the situation. If they sell for a good price, we can save money; otherwise, we will just lose the money we spent on the piglets. We just have to wait and see." This farmer is dependent more on luck than on knowledge.

Lack of sufficient machines for agricultural activities is also what farmers constantly raise as a source of their difficult life. In Long Tuyen Village, most farm work is done manually (*chan tay*) with handmade tools, such as sickles, spades, fruit catchers, and fishing nets, to name a few. For many farmers, doing all the work by hand is the cause of daily hardship. Youngest Brother often commented, as we worked in the field and garden of Uncle Bay that he would some day inherit, that the life of Vietnamese farmers is hard because all the work is done manually. His father and mother have had to work by hand all their whole lives. In making this comment the brother is obviously comparing the situation in Vietnam to that of other more developed countries, Japan in particular. He believes farmers in other countries have much better lives because they can use machines and do not have to work as hard as in his own country. When I asked other farmers whether their life was good or difficult, a number of them answered that life was difficult because their work required much manual labour. Many villagers say they have changed their rice fields into fruit gardens because rice requires more labour and growing fruit is easier (though it is not the only reason). Also, some parents do not wish their children to be farmers because they think farm work is physically too hard, and they do not wish their children to suffer the way they have.

Actually, agricultural machines (*may*) are found in the village of Long Tuyen. According to one owner, "Before, a farmer's life was difficult because everything was manual, but now it has become more mechanized." However, although machines have been introduced to the villagers and seem to have made the life of some easier, they are also causing problems. Not every villager can enjoy their use: some wealthy families in Binh Thuong B Hamlet have machines, but many villagers have little access to them. All machines are privately owned, and none are communal. Those who have machines lend them for money to other farmers in the hamlet and village. One morning, I saw a boat carrying a large machine to someone else's field, and asked the farmer on the boat about the rent. He explained the situation to me: "They are very expensive. If you rent equipment to use on one thousand square meters of rice field, you have to pay twenty kilograms of rice. In order to buy one machine, you will have to pay four hundred US dollars, which is four times the price of a TV, so it is still cheaper to rent a machine, but it is very expensive for us." Since this farmer cannot afford to rent every season, he cannot depend on rented machines regularly. The high cost of renting a machine often explains why other members of the village are discontented with those "rich" farmers who own such equipment.

We have seen that the farmers of Long Tuyen village feel a number of uncertainties associated with their agricultural activities. Some are natural causes, while others are brought about more by social and economic factors. Although it is not easy to assess exactly which phenomena are the direct result of the *doi moi* reform, villagers see their economic conditions and social situations as sources of anxieties they experience in both agricultural production and market sales.

LAND

Closely related to agriculture, another subject of constant discussion among the farmers of Binh Thuong B Hamlet is land (*dat*). When land is mentioned in the villagers' conversations, they are referring to two major concerns: a shortage of land, and inflation in land prices. Some of the problems associated with land are rooted in natural or "traditional" causes, but there are also social issues related to the economic situation and the national development.

Dividing a parent's land, equally or not, means that land parcels get smaller and smaller with each generation.[18] In fact, it is commonly said in Vietnam that a rich family can be poor after three generations because of such division.[19] Many farmers of Long Tuyen Village, too, think that their land has become smaller because of split inheritance from one generation to the next. One parent says, "we bought ten thousand square meters before 1975, but now we only have three thousand square meters because we have divided the land among our children", and another explains, "in the past my parents had a larger piece of land, but now we only have small plots, because the parents' land was divided among the children." As is generally thought, less land means a harder life for this farmer: "Land gets smaller and smaller with the generations, and life gets harder. In the past, life was easier and better when land portions were larger before division." It is quite common for farmers to complain that they do not have enough land.

It is not hard to imagine that land is generally a crucial asset for farmers. Long Tuyen Village is no exception. How much land one owns often determines how well off one is.[20] Though there are other determinants of wealth, land for agriculture is certainly an important source of income, and farmers value it for that reason, as the following comment shows: "There are people who sell their land for money, but we do not want to sell our land, because it is the source of income for us." Another farmer who sold his land confesses, "We sold our rice field several years ago, because our son joined the army and he was not going to be a farmer, but now we regret it because life was better when we had the rice field. Also, land was cheap at that time, and we did not get much money from selling it, so now our life is harder." His comments show how he associates land with wealth.

On the one hand there are farmers in the village who do not own land, or have a small plot sufficient only for their own consumption. These people are usually the poorest and least advantaged residents of the village, often living in shanty grass-made houses with no electricity. They normally have to find ways of earning money other than farming their land, the most common being working on other people's farms. Besides being labourers in the village, they also engage in other petty businesses, such as making cakes or rice paper and selling them in the market

On the other hand, some people with larger size of land use it not only for agriculture cultivation, but also for other ways of earning money. As mentioned above, they might sell their land.[21] It is quite customary for some farmers to sell and buy land, and some have traded land several times in the past and no longer remember how much they had in the beginning and how much they have sold or bought. One woman in another village told me that she was going to sell part of her family's land to buy a motorbike so her son can start a business as a motorbike taxi driver, a popular job for men in the village. Another farmer in the same village sold his land because all his children got jobs outside of agriculture, and needed to buy houses elsewhere. Some people also choose to sell their land and buy houses where they can have more stable jobs than farming.

Another common practice is pawning land for money. For instance, a widow had four thousand square metres of land in the past, but she pawned two thousand when her husband died two years ago, because life became harder and she needed money. Also, many farmers mortgage land in order to pay back the debt that they borrowed to buy fertilizer. However, it is not uncommon for farmers to have difficulty getting their land back because they cannot find the money. The widow has not gotten her land back after two years, nor does she have any prospect of doing so. Another woman told me in tears how hard her life has become since she mortgaged her land several years ago. Now that she has less land and income, she needs to borrow more money, and life gets harder and harder. In fact, pawning and mortgaging land can often lead farmers into poverty.

While those with less land and limited resources often lose their mortgaged land in the end, some privileged people with large land can reap an income from it. Among these families, it is common to lend land for money. One family in Binh Thuong B Hamlet has a rice field of twelve thousand square metres and rents out a big portion of it. Since the income from the rent is enough for the family to live on, the parents do not have to work in the field, and all the children have factory jobs outside the village, so no one from this family works as a full-time farmer.

In order to secure a living, farmers sometimes buy more land and expand the area of their own cultivation, too. Villagers remember that in the past it was easier to buy land. For example, Fourth Brother-in-Law inherited two thousand square metres in his native village next to Long Tuyen Village, and went to live there when he got married. A few years later, around 1990, the brother and Fourth Sister bought five thousand square metres in Binh Thuong B Hamlet from someone who was moving out of the village, and moved here. Now they cultivate three thousand square metres of fruit garden and two thousand of rice field. When they bought the land over ten years earlier, they paid an amount in gold bars equivalent to seven tons of rice (or about two million Vietnamese dongs) for one thousand square metres, using money they had saved after their marriage. The land was cheap at that time, so they could afford it.

However, acquiring new land has become much more difficult, and this is another major difficulty the farmers face. For example, Fourth Sister and Brother-in-Law estimate that if they wanted to buy the same piece of land now, it would cost ten to fifteen million Vietnamese dongs per one thousand square metres, five to eight times as much as it did over ten years ago. When we talked about land, the villagers often told me how rapidly the price of land has gone up in the last decade. Some villagers think that one of the main reasons is overpopulation. According to the chairman of the Long Tuyen Village People's Committee, the rate of population growth in the village is 1.4 per cent. Since there has been little migration into the village since 1975 when existing census data was first collected, the current population increase is basically due to natural causes. Because there are more people today, the chairman says, land is more expensive. As described earlier, land is split among children and divided into smaller and smaller pieces, so the increasing number of people in the village has led to land shortages.

However, population growth alone cannot account for such a rapid and dramatic rise in the price of land. Other factors also seem to have caused the land shortage. One of them is the development of irrigation systems such as digging new canals and arroyos. Accurate data on irrigation development in Long Tuyen Village is not available, but in a village in the neighbouring district, farmers recall that the irrigation system was developed in the late 1980s by the government and many families lost their land. One woman, who has no land now, laments that her mother had a small plot, but lost it because of irrigation construction, and life has been harder since. Another farmer says that in 1985 his grandmother decided to give their land to an irrigation project, and regrets that they did not receive enough compensation from the government. These farmers may be blaming governmental projects for their difficult lives, when other factors may also be responsible. However, their statements show how people associate the public irrigation project with the shortage of land.

In the last few decades, other development projects have emerged that farmers find potentially threatening to their land holdings. Second Brother tells me, "the government is planning to build an inter-provincial road in the back of our rice field, so if you come back here ten years later, you will see a road just over there, and our rice field may be gone." At the time the road construction was only a plan (it was constructed a few year later), but it is obvious that the brother feared losing his land due to a force beyond his control. In another village in the neighbouring district, some farmers lost their land when a road was built in 1986, and they complain they received little compensation in return. A farmer from this village thinks his life has become more difficult after he sold his rice field to the government. Not only did his income decrease, but he also has to buy rice now because he cannot grow any for his own family's consumption. Some farmers have given up farming after they lost their land. On the newly built road, there are a few grocery shops and cafes owned by former farmers whose land was used. In another village closer to the city of Can Tho, people have sold their land for another development programme, a hospital. When I visited the village, the hospital was not yet built, but I saw a large portion of land reserved for the project.

Besides building roads and hospitals as part of development projects, there are also plans to industrialize this rural region, the surrounding areas of Can Tho City in particular. To some villagers these projects may pose threats. In one village, I met a farmer who gave up three thousand square metres of land in 1987 for a state-run salt factory to be built. Along with industrial plans for the area, there are also plans for tourist attractions run by the government in some villages. Fruit orchards have become such an attraction locally and people come from Can Tho City by boat to enjoy a picnic under the fruit trees.[22] In one village I visited, a few farmers explained to me the problems they face:

> There are plans to turn this area into a touristic place, and we farmers have to follow. We have to plant different kinds of fruit trees. We will have no place to live, because the building of small huts will not be allowed. It is difficult for us, because we do not know what is going to happen and cannot make any plans for the future.

A neighbour agrees, saying due to the plans to turn the area into a tourist attraction by the year 2010, farmers cannot plant long-term trees, which could have brought more income. They think it is too risky to grow long-term trees when they are not sure what is going to happen in a few years' time. While the farmers do not necessarily oppose the idea of tourism in the area, they feel very confused and anxious due to the lack of sufficient information from the planning office, and they want to know the exact details of its plans so they can plan their future better.

Land shortage in the Mekong Delta may be similar to that experienced by a Thai village in the 1970s discussed by Foster. He describes how hard it was for people to find land that was for sale, and "even if available. It is so expensive that the farmers say they can scarcely meet expenses farming rented land. Purchasing significant quantities is beyond the means of all but the wealthy" (Foster 1978, p. 150). The sense of losing control over land felt by the farmers of Long Tuyen Village and other neighbouring villages is also similar to that described by Appell in Malaysia during modernization, even though the economic and historical backgrounds may differ. In a study on the Rungus people, Appell describes the situation in the 1960s:

> The Rungus believed in the 1960s that their political and economic futures lay in the hands of others. They were deeply concerned that they would lose control over their land and end up laboring for political control of the Coastal Muslims. This was their interpretation of the highly complex social situation that confronted them as the region was becoming modernized and integrated more closely to the national economy and foreign markets (Appell 1985, p. 127).

As we have seen, the Vietnamese farmers in the Mekong Delta often express similar anxiety about control of their own land, which is crucial to both their economic activities and well being.

AGRICULTURAL CONCERNS AND THE FAMILY

Agriculture and the sale of agricultural products are the biggest concerns shared by farmers in Long Tuyen Village. However, these economic activities cannot be understood fully if they are considered apart from the moral life of families, which is particularly important as they struggle to cope with the uncertainties of their lives.[23]

As in the case of rice harvest in Uncle Bay and Aunt Tam's field, farming is the family's job, and all members, except for young children, are responsible for working on the family farm. The father and mother are the main forces of family farming, with the father often taking the central role. There is no strict rule about who should be the leader and decision-maker of a household, although in many families, as in Uncle Bay and Aunt Tam's family, married couples say it is the husband who makes final decisions about farming. Since the father is considered the head of the family, many wives say they follow their husbands' decisions. Though fathers may discuss important decisions with their wives, they usually carry out minor agricultural activities without consulting them. When I asked Aunt Tam about the family's agricultural activities while Uncle Bay was out in the farm, she often told me to ask her husband when he came home.

However, this does not mean that the father makes all the decisions. With the introduction of new methods and technologies, and as lack of information is a serious problem, discussions and sharing of knowledge among family members are crucial. Both Uncle Bay and Aunt Tam take part in significant decisions. For example, I once saw them discussing whether they should buy more piglets, how many and at what price. Another farmer referred to the time when they converted part of their rice field into a fruit garden and chose what kind of fruit trees to plant as an example of discussing crucial agricultural choices with his wife. Since neither had any previous experience with fruit production, the couple discussed the matter together and pooled their knowledge. This farmer thinks it is better to discuss issues with his wife because they each have different experiences and knowledge they can share.

Fathers often discuss decisions with other family members as well. They consult their children, the sons in particular, who will care for the land in the future. Particularly when the father is old and the son has already taken over the major farming responsibilities, the two usually decide together how they will conduct business in the future. It is mostly through their father that children learn about farming, but today, the children's knowledge is also important. I often saw Youngest Brother go to the field to work with Uncle Bay on Sundays when he did not go to work in town, and they discussed their work when they came home.

Although most farm work is done by parents and their children, the contribution of younger generations such as grandchildren and nephews (and nieces) is also valuable (depending on the family development cycle). Most children start participating in agricultural activities when they are around fifteen years old. Before that age, children are considered too young. Fourth Sister's son is a thirteen-year-old secondary school student, but she does not let him work on their farm as he is not old enough. Instead, she sometimes asks Second Brother's eighteen-year-old son to help her and her husband with their work, particularly during the harvest season. For example, when I visited Fourth Sister's house one afternoon, Second Brother's son was in the front garden helping Fourth Brother-in-Law dry harvested rice before selling it to a mill. Since the family started harvesting three crops a year, this student's help has been highly valued in the busy seasons.

Many farmers' families consider education very important for the younger generations and the choice between the family farm and school has been a difficult one. Since Second Brother's son is a high school student, he does not take part in agriculture full-time, yet he is considered old enough to take some responsibility in family farming, and he divides his time between schoolwork and farming at home. In the afternoons, when he bicycles home from school in town, he waters his father's fruit garden. Afterwards, he usually comes to his grandfather and grandmother's to water their garden as well. Since Uncle Bay and Aunt Tam are too old to be active in farming, and their youngest son cannot help out regularly because he works in town, they depend on this grandson for some assistance. Then in the evening, when the day's farm work is completed, the grandson does his homework.

Families where there are not enough children or the children are still too young to work sometimes hire local labourers for special seasons if there is more work than they can cope themselves, and if they can afford the expense. (The rate of hiring varies, but Fourth Sister and her husband occasionally hired people for 25,000 dong per day in busy seasons.) However, except for rather wealthy families and particular seasons, family members are usually the only major source of labour. Adult relatives and siblings seldom help each other with farming tasks. Although they may exchange some ideas in daily brief conversations or on special occasions when they get together, they seldom cooperate in actual agricultural activities. I did not observe anyone other than children and grandchildren working on Uncle Bay's farm, nor did I see adult siblings helping each other on their farms. Since family members are the only source of labour, their absence often causes a problem. In one family I met, after the children married and left the village, the parents had no more labour to rely upon, so they changed their fruit garden into a vegetable farm, which brings less income but requires less labour. Therefore, most parents try to keep at least one child in their village to take care of their land.

It is not uncommon for younger generations to have jobs outside of agriculture, because agriculture does not always bring sufficient income for the family. In the family of Uncle Bay and Aunt Tam, Youngest Brother has a job in Can Tho City. However, he also takes part in family farming whenever he has the time. He takes care of the pigs and washes them in the morning before he goes to work, and after he comes home in the evening. On weekends, he goes out to the rice field to spray pesticides, to the fruit garden to pick ripe fruit, or to the market to buy fertilizers. He resides in his parents' house, commutes to work from the village, and is supposed to live there after he marries, because he is responsible for taking care of the parents and their land. Youngest Brother confesses that in his heart he wants to live in a city when he gets married, but he plans to stay and inherit the land and the house, because it is his duty as the youngest son.

While married children do not help each other much in cultivation, the task of going to the market to sell produce is often shared among them, and as we saw, sisters and sisters-in-law often work together. This is another crucial aspect of family cooperation in the market situation when prices fluctuate rapidly and may drop unexpectedly. When the family members go together, they share related expenses, such as the cost of oil for the boat's motor, and divide the income according to the amount of produce each one brought and sold. The family is important not only in the actual selling but also as a source of market information. After the sisters come back from the market, other members of the family come to learn about the daily market situation, and discuss their future sales.

Family moral is observed in land management and inheritance, too. As land becomes scarcer and more valuable, it seems even more important for the family members to keep and maintain their land. I met a few people who had left the village earlier, but returned in order to inherit land from their parents and care for it. For example, one forty-five-year-old farmer was a high school teacher in the city before, but returned to the village when his father passed away to take care of his mother and the family fruit orchard. In another case, a fifty-nine-year-old woman had trained to be a nurse in the city, but was also called back to the village to take care of the family garden. Another man says that because he was a good high school student, he was encouraged to go to Hanoi for further study, but had to return to the village and inherit his parents' land because he was their only son. In fact, some people graduate from colleges and universities but return to their home village because it is their responsibility to take care of the family land.

In general, inheritance and the division of land from one generation to another is a peaceful process. However, in a few cases there are conflicts among family members due to an increased value of land. I encountered such a case in another village closer to Can Tho City. In this family there are three children, two sons and one daughter, and I talked with the oldest brother. According to him, their father intended to divide his land among all three children, including the daughter. However, he died without leaving any written evidence of his will.[24] The daughter, in the meantime, married someone from another province and followed her husband to his native land, so she did not get any land from her father when she married. After she left, the father died, and the second son took the land that she was supposed to inherit and cultivated it as a fruit orchard of two thousand and five hundred square metres. The daughter and her husband fished for a living in the other province for ten years, but their life was very difficult, so they decided to return to the daughter's native village and survive by farming the land she would have inherited from her father.[25] They returned with their three children. However, the second son would not let his sister have the land their father said he would give to her. The son only agreed to give back a small portion of land for them to build their house on, but none for them to farm.

I was not able to talk with the second son who was not there at the time of my visit, but according to the oldest brother, the second brother claimed he did not want to return the land to his sister because he had been cultivating it for over ten years, and also because he thinks it is valuable. In this area, the government is planning to build a pork factory in a few years, so the second son thinks that if he holds onto the land, he can sell it for a high price to the government. Right now, the daughter's family lives with her oldest brother and the daughter earns her living by selling his fruit in the market. Her husband earns money as a construction worker. But the husband does not earn much because he is not experienced. The oldest son considers it his responsibility to solve the family problem, and he tries to persuade the second son to return the land to his sister. However, he is not sure he can succeed.

Another family is also experiencing a conflict as their land gains potential value. A forty-six-year-old woman wants to turn her family's land into a tourist attraction, but she says she cannot. She farms nine thousand square metres (two thousand square metres of rice field and seven thousand of fruit orchard) of land that her husband inherited from his parents, but she does not like living in the village because she dislikes farming and the low standard of rural life (before marriage, she lived in a province near Ho Chi Minh City, where her father ran a bus renting business). She wishes to sell part of their land and get enough capital to start some kind of business in tourism. However, she says, "I cannot sell or convert the land because my husband got it from his parents, and I have to listen to their opinion. They do not like my idea. I cannot sell our land because it was originally theirs." As I described earlier, children get their own land upon marriage and live independently of their parents, and in many cases people sell and buy land quite frequently. This woman's story, however, shows that people sometimes still have to listen to their parents and parents-in-law from whom they received land.[26]

CONCLUSION

The family, nuclear and extended (of parents, children and grandchildren), is at the centre of farmers' agricultural activities and is practically the only unit in which people exhibit cooperative behaviour. In cultivating rice fields, growing fruit orchards, and selling their products in the market, family members work together. Other people do not often help each other, unless they are hired labourers and farmers say that they do not like to share their agricultural knowledge with other people in the village, nor do they wish to cooperate with their neighbours because people have different ideas, and other people are not always trustworthy. They would rather depend on themselves and their own experiences. This means that a family has few outside people to depend on in times of difficulty or when faced with problems and the family plays an important role in farmers' struggles in agriculture. Family cooperation is often crucial in the cultivation of new rice crops or a greater number of crops, or in planting new kinds of fruit trees in orchards. The family is source of not only labour, but also information about new agricultural technologies.

We saw in this chapter that the Vietnamese family in Long Tuyen Village and the surrounding villages faces numerous agricultural difficulties that make life uncertain. It is not possible to designate which of these problems stem directly from social changes taking place under the *doi moi* reform, and which are inherent in agriculture in general. However, problems that may trouble peasants around the world are not simply natural difficulties for the farmers of Long Tuyen Village. Instead, they are compounded by a series of other economic and social problems that farmers experience in contemporary society: new technologies, poor information, competition in national and global markets, market price fluctuations, an increase in the cost of agricultural activities, land shortages and price hikes, and local and national plans for development.

The uncertainties that afflict agriculture have caused farmers to be unsure about the future. They often express serious worries about how long they can continue to farm as they believe their ancestors have for many, many generations. Faced with the uncertain future of agriculture, some farmers express resignation, seeing the problems that threaten their future as a fate they just have to accept. To them, life is a matter of luck, and there is little they can do to control it. Given how unpredictable their agricultural activities have been and how hard it has become to plan for the future, it seems natural that some farmers have this fatalistic view.

However, not all farmers simply accept the hand of fate. There are families who are seriously concerned about their future, and try to cope with problems and adjust to the larger society affecting their daily lives. Though it is hard to plan given the uncertainties, they struggle to make sure their future will be all right, if not ideal. And family cooperation is crucial in these struggles, too.

Families also struggle with uncertainties in other aspects of their lives. Because the future of agriculture seems rather gloomy, some families believe their children's generation may not be able to live on agriculture, or that it will not bring them a decent life. These families are taking serious measures to ensure their children's future, and they struggle for that purpose. In the next chapter, we will look at how these families are trying to make the lives of the next generation more stable.

Notes

1. Fifth Brother-in-Law did not join the brothers. The reason is not clear: it may be because he was busy working in his own farm, as Fifth Sister works in the People Committee and he is the only one to take care of their farm (when I walked in the field, I sometimes met him working in his rice field all by himself); it may be because he lived further from Uncle Bay's rice field than the other brothers; or it may be because of other reasons.
2. The farmers in the region use the unit called *cong* to measure the size of land. The area of one *cong* varies from one region to another within the Mekong Delta, and in Can Tho Province one *cong* is approximately 980 square mets.
3. According to the measures given by Brocheux (1995), the area of cultivation in Cochinchina (the colonial name for South Vietnam), which was below 400,000 hectares in 1879, rose to nearly 2,000,000 hectares in 1924.
4. At that time, however, a large part of the Delta was under water, so hydraulic measures, such as digging canals and building irrigation systems, were necessary. Although the colonial government acknowledged the need to solve these water problems, most of the work was left to the cultivators themselves; with the limited technology they had available, rice cultivation was often perturbed by natural disasters related to the water problem (Brocheux 1995, pp. 52–55). Nevertheless, struggling with these natural phenomena, the region developed into a rich rice-producing area and continues to be one today. Now the land is more developed than in the past and natural disasters tend to be less destructive, although farmers still need to grapple with the problems such as annual floods.
5. Le Xuan Sinh, Nguyen Thanh Toan, and Tran Thanh Be (1997) gives a quantitative survey of farming in the Mekong Delta.
6. Vietnam has been experiencing rapid inflation, and the prices of pigs as well as other products have changed over time.
7. In some parts of the Mekong Delta, more systematic fish and shrimp raising have been introduced as a development project (see Le Xuan Sinh 1995; West-East-South Program 1997; Yamazaki and Duong 1998), but they have not yet been introduced to Long Tuyen Village.
8. Yamazaki and Duong (1998) analyse the relation between class and diversified farming in the Delta, concluding that the upper-middle-class peasants are most active in it.
9. Nong Quoc Chan (1982) analyses both positive and negative cultural backgrounds to the Communist revolution in the Mekong Delta.
10. Sansom (1970) discusses land reforms carried out from the 1940s through the 1960s in the Mekong Delta by the Viet Minh, the Diem government, and the

Viet Cong, which targeted large landownership. Also, see Williams (1976) on landlordism and class relations during the revolution in North Vietnamese villages.

11. Ngo's (1988) study on cooperativization in the Mekong Delta also argue that household remained the production unit throughout the socialist period.
12. Officially, all land is a property of the state today, and the farmers only have the rights to cultivate the land and gain income from it.
13. The problem of market price fluctuations in the rural area has been noticed nationwide (see Trung Tam Khoa Hoc Xa Hoi va Nhan Van Quoc Gia and Thong Tin Khoa Hoc Xa Hoi 1999).
14. The boats in the Mekong Delta region are not rowed in a sitting position. You stand up on the end of a boat and use two long oars crossed in front of you, handing the left oar in your right hand and right one in your left hand.
15. Taussig's (1980) study of peasants in South America shows how the commercialization of agriculture interacts with the local cultural knowledge.
16. Leshkowich (2000) introduces women's market activities in Ben Thanh Market in Ho Chi Minh City.
17. Sansom (1970) show that fertilizers were used in South Vietnam in the 1950s and in the early 1960s, when development programmes such as USAID programme encouraged the use of fertilizers.
18. Geertz (1963) uses the term to explain the ecological situation of Javanese rice cultivation, which he contrasts to the swidden agriculture of other areas in Indonesia. According to him, the Java rice cultivation during both pre- and colonial periods saw intensification of traditional patterns used more as the population increased, and hence, more complex and complicated social systems in the village arose. The shortage of land that brings about intensified cooperation among family members in agricultural activities in the rural Mekong Delta may seem similar to the case in Java. However, there is more commercialization and diversification in the Delta.
19. Taken from Professor Tai's lecture at Harvard University in 1997.
20. In the Mekong Delta region, it is generally believed that households owning less than five thousand square metres of land live in poverty. In Binh Thuong B Hamlet, the size of the land each household owns varies, but most land plots are between one thousand and five thousands square metres. There are also people who have no land or who have as much as twelve thousand square metres.
21. In South Vietnam, cooperatives and production groups of the socialist era were completely abolished after 1988, and collective property was distributed or sold to the members (Grossheim 1999, p. 112). Although all

land is officially the government's property, and the farmers only have the rights to use it, they can sell it with some bureaucratic procedures.

22. A picnic to fruit orchards is a popular entertainment of urban dwellers of Can Tho City, among the young in particular.
23. Ebihara, in a study on Khmer peasant villages and residence patterns in Cambodia, introduces the idea that "a family is a primary kin unit in terms of both sentiment and functions, bound together by a variety of affective, economic, moral and legal ties", and that "within this group there are the strongest bonds in village life" (Ebihara 1977, p. 63). Ebihara also states, in discussing residence pattern decision-making in the Khmer villages, that "it is undeniable that...economic considerations are significant for the analysis of residence patterns because a family must have means to subsist. But it is also important to note that...villagers' perceptions of residence choices emphasize familial sentiment and morality rather than economic advantage or necessity" (ibid., p. 66). Essays in Medick and Sabean (1984) also stress the importance of understanding the correlation between emotion and interest that may create one sphere in the family, rather than cancelling each other out. See Lutz (1990) on emotions in social relations.
24. It should be noted that many farmers of his generation are illiterate because they did not receive any school education, which may explain why they did not leave a written will.
25. It is generally thought in Vietnam that fishing villages and fishermen are the poorest in the country.
26. Some studies indicate domestic violence as a potential family problem in Vietnam (Kwiatkowski 2011). Although I did not meet anyone who had experienced it, I occasionally heard about such problems in some villages.

5

WORKING OUTSIDE OF THE FAMILY

JOBS OUTSIDE OF AGRICULTURE

Though family farming remains the main livelihood of the rural Mekong Delta, some people spend much of their everyday lives in jobs outside of agriculture. It is difficult for farmers to earn enough income from agricultural activities, so some members of their families seek jobs outside of agriculture to provide enough earnings for the present as well as the future. The inhabitants of Long Tuyen and the neighbouring villages are engaged in a variety of occupations outside of agriculture, which at first seemed a little surprising to me. Many are part-time or seasonal jobs that supplement agricultural activities, the main source of their income. There are also full-time jobs which serve as the primary occupation.

Jobs outside of agriculture have a significant meaning for family life, because in one sense, they constitute a life beyond the family.

While agricultural activities are almost exclusively family-based (both nuclear and extended, including in-laws), jobs outside of agriculture are mostly conducted outside of the family sphere. They constitute a place in which people may experience other social relationships that affect family values. However, working outside of the family does not necessarily mean separation from the family. On the contrary, jobs are interconnected with family life in a number of ways. Most jobs create a social environment that incorporates members of the families.

The information I gathered on jobs outside of agriculture come from not only Long Tuyen Village, but also other villages, where these occupations are more common. I also visited a few workplaces in those villages.

SUPPLEMENTARY (PART-TIME) JOBS

One of the most popular part-time or seasonal jobs taken by Long Tuyen villagers is bricklaying (*tho ho*), a job that has been available to villagers for a long time. Those working as bricklayers are almost exclusively men. For example, one farmer has been working as a bricklayer since 1968. In order to be a bricklayer, he served his apprenticeship with another bricklayer for over three years and was trained before he started to work independently. He says it is not very difficult to become a bricklayer, because the job does not require a lot of education. In his opinion, "Whether you can become a bricklayer or not depends on determination. If you are determined to become one and work hard, you can be a layer."

Two of this farmer's sons are also bricklayers and have had the job since three to four years ago. They went to elementary school, but did not continue onto secondary school because they did not like to study, and decided to become bricklayers. The three men sometimes work in the surrounding villages, and sometimes go to other provinces in search of jobs. As we see in this farmer's family, it is common for a few members of one family to work as bricklayers. They find jobs through people they know, and go wherever people hire them. The father thinks having another job besides farming brings in much needed extra income, but it is not a lot and the main source of income remains their rice field, so life is hard and difficult when the harvest is not good. Income from bricklaying is considered only supplementary to farming.

For men, repairer (*sua xe*) of motorcycles is also a popular job to do in addition to farming. This was not a common job in Long Tuyen Village at the time of my research, but in other villages closer to Can Tho City, a number of men were engaged in such repair. In Can Tho City, the most common means of transportation are bicycles and motorcycles (mostly between fifty and one hundred cc), and there is a big demand for motorcycle repair services. Particularly because many roads in the area are bumpy, it is quite common for motorcycles to need repair. I myself often had to bring my motorcycle to repair shops. In order to be a vehicle repairer, men usually work as apprentices for a few years, often in a repair shop in Can Tho City, after which they open their own workshop. In one family, the mother sent her son, now twenty-two years old, to a friend of hers who owned a *Honda* (a Vietnamese term for motorcycle) repair shop. The son studied there for three years. The mother thinks it was expensive to support her son's apprenticeship for that long, but now he earns a good income, which he shares with his mother. Since there are fewer motorcycles in the villages, men often work on streets or in small shops closer to the city, where they can attract more customers.[1]

Many village women are part-time market sellers. This job is not very common among Long Tuyen villagers, but in other villages closer to Can Tho City, I met several women who work in the central market and smaller markets in the city. Women sell a variety of goods in the markets, but most commonly fruit products and vegetables that they grow on their farms. Farmers usually sell their products to wholesale merchants at floating markets or those who come to the villages to buy fruit, but these women sell their products directly to retail customers in the market because they can ask for a higher price. In order to sell at the markets, women have to rent a place where they can open their stalls, and pay tax to the government officer who manages the markets. Some women, however, do business on the streets around the markets, so they do not have to pay rent or taxes. According to these women, the board of the market sometimes tries to get rid of them, so their job is not stable, but since acquiring a stall in a market is not easy and is rather expensive, they prefer to stay on the streets, where they can run their business at a lower cost.

While village women most commonly sell their own agricultural produce, they also offer other goods at the market. For example, one village woman sells ice cream and frozen fruits, and another sells traditional cakes. A widowed woman who has no land has no agricultural products to offer, so she makes rice paper and dried banana cakes at home to sell in markets in Can Tho City and sometimes also Ho Chi Minh City. Her daughter helps her with the business, and during the Lunar New Year in particular, they go to Ho Chi Minh City (*thanh pho* meaning "city", the name villagers use) to sell cakes, since it is a good time of the year for such business. However, the mother says that sales are not that good because of increased competition. I also met an old woman in another village who makes sticky rice cakes to sell at the market. When I met her around two o'clock in the afternoon, she had just returned from the market. Every day, she wakes up at two in the morning, prepares cakes, and leaves for the market early in the morning around four. She sells the cakes all morning and then returns home to start preparations for the next day. The woman thinks her business is going all right at the moment, but life is difficult because she does not make a lot of money. She and her husband have only a small piece of land and live in a poorly equipped house with a dirt floor. When I visited their house they apologized to me that they were too poor and could not serve tea. The woman worries how they will earn their living in the future when the market situation becomes even more difficult.

Another job almost exclusively limited to women is tailoring (*may*). In Long Tuyen Village, tailoring is not commonly practised, but in a neighbouring village, tailoring is quite popular among women, and young women in particular.[2] To become tailors, women have to serve an apprenticeship with a professional tailor for a few years and learn the necessary skills. Some women decide to live with tailors in other villages or in Can Tho City to serve their apprenticeship, and come back to their villages to open a tailor shop of their own. There is also a tailoring school in the city, and some women from this village go there to study the craft. Regardless of whether they choose to serve an apprenticeship or go to school, studying to be a tailor can be quite expensive, and some families regret not being able to send their daughters to learn the skill as they were too poor even though they want them to acquire the skill to bring extra income to the family. Though not very common, I also observed one case of a different type of tailoring in this village. Normally, tailors sew clothes piece by piece on demand from village customers. An alternative approach is mass production. The woman I met is hired by garment factories and assigned to sew parts of clothes, such as sleeves, hundreds of the same pattern, which she will send to factories in town. The tailor is paid by the factory depending on the amount of work she does.

Besides tailoring, a few women also study to be hairdressers (*cat toc*). I met a thirty-four-year-old mother who has opened a small hair salon at her home in a village close to Long Tuyen. She is one of the few hairdressers in the village and started training to become one when she was seventeen years old. She lived in another hairdresser's house and served her apprenticeship there. While she worked with her teacher and learned the craft, she took care of the teacher's housework. When she was twenty-two, after a five-year apprenticeship, she returned to her native village and started her own business at home. The salon she has right now is a small one, with only one chair in the front living room of her house, but her mother believes the income is quite good, since it is difficult to be a hairdresser and there are not many in the area.[3] In local villages, while most of the old women wear their hair long and tied back, some middle-aged and younger women keep their hair short, which implies that the salon may attract the younger generations.

Other farmers open small cafes (*cafe*) or grocery shops (*tiem*) in addition to their agricultural activities. In Binh Thuong B Hamlet, there is one cafe on the way to the village market, run by a family in the front room of their house. This is an open-air cafe, where villagers come to drink tea, coffee, fresh fruit juice and soda such as Coke and Seven-Up, which became available a few years earlier. In the evening, they also serve alcoholic drinks such as beer and rice wine. Though most customers are men, women are also sometimes seen having soft drinks or juice during the day. I also occasionally went to this cafe with my female friends to enjoy a glass of iced coffee with sweet milk. The main attraction of this cafe is the video. Although many houses in the hamlet have TVs, few families own a video player, so people come to this cafe to watch videos of Chinese traditional dramas and Vietnamese operas. This is a popular form of entertainment for the villagers. In the morning, when we go to the village market for everyday shopping, we see several men and sometimes women drinking morning tea and coffee before they go to work, and watching videos. In another village, I met a couple who just opened a cafe four months earlier. They started it because they had only five hundred square metres of land, and they have to do something besides farming to earn a living. Before, they were fruit sellers in the market, but because the income was not good, they quit that business and opened a cafe. The couple likes the new job, because income is better than selling fruit in the market, work is less difficult and they can stay home while they work.

In Binh Thuong B Hamlet, people regularly go to the village market for most of their shopping, but there are families who sell small items at home. Uncle Bay and Aunt Tam have such a small shop. They sell tobacco, snacks for children, dried noodles, salt, sugar, packets of shampoo and other small daily items. Every morning when the mother goes to the village market, she goes to a grocery shop and buys a few of each item that she sells at home. For instance, she buys a few packets of tobacco at the shop, and sells them to the villagers piece by piece. In one village, I also met a woman who owns a small shop in front of the house where she was born and grew up. Because she left her village upon marriage, she did not inherit any land from her parents, and when she got divorced and returned, she had no land to live on. So she built a hut on the path in front of her family's house and started a small grocery shop where she sells a variety of daily necessities, such as soap, soy sauce, cooking oil, ice, and bottled drinks. Since it is a small shop, the income is not good, but the woman can earn enough for herself to live. In some cases, a cafe and a grocery shop are combined, or sometimes villagers sell noodle soup in front of their shops as well.

FULL-TIME JOBS

Although less common than part-time jobs, some villagers also have full-time jobs outside of agriculture. The most common full-time jobs are in the public sector, such as school teaching (*giao vien*). A vice principal of Long Tuyen elementary school lives in Binh Thuong B Hamlet. She usually teaches in the morning and early in the afternoon, and then helps her family on their farm in the late afternoon. To become a teacher, she studied at a teacher's college for two years, and then continued to study for another year after she signed a contract with the school. Usually fees at a teacher's college are low compared with other vocational colleges, and students can receive fellowships because they are going to teach at public schools in the future. For this reason, she did not find it too difficult to become a teacher.

However, teachers in rural areas earn a salary that is not sufficient to sustain a family. (The amount of the salary of a secondary school teacher in 2000 was 215,000 dongs per month for the first six months, 290,000 dongs afterward, with 30,000 dongs added every two years.) Third Brother, a secondary school teacher in another village, and his wife often complain that they are very busy with lots of work that they feel they need to do in order to make enough to support the family and educate their two children, who are college and secondary school students. Low salaries in the public sector are often seen as a social problem by the villages, particularly given the situation in which people find the cost of living high. Third Brother told me that because a teacher's salary is low, many of his colleagues are quitting their jobs and starting their own small businesses. He worries that it is a big problem for the school system that people can make more money from business than from teaching. Because teachers' salaries are not that high, the vice principal of Long Tuyen elementary school intends to stay single for now and save money before she gets married. She thinks that economic conditions are not good at present, and she and her fiancé, also a teacher, want to save enough money before they marry. She plans to continue working after they get married to keep earning money.

Another full-time occupation that people have in the public sector is government officer (*vien chuc*) at the People's Committee of the commune where they live. Fifth Sister works as an accountant for the village committee of Long Tuyen. She graduated from a vocational college in Can Tho City and has been working at the committee for ten years now. She works full time every day from seven in the morning until four in the afternoon. Although she is a full-time office worker, on weekends when she does not go to work, she works on the family farm. Her husband only farms, so he usually takes care of their rice field and fruit garden, and Fifth Sister helps him on weekends. She often complains that she is too busy working full-time everyday and taking care of the house and the farm at the same time. Income from her work at the office is not very good, she says, so she has to work hard on the farm to supplement her salary and earn enough to support her family and six-year-old son.[4] Some villagers are tax collectors for the People's Committee. As I strolled through the village, I often met a collector carrying a bag full of tax receipts and visiting each house to collect taxes. He graduated from high school, and served in the army for ten years, after which he began working for the committee. During the cooperative years after the war, he served as manager of a cooperative, and when the land was de-collectivized, he became a tax officer. Although he works full-time at the office, he also takes care of the family farm after work and on weekends, because income from the job is not sufficient for him to keep up with the rising cost of living.

One possible full-time position outside of the public sector in the rural area around Can Tho City is factory worker (*lao dong nha may*).[5] Although a growing number of factories have started operation in Can Tho City or in the areas surrounding it, many villagers lament the lack of sufficient industry, as is the case of Long Tuyen villagers, too. There is a widespread perception among the residents that the area is still industrially underdeveloped, and if there were a bigger industrial sector there would be more job opportunities. One villager explains his view on the situation: "There are not many companies and factories in the area close to this village. If there are more, life will be better, and I hope for that. The working condition of the area is not good right now, and the rate of unemployment is high. Seventy to eighty percent of the villagers are poor." When this villager refers to "unemployment" he does not mean agriculture, since most of the villagers are engaged in farming. What he implies is that there are not enough jobs available outside of agriculture, in the industrial sector in particular.

However, In Binh Thuong B Hamlet, I met a few villagers employed by factories. Hon is one of them. She has been working in a textile factory for six months. She is twenty-three years old, and went to school till ninth grade. Before she started working in the factory, she used to work with her father at the village People's Committee for three years. She got the job at the factory through an acquaintance of her father's. Since her father works on the committee, she explains, she had good political connections, and could get the job. She says there are two people from Long Tuyen Village who work in the same factory, and how easy it is to get a factory job depends on each company, but she thinks it is usually rather difficult.

This is how Hon describes her job at the textile factory and her life. The factory is jointly owned by a Vietnamese and a foreign investor. She thinks he is from Norway, but she is not sure, and has never checked as it does not matter much to her. In order to learn skills at the factory, women have to be trained from one-and-a-half to four-and-a-half months and get a licence, and Hon is proud that she finished the training in ten days. The working hours at the factory depend on the quantity of production. Sometimes Hon works all day, every day, and sometimes she gets days off. She works night shifts, too, and gets bonus wages when she works after hours or at night. Products are made to order, and most are exported to foreign countries. Sometimes products are returned, too, so the quantity of her work is not stable. She thinks that fluctuations in the work are important in making decisions about her current and future job, because they determine her salary.

At the moment, Hon feels the job is all right, but she is not sure if she will keep it in the future. Whether she will continue or not depends mainly on her family's economic condition. If it deteriorates, she may change to a job with more work and a higher salary. She earns about 650,000 to 800,000 Vietnamese dongs a month from the factory. She uses most of her salary for her family, and a smaller part for herself, mainly to buy clothes to go to work. In the beginning, she felt the work was interesting, but after working for a long time, she feels a little tired now. However, she tries her best, she stresses, for the sake of her family's livelihood.

She bikes to the factory, which is about seventy kilometres from her house. She sometimes stays for a couple of months with her uncle and his family who lives closer to the factory, and comes home when she gets some days off. When she stays at her uncle's, she sometimes misses home, but says she does not feel very lonely because she is with her uncle's family. Some of the workers at the factory are from Can Tho Province, and some are from other provinces. There are workers from Ho Chi Minh City, too. She has many acquaintances at the factory, but only a few close friends. The problem that she finds in working at the factory is that the manager is difficult and strict. Some workers like him, but she finds him difficult. Besides friends at the workplace, she has four other friends in the village. They are from the neighbourhood and not from the same class at school.

Before she started working in the factory, she sometimes helped her parents on the farm, but now they do not let her because she is busy working. They only ask her to cook for the family. She has one sister who is married and lives in another district. The sister returns to the village every two weeks or once a month, sometimes with her husband. Hon seldom visits her sister because she does not have the time. In the future, she can live either in a city or in the rural area, but the decision will depend on what her family thinks. As for marriage, her parents say she will be happier if she chooses her own husband, but Hon does not know at the moment if it is better to choose herself, or to have her parents choose for her.

Eager to learn more about factory jobs in the area and the life of factory workers, I visited C Shrimp factory which is a state-owned food processing factory located in another district next to Can Tho City. This company was established in 1987, and has been operated by the People's Committee of Can Tho Province. It specializes in shrimp, mostly cocktail and deep-fried.[6] C Shrimp factory hires one thousand and five hundred workers, including thirty office workers and administrative staff. In the villages near the factory, many women, young ones in particular, are hired. The managing staff includes both men and women, but over 90 per cent of the workers at the factory are women, and most come from neighbouring villages. The manager explains that the job is more suitable for women because it involves the careful use of hands and women are better at this.

Cho is twenty-three years old and has been working in C Shrimp factory for four years. She went to a food-processing high school, where she found out about the factory, and got the job by herself. None of her relatives or acquaintances works in the factory, and she was not introduced to the job by anyone. Before she went to the food-processing school in Can Tho City, she lived with her parents and worked hard on the family farm. While at school, she lived separately from her family, and after she started working in the factory, she lived with a friend until she got married. She thinks people in rural areas can receive a better education because there is less entertainment in the villages. The only thing to do in the countryside is to work on the farm, or to take care of the family and the elderly.

Cho works a different shift every week. Day shifts start at six in the morning and end at four in the afternoon, and night shifts are from three to eleven. The working shift switches every week. She works every day, including Sundays, and gets only about ten days off a year, including factory holidays, when everyone else is off. She thinks the salary from the factory is quite good, and life is all right, though her husband makes more, since he works in a foreign company producing chemicals. A part of her salary is fixed, but the rest depends on the production level. She also receives bonuses from time to time. She likes working at C Shrimp factory very much, because it is a good job, she gets a good salary, and she has good friends. She also feels that the work at the factory is less difficult than farming, and the income is better than in agriculture. She could live on her husband's income, but he does not make that much, and she has to work to save for her child's education. She also wants to have freedom and an independent life. She does not want to be financially dependent on her husband, so she thinks it is better to have her own source of income.

She grew up in a farmer's family far away from the factory. She has two sisters, a teacher and a market seller, and one brother, who is also a teacher. None of them followed their parents and became a farmer. Right now her parents live with her brother near Can Tho City and she visits them once a week. She got married two years ago, and lives on the other side of Can Tho City. She has one daughter who is twelve months old. The husband's parents work in the rice factory of a rice research institute in another district.[7] While she works in the company, she hires a nanny to take care of her child, and her older sister also helps her with the housework. The relationship with her parents-in-law is good, and they also help her take care of the house and the child.

The husband's family says they should have one more child, but she is not sure about this yet.

WORK CHOICE

What factors do people consider in deciding on a job outside of farming, either part-time or full-time? Money is certainly one of the most important ones, because they mainly work in order to support their families financially. Hon, for example, thinks the decision about whether she will continue in her job depends on her family's finances. Also, an increasing number of teachers quit and go into small businesses in search of money, because a teacher's salary is too low to meet the high cost of living. However, people cannot always choose how much money they can earn. With jobs that do not require high education or special skills, people usually have to take whatever is available, and do not have the opportunity to compare salaries, or the power to negotiate their wages. One of the bricklayers earns about 20,000 Vietnamese dongs per work day. He does not think this is enough for his family and he is not completely satisfied, but that is all he can earn now, and he considers it certainly better than not working at all.

For women in particular, another determinant of job choice is accessibility. It is especially important for women who work in factories to find jobs in places that are close enough for them to commute everyday. In villages near factories, factory buses transport workers to and from the villages, and that makes it easy for women workers to seek jobs in these places. In many other cases, women have to buy bicycles to commute to the factories where they work. Like Hon, if they are lucky, they have a relative's house near the factory where they can stay when they work and then return to the village on holidays. One of the reasons why few women in these villages go up to Ho Chi Minh City to work, where there are more jobs available, is that they have no place to stay. Some studies on Ho Chi Minh City point out that many families in the city are becoming extended in structure, as they accommodate relatives from rural areas who come to the city to work (Belanger 1998). In Long Tuyen and the surrounding villages, however, not many people seem to have relatives and acquaintances in the city, and hence, not many go there for jobs.[8]

In contrast, for men who work as bricklayers and in construction, accessibility may not be a major concern in choosing a job. Many of them often go to other provinces where jobs are available, and stay there for a few days, weeks, or up to a couple of months. For them, job availability is the most important factor, and accessibility is not usually a concern. They go wherever jobs are available. For them, being away from home usually does not cause a problem. Not only single young men, but also men who have families and who are fathers go to far away places and stay away from home for some time, while their wives and grown-up children take care of the house and their farms. In this sense, on the one hand, we can argue that men have more mobility in choosing jobs than women. On the other hand, factory jobs are usually limited to women, so men have fewer chances to get jobs in factories near their home, and are often forced to seek jobs in other areas.

Well-educated people often share the idea that it is best to find a job that suits their ability. In particular, for jobs that require special skills, people seek work that fits what they have learned. For instance, one of Second Brother's sons who is studying industrial technology, wants to get a job in foreign factories that requires his knowledge and ability. A young man who has taken training courses in electrical technology is seeking a job in that special field. Also, people who attend a teacher's college and study to be teachers generally seek positions in teaching, although this is not necessarily the case. Some who study foreign languages, such as English, at a teacher's college, sometimes seek jobs in the industrial sector where knowing English is valued. However, although this varies from one village to another, there are relatively few people who have higher education and have a choice about the jobs they can get with their skills, knowledge, and ability.

DECIDING TO WORK OUTSIDE OF THE FAMILY

How do villagers decide to have non-agricultural jobs? The family also plays a role. In the family of Uncle Bay and Aunt Tam, the members often discuss the education of the grandchildren or the job positions of the younger generation. Often the children, who live in different houses in the village or in other villages, come to consult their parents.

For example, Second Brother came a few times to talk about his son's future job, and he sought both Uncle Bay's and Aunt Tam's opinions. Siblings also often participate in these discussions and exchange ideas, as they usually get together at the parents' house in the evenings. The children listen to their parents' opinions and discuss matters with both their father and their mother. The mother is always there to talk with her children, but in the end, she often says they should listen to their father, as he is the head of the family. They sometimes have different opinions, but they seldom argue loudly or quarrel aggressively with one another. In fact, during my stay with the family, I never encountered a situation in which family members quarrelled with one another. This does not mean that they always arrive at an agreement easily, but it shows that in this family, the ideas of other family members, parents in particular, are considered.

Often, while children claim they respect and follow the ideas of their parents, parents also say that they respect the opinions of the young, even if they differ from their own. For example, a mother in another village comments, "if my children want to go out to cities for work, I respect their freedom. If they want to go there and earn more money, I have to respect their ideas." However, she also says, "my children respect their parents, and they obey and follow us. There is no argument or conflict in our family." She claims that the mother is the main character of the family, and the children always listen to her. Her comment suggests that she believes an ideal family is one in which both parents and children respect each other's opinions, but children listen to their parents. In fact, many families in the area share this mother's view of the ideal family: it is proper that parents and children exchange ideas about the children's future.

In many cases I investigated, people remember that they discussed the issue among the family, between parents and children (who seek jobs) in particular, before they decided to have jobs outside of family farming. A forty-five-year-old woman has a daughter who works in a medicine factory near their village. The mother describes their decision-making process this way: the daughter first had the idea of working in the factory and asked for the mother's advice. The mother always respects her daughter's ideas, so she did not oppose her working in the factory, and the daughter decided to get the job. According to the mother and the daughter, whenever there are problems, or differences of opinion, they have a discussion. However, when making an important choice, it is the father who makes the final decision after the family discussion.

However, the actual decision-making process may differ from what people perceive as ideal or common. In fact, the process sometimes varies from one family to another. In some cases, parents decide about their children's jobs. One mother has a son who is working in a factory near Ho Chi Minh City, and explains how she made a decision about his job. "I sent my son to a factory in Ho Chi Minh City, because I wanted my son to learn about society and to know how to use money. If my son were to return here and work on our farm, our income might be a little better, but if he had stayed here, he would have only known about the world here." She continues to explain why she sent her son to the city, "There are not many jobs for young people around this area, so I decided to send him to Ho Chi Minh City. Even though the factory salary is not too big, I want him to work there. I think it is better for my son."

This is a rather special case in the area, and shows how parents' own experiences may affect the jobs of their children. This forty-six-year-old mother lived in Ho Chi Minh City before she got married. Her family had moved to the south from North Vietnam in 1953, and settled in the city. After the war, she came to the village, which was the native place of her husband. But she plans to return to Ho Chi Minh City when all of her children are married. Having experienced life in the big city, this mother thinks it is better for her son to go there and learn about the world, and she decided he should work in the factory. She thinks her ideas are different from that of most people in the village and cherishes her own opinions. In the city, the son lives with his grandmother (the mother's mother) who still lives there. The mother visits the son once about every two months, and the son also returns home occasionally.

Sometimes children themselves decide on their jobs without consulting their parents very much. A twenty-nine-year-old daughter who works in a shrimp factory made the decision to work there on her own. She went to school up to the eighth grade, after which she stayed home and worked on the family farm. However, her family's garden is small, and when her parents work there, there is not much work left for her, so she started to work in the factory eight years ago. Some other women in this village also work in the same factory, so she heard about the job from her friend. She went to the factory herself, asked for a job, and got one. She did not particularly seek her parents' opinion about working outside of the family, but when she got the job she told them, and they agreed to her decision. The mother, who was also there when I spoke with the daughter, confirmed this story. According to the daughter, it is a small factory and the salary is not very good. Yet she does not think she can change her job, because she has no school certificate as she did not graduate from high school, and without a high school diploma, it is hard to get better jobs. For the time being, she is quite content with this job, though it is not ideal, and feels happy about her decision.

FINDING JOBS

How do people find jobs in sectors other than agriculture? In many cases, family members play a role in introducing people to jobs. For example, one worker at C Shrimp factory got the job because she was introduced to the factory by her sister-in-law who was already working there. Although this does not necessarily mean that having a family member in the workplace assures a job in a factory or a company, it is a good source of information, and often facilitates the employment process. Getting a job is often difficult without some connections, and having family members at the workplace certainly serves as a connection that people can utilize in getting new jobs. In another family in a neighbouring village, three daughters work for the same garment factory. One daughter quit school at ninth grade and did not graduate from high school. Getting a job in this factory usually requires a high school diploma, but she was able to get the job because she was introduced to the factory by her sister. It may have been easier for her to get the job that way than by applying on her own without a diploma.

Parents and siblings are not the only people who introduce jobs to other members of the family. In some cases, people outside of immediate family help one another, too. Relatives such as cousins or aunts and uncles also play such a role. In the case of a man who works in the chicken-raising factory of a joint company between the state and foreign management of a Taiwanese private corporation near Can Tho City, he got the job when he was introduced by his uncle who also worked at the factory. He says he was lucky, because it is usually difficult to get a job in the factory. He thinks he was able to get the job because of good timing: the factory needed more employees and he was introduced by another worker. In general, he says, getting jobs in the area is difficult and one needs good education and skills to be hired at this factory. His story suggests that relationships with relatives outside of the immediate family are also important.

However, family is not the only means when it comes to finding jobs outside of agriculture. School also plays a role in some special cases for getting jobs that require higher education: people are introduced to jobs at the school where they study. For example, when students graduate from teacher's college, acquire a teacher's licence and decide to become teachers, they are appointed by the Ministry of Education to the school where they are to teach. Regardless of whether the graduating students are from the city or from the rural areas, they are usually appointed to work in rural areas, as that is where most of the population live and many elementary and secondary schools are located. Most teachers both from the city and rural areas are assigned to schools that are close enough for them to commute from their home, but those from rural areas do not necessarily work in their own village. Like Third Brother, many teachers teach in other villages near their own. In the case of Long Tuyen Village secondary school, a couple of teachers are from the village, but the majority of about fifteen other teachers commute from other villages or Can Tho City. Sometimes, teachers are assigned to schools far away from their home, and in that case, they move to those villages in order to teach. I never encountered such a case, but Third Brother told me that there is a possibility that he may be appointed to other villages, and then he might have to move.

As for other vocational schools, students are not often introduced to jobs by the school. Unlike teachers, they are not assured of jobs after graduation, and they have to find employment by themselves however they can. Sometimes, going to school may help them learn more about the local industry, which proves useful in finding jobs: for example, the young woman who went to a food-processing vocational school in Can Tho City, learned about C Shrimp factory at the school and then got a job. For many people, however, it is more difficult to find jobs appropriate for their knowledge and ability. As one mother whose son is an electrician explains, "it is hard for my son to find jobs. Although he studied to be an electrician, there is not much information on jobs available for him in the area. So now he works more in construction and he works on the family farm when he does not go to work." Second Brother often expresses his worry that it is difficult for his oldest son, a student at the vocational college of industrial technology, to find jobs. Both hope that the son will get a position that will match the abilities he has developed in school. Since the school does not introduce its students to many jobs, the son has to look for a job himself, but with not many industries in the area and with little information it is not easy to find a suitable job. If he can get a good job in the industrial sector, they think he will be able to earn good income; otherwise, he will probably seek jobs in construction work like many other young men from the village and work on the farm at the same time.

Second Brother often asked me if I could introduce his son to a Japanese company in Vietnam so that he can get a job there. This is an indication that people find jobs through acquaintances and friends, too. For example, the twenty-two-year-old man introduced earlier who works as a motorcycle repairer served his apprenticeship at the shop of a friend of his mother's in Can Tho City. One of the few women who work in Ho Chi Minh City also got a job in a garment factory through her friend. She looked for a job in the area around Can Tho City, near her village, but she could not find one, and as her friend introduced her to a job in Ho Chi Minh City, she decided to go there. Friends, even if they do not actually introduce jobs, are often a good source of information. One woman who works at C shrimp factory heard about the factory from her friend who was also working there. The friend did not introduce her to the job, but she went to the factory herself, asked for a job and got one.[9]

Finally, some people also find jobs by themselves without the help of school, friends or relatives. Six out of eight workers interviewed at the C Shrimp factory say that they found the job by themselves. They do not live too far from the factory, about thirty minutes by bicycle, so they knew about the institution, or had heard about it in their daily conversations with other villagers. They then came to the factory and applied for jobs directly at the factory, without anyone introducing them. Some of these workers had high education, as one of them was a teacher before she started working in the factory, and another was an officer of a local authority. While there are variations in answers when asked whether getting jobs in the factory was hard for these women or not, securing the job was hard for most of them. The first year after they were hired, they had to serve their apprenticeship on a contract, during which time they were not officially employed. During that period work was hard and pay was low. It is only after the apprenticeship that they had proved their ability and competence and could be officially hired as employees. In other words, these women sought jobs by themselves, and then secured themselves stable jobs by their own efforts and ability.

INCOME AND FAMILY

Hon's and Cho's stories about their factory work illustrated earlier suggest a couple of interesting points about how they perceive their own work particularly in relation to their family life. How are the relationships of people who earn money from jobs outside of farming with other members of their family? As one way of investigating this question, I now look at how income from jobs is spent.

In the rural Mekong Delta, the work outside of farming is also considered to be for the sake of their family's finance. People do not work mainly to earn their own money.[10] While Hon works to financially help her parents who live on farming, the primary purpose of Cho's job is to supplement her husband's salary and save for their child's future.

In the case of single children who live with their parents, like Hon, it is commonly expected that they share their income with their parents regularly.[11] For example, a female worker at C Shrimp factory gives most of her income to her parents to be used by the family, and she uses only a little bit of it to pay for transportation to go to work. Also Hon, the female factory worker from Long Tuyen Village, says she keeps part of her salary for herself, mainly to buy clothes to go to work, but then gives the rest of the money to her parents. As she says, "because I work for my family". It is not for herself, but for her family that she works, so it is natural for her to give the money to her parents and spend it together with other family members. (When married, people usually spend their income for their own family and rarely share it with their parents except in the case of the youngest son who lives with his own parents after marriage so he shares his income with them.) These comments by working daughters concur with the perception of Taiwanese factory women studied by Kung (1983), who perceive their jobs as a part of their family obligations, and hence they strongly consider it their responsibility to contribute their income to their family.[12]

It is not only daughters who bring their income home and spend it with their parents. The three sons who work as bricklayers sometimes go to other provinces and work there for a few weeks. However, the oldest son, who was at home when I visited them, told me they bring most of their income to their mother, after they use part of it to cover necessary expenses such as transportation fees to go to work sites. Their mother is very proud of her sons: "Of course, my sons always bring their income to me, because I am the mother of the family!" Whether the sons actually give all their income to their mother in reality cannot be confirmed, but statements by both son and mother show that they both think sons should bring money to their mother, even when they work away from home. Just like income from agricultural activities, which is spent for the household, any income from other jobs is also supposed to be shared, rather than spent individually by each worker.

Sometimes, whether children share their income with their parents also depends on whether or not they live with them. There are children who do not live with their parents but send money home regularly. In one family in another village, two daughters work as seamstresses in a garment factory near Ho Chi Minh City, and they send money home regularly every month when they receive their salary. The mother says the daughters went to work in order to help the family, so they should share their income with the family. I never had a chance to meet the daughters, who returned to the village only once or twice a year, so it is not clear what portion of their whole salary they keep for their own living expenses and needs and how much they send to their parents. However, according to the mother, the money that the daughters send back is enough to help with the family finances.

In other cases, working children do not always share their income with their parents, if they live separately. For example, in the case of one family, one twenty-two-year-old son works in a cake factory in another province, and a twenty-year-old daughter works in a cigarette factory near Ho Chi Minh City. Both children are single but since they work in different provinces and cannot live with the parents, it is not expected that they share their income with the parents regularly. The son's salary is low, and not much is left after he pays for his own living expenses.[13] However, although the children do not send their salary regularly for the family, they sometimes send money back home, to help the parents and their younger siblings. In other cases, children bring money home when they return. In fact, it is rare for single children not to give any part of their salaries to their parents, even if they do not live with them.

There are also parents who say they feel uncomfortable when children living and working in the city help their parents with money because the children also have difficult lives. The sixty-five and sixty-three-year-old couple find it inconvenient living by themselves, with no one to take care of them, especially when they are sick. However, rather than living in the city with their children, they prefer to live in the village where they have their own piece of land (one thousand square metres). The land is not sufficient to support the whole family including the children, and there are no jobs available in the village, so the couple accepts that their children have to live in the city. They consider it better for the children to live in the city where they can get jobs (the daughter works for the local government there and the son works in a factory), and think they have to endure the inconvenience and hardship of living by themselves. The mother says, "At our age, people usually have their children cook and wash for them, and take care of them. But we have to endure separate lives. We have to compromise, because we have to let our daughter and son live in the city where they can find better jobs." The old couple somehow manage on their own relying upon income from their land and with occasional help from the children, if they economize in other ways, for example by attending fewer weddings.

There are also some cases, although they are relatively special, in which workers spend their salary more independently. There are some young men who use their income for their own sake. In one family, a son helps the family with a wholesale business, and at the same time, has a job in a bread factory. He lives in town, in the family's warehouse near a wholesale market, and takes care of the family business. In his case, since the wholesaling business is a family business, he gives all the income from this job to his parents, to be used for the household. However, the money he earns from the bread factory he keeps for himself. He was raised by his aunt, and he gives a part of his own salary from the factory job to the aunt, but he does not spend it for his own family. He keeps the rest of the money for himself, and has bought a motorcycle with part of it. He saves the rest for the future. However, saving his income for his own use does not necessarily mean that he is more detached from his parents. Although the son earns his own income, which he can use for himself, he says he wants to stay single until he is around thirty-two, because he wants to help his parents in the family business. Once he gets married, he will build an independent household, and will not be able to work for his parents, so he wants to make sure that the business goes all right, before he becomes independent. His mother is happy that her son is very obedient.

Unlike this son, who tries to be a good son for the family, even when he has his own salary to spend for himself, there are other young men who spend their income only for fun. In one village, a mother lives alone, and says her son is now in Ho Chi Minh City. According to the mother the son used to live in the village with her and worked in construction. However, he used his income for gambling and playing cards, and went in debt. Since he could not pay the debt, he had to flee to the city to hide from the moneylenders in the neighbouring villages. Right now, the mother sometimes receives letters from her son, but she is not sure exactly where he is, how he lives, and when he will return to the village. In another village, a father complains that his son plays too much, and spends his money only to have fun. I only have the father's side of the story, but according to him, the son gambles away all his money from his construction jobs. The son also tries to persuade the father to sell a part of his land for money, but the father disagrees and the son is frustrated. The two are always arguing, and the father regrets that there are always conflicts in the family, which he sees as a big problem. The father does not know what to do about this problem, and how he can change the way his son thinks.

However, in some cases children's spending the income as they please does not cause conflicts with their families. One female worker at C Shrimp factory is thirty-one years old, and has been working in the factory for six years. She was married once but got divorced eight years ago, and now lives with her own parents. She has no child. When she got divorced and came back to the village, her mother wanted her to be a tailor, so she worked as a tailor for one year. Then she found the job at C Shrimp factory. In the beginning, the salary from the factory was lower than the income from tailoring, but tailoring is a seasonal job and she has a more stable income from the factory, so she has continued working there. Though she lives with her parents, she spends only a small part of her salary on them because she says they can support themselves and do not need much money from her. She saves most of her income to buy a used motorcycle to commute to the factory (right now she rides a bicycle, which takes nearly one hour), and she thinks she can buy one soon. It may be easier for this woman to spend her income independently, because she was once married and lived on a separate income from her parents. When she got divorced and came back to her natal home, she had to earn her own living, but may not have been expected to contribute to the family finances. In this sense, her situation may differ from that of many single women who work for their natal family, or married women who work in order to raise their children.

Although this may be a rather special case, some other women's stories also reveal that they may be able to have more freedom and independence by working at the factories than working only in the family farm. Hon spends a part, though small, of her salary for her own use, and Cho says she enjoys some independence from her husband.[14]

Some studies in Asia have pointed out different expectations between working sons and daughters.[15] However, there is not a big difference between males and females in rural Mekong Delta in terms of what they are expected to contribute to their families through working outside of family farming.[16] There is a slightly higher expectation of daughters that they should help the family, than of sons, and people may be more tolerant with men when it comes to spending their income for their own purposes. However, many sons are also often expected or required to share their income with the parents, and spend all or most of it on other members of their families, including their mothers and other female members. By contrast, some (though not many) daughters can keep their income for themselves and spend it on their own instead of on male members of their families.

Most examples that we have seen from the Mekong Delta show that the power and ability of the young in particular to work outside of family farming do not break the family bonds or lessen their responsibility and loyalty to the family welfare. In many families, sons and daughters work in order to help their family financially, mainly to supplement the income that their parents earn from agriculture. As it becomes more and more difficult to live only by farming, many of the young use their capabilities to work in other sectors so that they can fulfill their obligation and responsibility to their parents and other family members.

VALUES AND BELIEFS

How do the workers of the rural Mekong Delta experience cultural differences and cultural transformations as they leave agriculture and enter other sectors of economic activities? Studies on working women in Asia have given different conclusions: for instance, Salaff sees little change in the cultural values of female workers in Hong Kong, and argues that they are being reintegrated into the existing cultural norms of the family; in contrast, Ong believes that factory women workers of Malaysia are caught between two different cultures, that of traditional peasant society and that of capitalist discipline, both of which she interprets as different forms of patriarchy.[17]

The stories of Hon and Chon in the rural Mekong Delta suggest that these women have developed social relationships with people other than their family members: Hon is experiencing difficulty with her manager while Cho is enjoying good relationship with her colleagues at the shrimp factory. Does working in a social sphere outside of the family affect the family values of the working people? I attempt to look at how existing family values may (or may not) be influenced by the social relationships at the workplace that some people are now being exposed to.

One area to investigate ongoing cultural transition is whether there exist different opinions of family members. In families in Long Tuyen Village and the neighbouring villages, most members of the younger generation do not necessarily develop independent thinking while working at jobs outside of farming. In my experience with the daily life of Long Tuyen Village families, major conflicts of ideas between different family members were not frequent except in a few cases. I seldom encountered conflicting relationships in the family of Uncle Bay and Aunt Tam. Youngest Brother who lives with the parents but works in the security office in the city rarely quarrels with his parents, or disobeys them. Although he says he would prefer to live in the city rather than in this rural village, he still plans to stay in the village and take care of his aging parents. However, not quarrelling or not having conflicts do not necessarily mean that there are no differences of opinion. Youngest Brother jokingly says, "I want to marry a woman from the city, but my parents want me to marry someone from the village, an ordinary village girl." The son's wish to marry a woman from the city comes from his work experience there, which his parents are not very familiar with. He sees the parents' hope for him to marry a village woman as traditional, something he does not necessarily oppose, but feels somewhat uncomfortable with.

In some cases, though relatively minor, new cultural values may conflict with existing values. This is particularly found between the daughter-in-law and the mother-in-law. Mai, a working woman at C Shrimp factory, complains, "elderly people have old ideas, and do not understand our jobs. I have a problem with my mother-in-law in particular. She thinks I should stay home, have more children, and take care of them at home. I feel confused. I work at this factory because the salary is good, and it is for my family, but my mother-in-law does not understand. I think some other women who are working here have a similar problem." She can receive understanding and help from her natal family members (while she works in the factory, her own mother usually takes care of her children), but she cannot gain the support of her mother-in-law. She says her husband also held "old male ideas" before and was not understanding in the beginning. According to Mai, he stays home to work on the family farm, because the factory job is not fit for men, so he was not happy in the beginning about her working outside. However, he gradually understood, and began to help her by taking care of the children. Now it is easier because her husband is cooperative, she says.

In the case of another woman also working in C Shrimp factory, the conflict with her mother-in-law was more severe, and grew into a more serious situation. Thuy says she got divorced because of it. At that time, she lived in her husband's village, and worked in another factory, but her mother-in-law, she says, had very old-fashioned opinions and disapproved of her working outside. In Thuy's view, the mother-in-law felt that the daughter-in-law's duty was to take care of the farm and the house, and she did not consider her salary from the factory as a main source of income for the family. The problem, Thuy says, was that her husband shared his mother-in-law's beliefs and did not support her. "So I decided to divorce him and came back to my native village. Now I live with my parents." Whether divorces like this are common among working women is not known. However, another worker who was there with Thuy commented that there are some young women who leave their jobs when they get married, because of their mothers-in-law's old-fashioned way of thinking.

Like Mai and Thuy, some working women are caught up in conflicts of ideas as they leave "traditional" domestic space, where women were supposed to spend their lives, and enter the industrial workplace, like working women in Malaysia. However, these conflicts appear to be relatively rare. I had a chance to interview eight workers at C Shrimp factory, and Mai and Thuy were the only two who said they had problems with other members of their families because of different opinions. The other six workers, when I referred to stories like those of Mai and Thuy, said they had no such problems.

While for some women, the new experiences in workplaces cause problems and conflicts in the traditional family, other women utilize the new social experiences for the sake of the traditional one, and successfully incorporate both into their lives, crossing the boundaries between the two without much conflict. Working outside of family farming and entering the new social sphere of the workplace is a new experience for most women of the rural Mekong Delta. Whether and how their ideas will change and what conflicts they may have with existing ideas are yet to be seen.[18]

CONCLUSION

Given the problems in agriculture, it is often important, and sometimes necessary, for people to seek jobs outside of agriculture to supplement their income from family farming. However, there are a variety of jobs and their roles often differ from one family to another. For example, for some families who have little or no land, having outside jobs is crucial, although they may earn some money by working on their neighbour's farms as well. For these families, jobs outside of agriculture are often the main source of income, but getting high-paid jobs is usually difficult, due to lack of education, information, and connections. Even for those with average land areas, it is important to have other jobs, so that they can add more income to their agricultural earnings and meet their everyday life expenses as well as agricultural costs, which are rising.

There are several jobs that are common among the villagers. While some jobs are relatively easy for many people to obtain, other jobs are limited to those with higher education and special skills and sometimes good connections. It does not always follow, however, that jobs that require special skills or certificates are better paid. For instance, a teacher's salary is kept low, although it requires a teachers' college diploma, yet a teaching job is one of the most secure as well as respectful jobs that bring a regular and stable income to the family.[19]

Although both old and young are engaged in a variety of jobs outside of agriculture, it is more common for the younger generation to be employed, while the older ones stay in the house and take care of the farm. One reason is that many jobs are suitable for younger people and it is easier for them to be employed. It is also considered more crucial for the younger generation to have jobs, since competition in agriculture is becoming more severe and the available new land is decreasing. The parents worry that their children's generation may not be able to live on agriculture so they think it is better for them to have other jobs. There are two major reasons why parents wish their children will find jobs outside of agriculture. On reason is about the present: they want the children to support the family by supplementing its income from agriculture with job income. The other concerns the future: many parents hope that their children will have a secure life in the future, and a better life than their own, and they think having a good job is one of the few ways to achieve that goal.

Family plays an important role in job choices. In making decisions about jobs, most, though not all, people consult other family members (parents in particular in the case of unmarried people) and they make decisions with the agreement of other members. Family members are often a good source of information, and often introduce people to jobs. However, other people such as relatives and friends also play a role in offering information about jobs, which suggests that other social relationships are also becoming important, although this does not seem to lessen the role of the family at the moment. It is generally the family that people first turn to when finding jobs, particularly because they often have jobs for the sake of the family and not for themselves.

In some rare cases, however, we can observe that family roles change and family ties are affected by people's experiences of working outside. For instance, conflicts in ideas arise between the old and young generations. Some young men spend their money for themselves, for fun or on gambling, instead of for their family and they do not listen to or follow their parents' ideas. Some women experience conflicts with their mother-in-law when they work outside. It is commonly believed that there has generally been conflict between mother-in-law and daughter-in-law in the past. However, the conflict these women are experiencing is unique because it is a problem of social space: whether they should stay inside the family or go outside.

Notes

1. In a study on urban China in the reform era, Ikels (1996) states that some families are successful enough in their entrepreneurship to expand their business. In Long Tuyen Village, such large-scale entrepreneurship is not found, and all family-run or individually managed businesses remain petty.
2. In another village not far from Long Tuyen, women are known to be engaged in straw crafts, such as Vietnamese conical hats, baskets, and bags. These activities started as a project with a foreign aid. However, such project never took place in Long Tuyen Village.

3. In Can Tho City, a haircut normally costs around five thousand dongs (fifty cents), although it varies greatly depending on the place. Although the price of cut this woman charges is not known, it is likely to be much less than the price in the city.
4. Salaries of public sectors are generally known to be quite low by the standards of living expense at the moment. The salary of Youngest Brother who works in the district security office was 38 US dollars (in 2000), and the salary of the Village Committee officers are most likely lower than that.
5. There are both state-run and private factories. In the reform era, more private factories are emerging throughout the country (see World Bank Report 1994).
6. A large part of its output is exported to foreign countries, such as Japan, the United States, UK, France, Belgium, Italy, Spain, Hong Kong, Singapore and Korea. In 1997, the main importer was Japan, whose share was 50 per cent of production, with the United States second with 30 per cent. The company grew quite rapidly in the 1990s, and according to their report, export turnover, which was twenty-six million and five hundred thousand US dollars in 1994, grew to forty-two million US dollars in 1997. This growth is mainly due to the increase in exports to major foreign countries.
7. There is a national rice research institute in Omon district, next to the district of Can Tho City.
8. Belanger suggests, based on a survey analysis on the households in Vietnam, that the rate of extended family is highest in the Mekong Delta region including Ho Chi Minh City. She attributes this to migration of the young from the rural area to the city.
9. Yan (2009) discusses the increased importance of friends for Chinese rural residents under socialism, which dismantled the traditional patriarchal kinship system. Although residents of the rural Mekong Delta did not experience the effect of socialism to the same degree, friends seem to be gaining more significance in the late socialist era when more people are seeking cash income from jobs outside of family farming.
10. Thai Thi Ngoc Du's (1995) study on intellectual working women in Ho Chi Minh City offers a comparison with these working women in the rural Mekong Delta.
11. Gallup (1997) discusses that children in Vietnam have more economic values for their family enterprises as family labour than as wage earner.
12. Kung argues that earning money has not given the Taiwanese women the right to control their own incomes. According to Kung, many daughters are expected to give at least 50-80 per cent (or sometimes all) of their earnings to their families. Kung argues that the reason why these women are less likely to challenge their subordinate positions in their families is because

the family is the only place of warmth and security that the young women know (Kung 1983).

13. In a sociological study on urban Taiwan, Sun and Liu (1994) argue that intergenerational flow of money strengthens the parent-children bond that has been weakened by separate living arrangements.
14. However, these working women may not have gained as much freedom as the Javanese factory daughters studied by Wolf, who "control their own wage and do not automatically give it to their families; they also control their expenditures" (Wolf 1992, p. 186). Most of the factory daughters in Java, Wolf argues, spend their money as they choose, and may afford luxury goods (such as clothes) or leisure, and spend little for their families. Moreover, some working women ask for money from their parents to supplement their income from the jobs. Parents' expectations about their daughters' contribution to the family finances vary, and some parents, according to Wolf, show dissatisfaction with their daughters spending all their money as they please and not sharing it with the families. However, many parents accept the situation and continue to financially support their daughters, because, the author argues, there are no other economic activities for women that offer a comparable stable income.
15. In a study of working women in Hong Kong, Salaff argues that working outside of the family does not free women from their family responsibilities, and on the contrary, their ability to work is put towards the family welfare. She states: "Generalized reciprocity within an ongoing circle of friends, colleagues, relatives, and patron is valued to meet family economic needs, and sons are the main recipients of family benefits. The unmarried daughter, like other family members, abides by these strictures, which demand her loyalty to her family of origin before marriage and devotion to her husband's family thereafter" (Salaff 1995, p. 258). The author suggests that the working women's financial contributions are used mainly for the male members of the family. For instance, Salaff argues, the daughters' income is used for the bride price that their brothers pay, and therefore the women are pressured to stay in their jobs longer before getting married. Salaff uses the term "modified centripetal family" to refer to the Hong Kong family that requires women to work for their families, and particularly for their male members. She goes on to argue that "the ability of the working daughter to sell her labor power for a price does not attenuate the bonds of familism" (ibid., p. 259). In her view, the economic power the younger generation has gained does not let them be independent, but ironically reintegrates them into the existing family system. Chan and Lee (1995) also investigate how families in Hong Kong are caught between two values:

modernization and traditionalism, under cultural influences from the West in particular.

16. See Arnold and Kuo (1984) for discussions on the differences between the son and the daughter regarding their economic contributions to the family in Korea. The authors argue that the son is preferred because they contribute more to their family.
17. Ong discusses how the women and their families are caught in cultural ambivalences as they move from one kind of society to another. Referring to the family relationships of the working women, Ong suggests that their "labor power enables [them] to challenge male authority at home", but this power ironically subjects them to another form of oppression at the workplace (Ong 1987, p. 113). It is the author's belief that the women are in transition from a traditional form of dominance at home to new power relations in the workplace, and women's spirit possession at the factory is a manifestation of their resistance to the new form of oppression.
18. Though not focusing specifically on women working outside family farming, studies in Drummond and Rydstrom (2004) examine the impacts of contemporary modernization and globalization on gender relations in Vietnam. These studies show that gender relations in Vietnam have not only been "traditional" but have historically undergone many influences of the time such as colonialism and socialism before contemporary effects of modernization and globalization.
19. The average monthly salary of a teacher was about US$30 in 1999 (Grossheim and Endres 1999, p. 183).

6

EDUCATION OF CHILDREN AND THE FUTURE

EDUCATION IN VIETNAM

How do the villagers of Long Tuyen pursue education?[1] What is its purpose and what role does it play in their lives, particularly in the midst of uncertainties associated with their family farming? In fact, education is one of the few means people have to secure a better future.

When talking about education (*giao duc*), villagers often refer to two kinds of education: one in family and the other at school. Education in the family setting is generally considered important. Within the family, people explain, education determines the relationships among members, particularly parents and children, and determines each family's way of life. Many parents talk, sometimes proudly, about how they educate their children. Some parents, by contrast, lament the difficulty of educating their children well at home. The importance of family education is recognized not only by each family, but also by the whole society. The family is once again recognized as the main social unit in contemporary Vietnam, so education is seen as crucial also to the development of the whole society. Through education family and society are closely connected. Thus, education at home is not only familial, but also social.

Education at school is also both familial and social. Especially, many families consider school education important for the children in the face of difficult social conditions. However there exist many problems that villagers are now facing in providing their children with a school education and people are struggling to secure a stable future through education for themselves and their children. Although school lies outside of the family space, it is closely interrelated with the family and its existence in contemporary society. Family views of the future as well as the present are often manifested in school education.

FAMILY EDUCATION

Education at home is thought to affect the children's lives. Uncle Bay tells me, "I taught my children to be honest, so they have no problem in their lives right now." He thinks that some of his children are doing quite well in agriculture and others have good jobs because they are good people and they work diligently. In his opinion, good family education has helped his children to be good people and have good life. He believes one of the major purposes of family education is to teach children good morality and values, and honesty is especially important. He recalls how, when he was young, his father tried to teach him to be a good person, although it was difficult during the war for parents to educate their children well. His mother died in 1954 when he was still a young child, so his father took on the responsibility of educating him and his elder brother. Now a father himself, Uncle Bay has tried to be strict enough in teaching his children so they will become good people.

Uncle Bay often stresses the importance of educating children well not only for their own good, but also for the whole family. He says that in other families, people have conflicts and problems because they are dishonest. In the rural Mekong Delta, one of the main reasons parents educate their children is to teach them to be morally good individuals within the family.[2] When people say "good children", they often mean such things as being obedient (*ngoan*) to parents and respectful (*kinh trong*) to the old. For example, when asked about the relationship between parents and children, one female neighbour of Uncle Bay said, "Our children respect and obey us, so there is no conflict in our family. Mothers are very important to teaching children to obey and respect their parents." Another says, "Younger generations have different ideas, and there are different ideas in the family, too. The younger generation likes to drink and play cards. But in the end, the children listen to and obey the father. The father is very strict with the children. So our family is good."

As these comments demonstrate, one goal of family education is making children obedient, so good children are expected to listen to and follow their parents. Obedient children make good members of the family. For instance, a forty-five-year-old female neighbour expresses her expectation about her twenty-three-year-old son: "my son always obeys me, although he is grown up and earns his own income. He always listens to me. Sometimes I get angry at his wrong doings, such as drinking, but when I scold him, my son keeps silent and does not talk back, and obeys me. Sometimes, when my son does something wrong, I even beat him, and my husband and neighbors try to stop me. But I think my son has to stand it and understand what is right and what is wrong." This mother's statement shows what she considers to be a "good child" and how she tries to educate her son.

Children consider it their obligation to obey their parents, too. A forty-one-year-old male farmer in a neighbouring village told me his story. He studied chemistry at a college in the city, but when he graduated, he had to return to the village because he was a good son and his father loved him, and the father gave him land. He had to "obey his father's orders" to return and take care of the fruit garden. He is now married, but his father is very strict, and although the farmer has enough money to buy a TV, his father does not allow him to do so, saying that the grandchildren can study better without it. His father does not allow him to drink or smoke, and he has to share any income from the garden with his father. This is rather an unusual case since in many families children have more independence from their parents after they marry, such as to buy a TV. However, this story shows how some children feel they must obey their parents, even to the extent of sacrificing their own will or independence for the sake of the family.

Respect for parents is also considered a significant factor in judging children and the education of the whole family. Reasons for respecting their parents are often based on their life experiences, rather than just an idea or philosophy, that parents have more experiences in life. For example, some children say, in reference to farming, that they respect their father's ideas because he has more experience.

Another reason often mentioned for respecting parents in some cases is that a parent has remained unmarried after a spouse has died. For example, one daughter in her early twenties says, "I respect my mother because she stayed single after my father died seventeen years ago, so I help her make and sell banana cakes at the market." Widowhood is not uncommon in this area, not only because of the long war, but also due to disease or accident. Two daughters from another family also told me, "we support our father, who is now old, because he stayed single after our mother died, and we respect him for that." Also, the father himself expresses his pride in staying single and being respected by his children as a result. In another family, children take turns taking care of their widowed mother, because she stayed single after her husband died and the children respect this. One father is very proud that his children, who live in the city, bought a rice cooker and a washing machine for him, because, he believes, all of his children respect him for not remarrying after his wife died thirty years ago. Rice cookers and washing machines are rarely found in the villages, and they are luxuries by the villagers' standards, but the children thought it would be easier for their father as he does not have a wife who cooks and washes for him.

As seen in these comments, respect and support for parents are often tightly connected. In fact, filial piety is one of the most valued moral in the relationship between parents and children, and taking good care of parents is a particularly important trait that people expect from good children, as indicated by a mother's claim: "My daughter is a very good daughter and takes care of me very carefully." This mother's prospects for the future depend on the "goodness" of her daughter. She says, "Right now my daughter goes to a nursing school, and when she graduates and gets a job, our life will be better, because she will be able to support me." Another male farmer says, "When I was a young man, I used to go out and play a lot, but after I got married, I stay on my farm, obey my father, and take care of my parents", suggesting that he thinks he was a "bad child" before but now he is a "good son" who looks after his parents.[3]

Besides taking care of parents, good children are also expected to help their parents by taking care of their siblings, and participating in housework and farm work. It is commonly observed that older children take care of younger ones, while their parents work in the field or go to the market to sell their products. While children are rarely asked to take part in farming until they are about fifteen to sixteen years old, they are supposed to start young helping their parents take care of younger children and do some of the housework, especially for the mother. Daughters in particular, though not exclusively, are expected to take care of younger siblings and do housework. Often as I walked around the village, I encountered young girls about ten years of age, holding small children and playing with them. These girls were looking after their younger siblings after school, and they also did the housework, such as cleaning and cooking, while their parents were out in the field. By contrast sons do not always help with housework, but are sometimes asked to participate in relatively simple and easy farming chores, such as running errands, buying agricultural equipment at the market or feeding the ducklings the family raises.[4]

Not spending time playing or hanging out with friends is also considered good traits of children. For instance, one father is proud that his daughters rarely go out to have fun, because he is strict with them. They have to ask for his permission when they want to go out with friends. This father is proud of his daughters and tries to make sure their friends are good and not bad influences. He makes sure that they have many girlfriends but not boyfriends, since he thinks playing with boys will not be good for his daughters. In contrast to this father, some people complain that their children play too much, which also shows that spending time on games is considered a bad trait. For example, one father laments that his son lives a dissipated life. It is more often the sons, rather than daughters, that tend to indulge in drinking, playing, and gambling and cause problems in the family. Most of the complaints I heard from the parents were about their sons rather than their daughters.

Closely related, children are supposed to be industrious (*can lao*). When asked what kind of woman would be an ideal wife or daughter-in-law, many villagers answer that she must be hardworking. And when asked what kind of man would be ideal as a husband, industriousness is again mentioned as one of the most important characteristics. In fact, being industrious is generally thought to be a more important trait for marriage than physical attractiveness or wealth and property. It is the ideal trait sought for in future spouses. I knew one woman in a neighbouring village who chose to stay single because she was afraid of marrying a man who would not work hard, and she preferred living by herself to having to endure a "playful" husband.

Living a simple life is also mentioned as a good characteristic of children. Living simply means not being extravagant and not spending a lot of money like those who play around. In fact, people are often praised for "being simple (*gian di*)".[5] Aunt Tam thinks it was relatively easy to raise her children because they lived a simple life when they were young and single. I was usually dressed in simple clothes (a white shirt and a navy pants, for example), and villagers often commented to me, "you are a good daughter because you are very simple." Being simple or living simple life is associated with being serious, industrious and not playful.

As we have seen, in many village families, parents consider themselves responsible for educating their children to be good, to have certain characteristics such as honesty, obedience, and industriousness, and to be eager to support their parents and take part in family work. This is not surprising when one considers the significance of family cooperation in agriculture as we have seen in the previous chapter. This view is shared widely in Vietnam. A number of Vietnamese scholars point to the importance of family education in the development of children's personalities, and since the mid-1990s, its significance has been strongly emphasized. Vo Thi Cuc, for example, stresses the role of parents in children's moral development. She argues, "many moral families believe that the best morality is developed when adults are mirrors to the young, so that the youth will naturally develop a good heart", and hence, "father and mother who do not have morality cannot raise obedient children" (Vo Thi Cuc 1997, p. 106). Besides morality, Vo also refers to the emotional development of children and particularly stresses the role of family culture in the development of children's emotions. She states, "Family culture mainly influences the emotion of the young through the relationships among family members and through family education" (ibid., p. 97). She argues that emotion does not develop naturally, but is developed and nurtured through family education.

Apart from its role in educating children to be good family members, the family is also considered important for training children to be good citizens of society that will lead to the development of the whole nation. Some scholars discuss this role of family. For instance, Nguyen states,

> Another function of the family that comrade Le Thi also mentions is to maintain and convey cultural values, traditional culture and spirituality. In fact, to convey culture is to educate, and nurture personality and soul, and we want to emphasize another factor, that is, families teach personality and train children. Yet another factor is that families maintain and transmit the traditional culture of the nation and the country (Nguyen Khanh 1995, p. 17) (translation by the author).

Although it is not clear from his argument what he means by "traditional culture", Nguyen continues to argue that good family education is crucial for the country's social development. In his view, strengthening the family as a unit of the whole society through education will make social relationships strong. As a strong Vietnamese family is developed, a firm and stable society will result.

The following passage by Tran Dinh Huou also stresses the function of the family in the cultural development of the nation:

> [The] Family has been both a social system with national characteristics and a symbol of cultural development. It is one particular phenomenon of national culture. Since families departed from the primitive lifestyle,

> the relationship among the family members as well as with other social systems have been consolidated. With talents and intelligence, people have gradually confirmed their positions as well as properties in society. In this way, people were able to widen their nation (Tran Dinh Huou 1996, p. 70) (translation by the author).

Although this sociologist does not refer directly to family education, he argues that as a basic unit, the family and characteristics of family members determine the nature of the whole society. He emphasizes that by building a good family, we can build an ideal society in which everyone can live in peace and happiness.[6] While Tran Dinh Huou discusses family and society in a general context, Hong Ha, referring to the traditional Vietnamese family, pays special attention to the role of family education in socializing children in contemporary society. In an article entitled, "Family in the contemporary renovation project", she stresses the importance of family in the development of society. The family is responsible for society, because the "family is not only an essential economic unit, but also a fundamental social unit" where people's socialization takes place and a large part of people's social life is conducted (Hong Ha 1994, p. 49; Le Thi 1999, p. 5). With families that have a good nature, Hong Ha stresses, the whole society will be well developed, and by playing a more social as well as economic role, the family in contemporary Vietnam will increasingly contribute to the development of the whole nation.[7]

In fact, many farmers in Long Tuyen Village as well as other neighbouring villages think of education not only in relation to their families, but also in the context of the whole society and its development. A seventy-three-year-old male neighbour of Uncle Bay thinks "Education is important for the whole society because it develops the country. If the old generation does not have enough knowledge to teach younger generations, you can ruin the next generation and hence society in the future. Now social values are changing, but in order to keep a certain level of morality in society, we need to educate the young well." People also say that they educate their children so that the next generation will give good citizens (*cong dan*) to society. Fifth Sister explains her view that "It is a responsibility of the parents to educate our children how to behave and what is good morally, so that they will be good citizens when they are grown up, and can contribute to the development of whole society." Many people think that the family, as a basic social unit, is the place where children are socialized, and it is the duty of the family not just to teach younger generations to be good family members, but also good members of society in the future.

Family education not only directly influences society. It is also influenced by society as it responds to changes in everyday life and different social demands. Sometimes, newly emerging social values are seen negative and they cause conflicts of ideas in family and village settings. Some people, the elderly in particular, lament that the younger generations have lost traditional morality and do not behave properly. Uncle Bay, for example, is concerned about the younger generation's lack of morality. He recalls that in the past when his children were still young, kids used to greet older villagers whenever they met on the village paths and showed respect to the old, but nowadays, he laments, children have become naughty and selfish. His understanding of the present situation might be coloured by nostalgia, but he blames new social values that no longer emphasize family and village hierarchy and stress individualism.

The question of new and old moralities has often been approached in the context of the dichotomy between tradition and modernism in Vietnam, and individualism is seen as one of the major social characteristics of the modern era.[8] As Vu (1959) argues, the "traditional" way of life is often valued in Vietnam and "traditional" thinking is considered ideal. When tradition is neglected, it is often thought that morality is ruined. For example, when I occasionally talked with the seventy-three-year-old neighbour, I often heard him say that people should respect more traditional customs. In particular, he complained that young people in the village did not dress properly. While I do not intend to analyse the relationship between individualism and modernism in Vietnam or trace its history, I would like to stress that the villagers often see individualistic tendencies of younger people as a relatively recent social phenomena. They are commonly considered as ruining traditional family values.

Thus, family education and society are closely related to each other in contemporary Vietnam. While the family plays the role of socializing younger generations, social conditions affect family education, too.

Sometimes, changing family values as well as social values cause conflicts of ideas.

SCHOOL

A significant part of children's education also takes place in the social context of school (*truong hoc*). There are three public schools in Long Tuyen Village: two elementary and one secondary. Students in the first to fifth grade go to elementary schools, and from the sixth to ninth grade they go to the secondary school. There is no high school so students have to go to Can Tho City usually on bicycles. Also, there are no private or missionary schools in Long Tuyen.

I had the opportunities to visit the secondary school attended by the sons of Fourth Sister and Fifth Sister and where I came to know some of the teachers. The school was founded during the war, and has undergone renovations and restructuring several times as social and political situations have changed in the past several decades. It is located near one of the village markets on the main road, and at the time of my research, there were 36 teachers and 798 students studying at the school. There are seven classes in the sixth grade and four in the ninth. The number of classes as well students decreases as you move up a grade. For instance, there are about 45 students in one class in sixth grade, but only around 38 in a ninth grade class. This shows that around 50 to 60 per cent of the students drop out while they are in secondary school.[9] Classes are divided into morning and afternoon sessions: sixth and ninth grades study in the morning, while seventh and eighth grades come to school in the afternoon.

In addition to talking to the schoolteachers, I also learned about schools in Long Tuyen Village and the surrounding villages from Third Brother of my host family, who is an elementary school teacher in a neighbouring village. I often met him late in the afternoon when he came back from his work, and we spoke about school education in the village as well as in the region. He started teaching when he was twenty-five. I asked him how he became a teacher. To become a teacher, he went to a vocational school in a neighbouring province for three years after he graduated from high school. He did not particularly want to be a teacher at that time, but there were only two possible jobs for him, banking and teaching. Although he wanted to become a banker, as he recalls, the banking course was not well established so he decided to become a teacher. In the beginning, he did not particularly like teaching, but he has gotten used to it now. The Department of Education assigns teachers to schools, and he has been assigned to several other schools in the province.

Officially, children are supposed to start school at six. There is a national law that children have to start school at six years old, so the village committee sends information to every family who has children at school age by order of the national government. Every child is registered with the village committee according to his/her birth certificate, so the village committee knows which families they have to inform. The chairman of the committee claims it is their responsibility to inform families and make sure village children attend school properly.[10] In reality, according to teachers, 80 per cent of the students who enter elementary school are six years old, and the rest are seven, eight or nine years old. Some parents think their children are too young to go to school at six, so they wait. For example, Fourth Sister's daughter is eight years old, but she has not started school yet. The sister says her daughter is too young to go to school, so she will wait another year. Third Brother gives other reasons why some parents cannot send their children to school when they are six years old: they may be too poor, live too far from the school, or there may be a discrepancy between the actual age and the age on the birth certificate.

Students in fifth grade have to take a final exam to graduate from elementary school. In the village school in normal years about 97 per cent of the students pass while the remaining 3 per cent fail the exam. Before, the rate of success was much lower, with only about 60 per cent of the students completing the programme. Teachers attribute the improving rate to a number of factors: management has become better, teaching methods have been transformed, and parents and students' attitudes toward school have changed.[11] Around 95 per cent of the students who finish elementary school proceed to the secondary level, but 5 per cent leave school because of their family's economic condition, or sometimes because they are already over fifteen years old by the time they finish fifth grade, and they would rather start farming on their family farm than spend a few more years in school.[12]

According to teachers at the secondary school in Long Tuyen Village, about half the students who enter secondary school reach ninth grade, and around 90 per cent of ninth graders graduate successfully, with 10-20 per cent proceeding to a high school after they graduate. The village has a higher secondary school graduation rate than other villages in the area.[13] Although the percentages presented here for the elementary school in the neighbouring village and the secondary school in Long Tuyen Village may not be accurate because there is no formal census or records,[14] they give a general idea of the situation in the region. Since there is no high school in Long Tuyen Village or in the neighbouring villages, the fraction of students who go to high school is notably small when compared to the fraction of those who finish secondary school.

A few students go to college in Can Tho City or vocational school in the province and other provinces after high school. For example, members of my host family are very well educated by village standards, and one of Second Brother's sons was a student at a technological vocational school at the time of my research. Another was at high school planning to go to a higher educational institute. A daughter of Third Brother was a student at a teacher's college in Can Tho City. There are actually very few people from Long Tuyen Village who go to college or university in Can Tho City. Third Brother's daughter in fact wanted to go to a university in the city, but she failed the entrance exam, and decided to go to the teacher's college and is now studying to become a teacher. She lives in a school dormitory in town, and returns home on the weekend. It was on those weekends that I usually met and talked with her, when she would accompany me to the market in the morning for breakfast or when she would come to help her grandmother with cooking.

The family of Uncle Bay and Aunt Tam is rather unusual in Long Tuyen Village for having children and grandchildren with more than a high school education. Not everyone has a chance to attend schools like some of these family members, because much depends on the family's situation.[15] For instance, Second Brother has no school education. It is sometimes imagined in Vietnam that the oldest son gets the most education, but this is not always the case. Why Second Brother, who is the oldest son, did not go to school is not very clear from his life story, but it is likely that he grew up when war was intense in the area and the family had to flee to other places, so he had no chance to attend school. Fourth Sister has also not had much education; she went to school only for a couple of years. She always comments that it is hard for her to educate her own children well and help them with schoolwork, because neither she nor her husband is well educated themselves.

In the past, it was not easy for the people of Long Tuyen Village to pursue higher education. Fifth Sister told me about her education as we walked together through the village one evening. She graduated from a vocational college in Can Tho City and is now an accountant for the People's Committee of Long Tuyen Village. "I could go to a college because I received a fellowship from the school. Without the fellowship, I would not have been able to pursue studying. My family had a very difficult life, and my parents had to work very hard." At that time it was not easy to go to school from the village. "I rode a bicycle to school from the village, but at that time the road from the village center to Can Tho City was not paved like it is now, so it was very difficult to ride my bicycle. And there was no light on the road because there was no electricity, and sometimes I came home late at night after studying at school, and I was scared to walk alone on the village paths." But she believes that as result of her efforts and those of her parents, and thanks to the fellowship, she graduated from college and got a job as an accountant at the People's Committee, where she has been working since she finished school.

While many students leave school at fifth or seventh grade and start farming, some families choose to give their children higher education because they think other knowledge and skills are important in contemporary society. Giving children more opportunities to get jobs outside of agriculture is one of the reasons why parents send children to school. They think that going to school not only gives their children credentials like certificates, but also the knowledge and skills that will help them find good jobs.[16] Fourth Daughter often mentions the importance of education for getting jobs outside of agriculture. She says, "If you are educated, it is good to live in a city, because you can get a job. But if you do not have education, it is better to live in a rural area, because if you live in a city, you cannot live by farming and it is hard to find a job without education."

Although Second Brother has had no formal school education, he thinks if his children acquire a good school education, they can get jobs outside of agriculture that are easier than farming. He says he and his father both think education is very important for children to have a better life. He thinks a farmer's life is hard, because he has to work all day long and all the time, and if his children have a good education, they can have other kinds of jobs. He comments, "If you have jobs other than farming, you can rest after work, and life is not as hard as for farmers. It is better for my children." Second Brother believes children can develop useful job skills and abilities at school. He wants his son to find a job suitable for his preparation in the Can Tho City technological school, probably in industrial electricity.

In fact, Second Brother has experienced non-agricultural jobs. When he was sixteen years old, he started to work at a rice mill in the town of Cai Rang and he lived and worked there for seven years. He earned ten million Vietnamese dong every month, and he liked the job. However, in 1975 when he was twenty-three, South Vietnam was liberated by the north, and the mill stopped operation. The communist force captured the owner of the mill, and Second Brother was also caught, but was later freed. After that, he returned to the village and worked as a farmer. From 1989 to 1992, he took another job as a traffic policeman. He did not like the job very much but he thought it was better than being a farmer. But he fell ill and could not continue the job, so he resumed farming instead. Based on his own experiences, he does not want his sons to follow his path as a farmer and wishes to give them more opportunities.

Moreover, the economic conditions and development plans have made him recognize the increasing importance of school education. He says, "In the future, there may be no land in this area, because the land is a property of the government and they are planning to build an inter-provincial road around here. The government may take our farm away, and then my children cannot live on farming, so it is important for them to have other jobs." Second Brother is seriously worried that his children may need other sources of income if his land is taken away, and he thinks education is important for that purpose.

While many farmers expect their children to help them in family farming, I met a few farmers who share Second Brother's view and consider going to school more important for their children. A mother of a neighbouring family does not want her children to help her with farming, because she wants them to study hard and be well educated, so they can work for the government or become teachers. A father in another village also comments, "my youngest daughter is now in tenth grade, and I want to send her to a university. I do not want her to be a farmer. I want to provide her with good opportunities." The family lives in a village closer to Can Tho City and Can Tho University in particular, so they do not think it will be too expensive for them to send the daughter to the university if she can commute to school from home and does not have to stay in a dormitory. The father also thinks that a good education will give his children the ability to do many things in society and withstand the difficulties of life.

He considers it important to educate both sons and daughters. Although there sometimes seems to be a slight preference for giving sons more education or a tendency to think that women do not need high education, most families that provide their children with higher education educate both sons and daughters equally. These families generally think that women also may need job skills in the future society. Also in many families, whether children go to school or not often depends on the children's willingness in addition to the parents' attitudes, and in some families daughters have more education than sons because they like studying more, while in other families the situation is reversed.

As a teacher, Third Brother also recognizes the increased importance of school education for getting jobs. Students' learning has improved compared to about six years ago, and the brother attributes this to both parents and children being more motivated under the social conditions. The brother thinks that motivation for education has been lower than during the socialist era, but has increased since the 1990s. He refers to parent-teacher meetings as an indicator of parental attitudes towards their children's education. The school holds three such meetings a year: at the beginning, middle, and toward the end of each year, and the brother estimates that about 50 to 60 per cent of the parents attend the meetings. The rate of attendance at the brother's school has been increasing, suggesting a greater interest in children's education among parents. (In his opinion, there are a few reasons why some parents do not come: some might be busy with their farm work or other work, while others are not serious about education. In order to motivate the parents to attend, the school sends out invitations, but the brother thinks that some parents do not come because they do not care. There was a couple in the past who refused to come, however hard the school tried, saying they were not interested in school.) Third Brother thinks the motivation is higher because people now recognize the difficulty of finding jobs and the importance of studying for getting good ones. Society requires educational backgrounds if the young seek jobs outside of agriculture and with a high school diploma, it is easier to get jobs in small factories and other occupations.

Another purpose of school education commonly pointed out by parents is teaching children to be good citizens (*cong dan*), the same goal as in family education. For example, a thirty-eight-year-old mother has four children, three of whom are students. Her children do not like to go to school, but she says she tries to encourage them to continue studying, because she thinks education is important for them as they can learn good opinions. The more they study, she thinks, the better they will become as contributors to society. Many other parents told me that they wanted to send their children to school, because they thought the younger generation would be good citizens if they got a good education. Thus, the socialization of children is thought to take place not only in families, but also in school, and parents are often considered responsible for giving their children an opportunity to attend school so that they can learn what they need to be good members of society and the nation.

Teaching about the society and the nation is one of the responsibilities of schools in Vietnam. Third Brother took a training course on a civil subject at a branch of the Ministry of Education in Hanoi for three years. The training programme is a national project that he was told to participate in by the school where he teaches. All of the teachers are expected to take the training course at some point in their career. There are other occasions as well when students develop a national identity. For example, every year on the National Unification Day,[17] which is a holiday, secondary school students of Long Tuyen Village gather in the schoolyard and experience camping. This is a one-day event, and the students learn to build a campsite, and listen to the stories of war veterans. The goal is for the students to experience what the soldiers experienced during the war before the socialist government won and the country was reunited in 1975 after many years of struggle for national independence. This is not only an occasion for students to learn their history, but also to feel patriotism and appreciate the efforts of the former generation to bring about national independence and a strong socialist government.[18]

Besides teaching children to be good members of society and the nation, parents also hope that going to school will teach their children how to behave and make them good human beings. School is often considered not only a place for students to acquire knowledge and learn new things, but also where they will be trained to behave properly. One mother expresses her wish this way: "If I had money, I would want to send my children to school, so that they will learn to be polite, but I do not have enough money to do that." Third Brother also thinks that it is the responsibility of school to teach morality. He comments, "Morality in school is not good these days. Students used to have more respect for teachers and the old, but now they do not. Some parents are not well educated. But we try to teach morality to students in our school. We do not teach only subjects, and now some students behave well." The brother's comment suggests that he thinks parents are primarily responsible for teaching morality to children, but the school has to participate as well.

SCHOOL, FAMILY, AND DECISIONS

School education and family are tightly connected in the lives of Long Tuyen villagers, and it has a particular significance in the context of social conditions and uncertainties that the people are faced with. When I talked with villagers about their families and family life, many people voluntarily talked about the education of their children even when I did not refer to the topic or initiate a conversation about it. Children's education is one of the major concerns for many families in the rural area.

The families' decision to send their children to school is based on several factors. One of them is expense. The cost of sending children to school is often the biggest problem that many farmers' families face. During the socialist or collectivization period, school was free. Cooperatives underwrote much of the expense for education, subsidizing basic salaries and supporting other programmes that derived from the provincial and central government. However, since the reform, the subsidies that were underwritten by cooperatives under the socialist economy have been disappearing, and in the late 1980s fees for primary and secondary school were introduced. School fees that are not covered by the government and hence have to be shouldered by individual families have been increasing rapidly, having impacts on school enrolment (see Belanger and Liu 2004).[19]

As Tran Thi Van Anh and Nguyen Manh Huan state, "The switch in...educational services from state subsidization to liberalization has had mixed consequences. On the one hand, services are better for those who can afford to pay. On the other hand, education has become less accessible, particularly to poor women and children" (Tran Thi Van Anh and Nguyen Manh Huan 1995, p. 213). In fact, whether parents find it expensive to send their children to school varies with the financial situation of the family: some say it is all right, while others say it is very difficult. Third Brother analyses that it is easier for farmers' children to go to elementary school than to obtain a higher education, "because the government does not ask for any school fee for elementary school". However, even in elementary school, though no official fee is collected, there are many small fees that parents are asked for on various occasions, and there are expenses on school supplies such as notebooks, pencils and carrying bags that parents have to pay.

In Long Tuyen Secondary School, the school fee was 54,000 dongs per year for six, seventh and eighth graders and 90,000 dongs for ninth graders in 2000 (the school fee for high school in Can Tho City was 180,000 dongs). In one year, in addition to the school fees, students' families were required to pay 50,000 dongs for school construction (*tien xay dung*) and 20,000–28,000 dongs for school insurance (*tien bao hiem*), and also asked to make other contributions. Villagers complain that the school fees for the secondary and higher schools change all the time and they have been going up every year over the past several years.

For many families, school expenses are a financial burden, and some students give up studying early on because expenses are too high for their families to afford. For instance, in one landless family that lives by selling cakes in town, one child entered school but stopped in the first year because there was no way for the single mother to afford the school fee and other expenses. Besides, her children have to either help the mother make and sell cakes, or tend younger siblings while the mother goes out to work. It is not possible for this mother to afford the luxury of sending her children to school. Another family faced a similar problem. Their son had to stop school a few months ago with sixth grade after one year in secondary school because fees were higher than in elementary school. The family does not have enough money to support his education any more and this child had to give up studying, although he would have liked to study and wanted to continue school. His parents understand that it is difficult for the child to give up school, and blame the school for not helping them out. They are angry that the school does not pay attention to families with such problems. In another family, their daughter liked studying very much, but she had to stop at seventh grade because her family had financial problems and could not pay school fees and expenses. Now she works in a small food-processing factory.

If the children were to continue in school, the family would not only have to pay school fees but also lose labour wages, which would create a double financial burden for the family. As we have seen, while younger children are not considered major labourers for the family, as they get older, they become important workers for their family economy. In poor families in particular, members are required not only to farm their own land, but also to work as labourers for the neighbours in order to earn enough money. Pursuing higher education requires considerable effort and sacrifice by children and their families. Second Brother has three sons, one in secondary school, one in high school and one in a vocational school in Can Tho City. Since he got divorced he has been raising the children by himself. Whenever I talked with Fifth Sister about her natal family, she commented about the brother, "he has to raise three children by himself, and it is very difficult for him." Though life is not easy for him, Second Brother is serious about his children's education. He knows his sons like to study and he wants to encourage them to study hard, so he supplies books for them. When one of his sons spends most of the day in high school, it means there are fewer hands to work on the family farm. Considering that Second Brother has no wife to farm with, one can imagine how much effort and sacrifice are required for him to send his sons to schools.

Thus, it is not only the situation and conditions of the family finance that determine children's access to school education, but also the attitudes of parents and children. To go to the high school in Can Tho City, the second son of Second Brother has to bike for about an hour every day. He is actually one of the few students in the hamlet of Binh Thuong B who goes to high school. He leaves home early in the morning before six o'clock, and comes back around three in the afternoon. After he works on the farms of his father and grandfather he usually spends most of the evening studying. Every night he comes to the house of his grandparents, where he spends the night studying. Since Second Brother's house is small and dark, the son comes to study and sleep at his grandparents' house. He spends a few hours studying either in the living room in front, or in the kitchen-bedroom at the back. Almost every night, he asked me to help him study English as he was especially eager to practise speaking. (In return, he helped me learn Vietnamese by reading his literature book to me.) He is very diligent and enthusiastic about studying and learning. He wants to become a businessman in the future, and wishes to go to a university or college.

Some parents particularly encourage their children to attend school. In one family I met, only the youngest daughter went to school and was in secondary school. According to her mother, the daughter likes to study, while the other children do not, so only the daughter has remained in school. However, the mother is worried that the daughter has been having some problems in school, and she does not like to study as much as she used to. Both parents want her to continue her school education and encourage her not to give up her study. Like this mother, some parents encourage their children to study, even when the children do not enjoy it. Another mother says her children do not like to go to school, but she encourages them to study, because she thinks education is important. She has three sons and one daughter, and the older son stopped school at sixth grade. Right now two other sons are in the first and fifth grades. The daughter is not yet of school age. This mother thinks education is important for her children and in order to make it easier for her children to pursue their studies, she has bought them a bicycle.

In contrast, there are also parents who do not regard school education as important for their children. Some farmers do not think school education will help their children's future if they are going to be farmers like themselves. They think it is better for the children to stop school and work on the family farm. Particularly in the situation when competition in agriculture is severe and making enough money is difficult, children's labour for farming is considered precious by these families. Some other parents claim that their children have had little education because they do not like to study and do not go want to go to school. These parents are not particularly concerned about their children's school education.

There is a tendency for well-educated parents to be eager to provide their children with good educational opportunities.[20] For example, Third Brother went to a teacher's school, and now his daughter also studies at a teacher's college in Can Tho City. As already mentioned, going to college is quite rare in Long Tuyen Village, and can show how serious the family is about their children's education. In another family in a different village, both the father and the mother graduated from high school and now work as clerks at a hospital in a nearby town, and one of their daughters is a student in the English department at a college and another is at high school. In many families with parents or a parent who has had much school education, the children have higher education.

However, this does not mean that the reverse is also true, for some parents of children who attend high school and college have often had little school education themselves. As the importance of education is recognized for surviving in society, many uneducated or little-educated parents also take school education seriously. As we have seen, Second Brother has had no school education, but sends his three sons to schools. He recognizes the importance of a school education and encourages his sons to continue studying, although it may mean a sacrifice on his part. A mother of the family in another village, with whom I spent one day and shared a meal, was very enthusiastic about expressing her ideas about her children's education as we talked. She claims she is open-minded, so she is eager to provide her children with a school education. Her oldest daughter is twenty-two years old, and she is a student at the English Department of a teacher's college in Can Tho City. Her son is in twelfth grade in high school, and he also wants to go to a college or a university.

The mother, who is forty-five years old and works as a rice seller in town, had little education herself. She says, because it was not easy to go to school in this area in the past when she was young. The mother finds it very expensive to send her children to school, but her children are eager to study, and she and her husband agree:

> We know that today, our children need good certificates of education to get good jobs. I work as a rice seller in the city, so I know many things. I am open-minded, and do not stick to traditional ideas, so I think school education is important for my children. Some traditional people think that farmer's children should learn to help their parents in the farm, instead of wasting time and money in school. But I know about outside society, and know the importance of education. I do not want my children to follow us and become farmers and rice sellers. I want them to have better jobs and better life.

However, in the past, there was some disagreement in the family about the children's education. The father wanted the oldest daughter to find a stable job when she graduated from high school, and he found an accountant position for her in a small company. However, the daughter did not want to take the job, because she wanted to continue studying. After discussing the matter with his daughter and learning of her wishes, the father agreed to send her to college. The daughter now very much appreciates her parents' efforts to send her to the college, and says "I am very proud of my parents, because they work very hard for us to study." (She said these words to me in English, which her parents did not understand. It suggests that she was not merely trying to please her parents, and she wanted to show me how hard she studies.) The daughter actually wanted to go to a university, but since she did not pass the entrance examination, she decided to go to a teacher's college instead. She wants to concentrate on her studies for the time being, and does not want to get married yet. She thinks studying is the most important thing for her to do at the moment and says, "I will think about marriage later, after I become a teacher. I am still very young." A few weeks later, she visited me in my room in Can Tho City to practise her English.

The family's neighbour, who spent the afternoon with us, agrees on the topic of children's education. The mother of this neighbouring family is forty-six years old, and although she has had little education herself, the elder of her two sons is in twelfth grade. The mother thinks that she can only do manual labour, because of her low level of education, so she considers it better for her children to have higher education. She encourages her children to study well, and now the elder son wants to go to college after high school. She is also a rice seller, and when she goes to the city for a few days to sell rice, her parents usually take care of her children. Whenever she returns home to the village, she encourages her children to study hard, and she occasionally returns home just for that purpose.

Even if children are eager to study and parents encourage that, some families face a moral conflict with the widespread belief that children should help with the family farming. Some people regard children's going to school after they are old enough to work in the farm as a waste of time and money. One mother finds it extremely difficult to send her daughters to school because of conflicting ideas. The mother thinks "traditional" ideas in the rural area are a big problem. In the rural area, she says, girls are usually expected to work on the farm, boys are supposed to have jobs in construction, and going to school is not valued much. She particularly faces a problem with her parents-in-law because they do not approve of her sending her children to school. They insist that the children should quit school and work for the family. In the mother's view, her parents-in-law have very traditional ideas and they think sending children to school is a waste of money. If her children quit school and worked on the farm or got other jobs, they would bring income to the family. However, the mother believes school education gives them opportunities for better jobs, so she does her best for her children to attend school, although it may be "against some Vietnamese traditional convictions". I never had a chance to meet her children, but the mother tells me, they understand the difficulty their mother is coping with, so they help her with the farm work, too. They go to school in the morning, and work in the garden in the afternoon. Her oldest daughter goes to high school, and since it is very far, the mother bought a used bicycle for her to bike to school.

This mother is thirty-seven years old and has four children. She herself went to school up to the fifth grade. She grew up in Can To City, helping her mother who had a small stall where she sold sticky rice for breakfast. She had to quit school at fifth grade to help her mother because they lived in poverty. Her father died when she was four years old, and she says her mother's life and her own were difficult because they were very poor and had to work hard in order to earn enough income to eat. (She moved to this village when she married at eighteen.) Because she had a difficult childhood and could not continue with school after fifth grade, she does not want her children to follow her path. She thinks it is important for her children to be well educated to secure a better life particularly now that society is changing. She says, "It is very difficult to send children to school, but I have to do it, because I do not want my children to have a life like my own." She is determined to do anything to secure enough money to send her children to school, and she is always in debt. On the day I talked with her for the first time, she was working as a labourer in a neighbour's rice field for money, and I met her in a small restaurant where she came to have a bowl of noodle soup for lunch with other farmers.

In another family, the father experiences conflicts with the grandparents (the mother's parents) about the children's education. His story is as follows: The father wanted to send his son to high school, because he knows how important education is in contemporary society. But the grandparents thought education was a waste of time and money, and they wanted the grandchild to earn money so that they could have a comfortable life. The father tried to encourage the son to continue education, but the son followed the grandparents' idea and quit school in the eighth grade. Now the son is a construction worker and wants to make money quickly. The father is sorry that his son does not obey him and disagrees with his ideas. Only the father works in the family fruit garden now, and when the son occasionally returns home from his work, he tries to persuade the father to sell his garden for money. Because of this conflict between the father and mother's parents, the mother has left home and returned to Cambodia where they used to live and where she makes a living by selling vegetables. In the father's view, his two daughters are better than his son, because they have a good opinion of education and finished the twelfth grade in high school. He thinks education is most important in shaping children's characters and futures, but in the case of his son, he thinks the situation was difficult because of differences in opinion between him and the grandparents. We can see that some values conflict with others, in this case, the importance of education on the one hand and the value of money on the other.

According to the Long Tuyen secondary school's records, the number of students drops quite dramatically from sixth grade to ninth grade.[21] Continuing school education is not always easy for the reasons we have seen.[22]

EDUCATION AND THE FUTURE

For the villagers of Long Tuyen, school education and jobs outside farming are closely related to each other. Many parents and children take education seriously as it is useful for getting a better job in the future, which will secure a more stable life. There is a common belief that without a good education you cannot get a good job, and recognition that school education is crucial for employment.

However, education does not necessarily assure good future. There are not many job prospects, and education does not seem to give villagers the security of having one. Even with a high school diploma, which is not a very common achievement in the village, it is not easy to find a job outside of agriculture. In a village closer to Can Tho City, I met one family whose son graduated from Can Tho University with a degree in food processing. After he graduated, however, he could not find a job, so he came back to the village and now he is engaged in farming while he continues to search for employment. He says that if you go up to Ho Chi Minh City, there are more industries and more jobs, but in Can Tho fewer are available.

The villagers of Long Tuyen face two seemingly contradictory problems. On the one hand, the prospect of industrialization of the area in the coming years makes them worry that they may lose their land and no longer be able to live by farming. On the other hand, seeking jobs in the industrial sector is still difficult. Second Brother is constantly worried that his land may be taken for development projects and his children may not be able to live on farming in the future. He hopes that his son, a student at an industrial college, will get a job preferably in industrial electricity. However, he knows that even with a good education, it is not easy to find jobs.

Unemployment in non-agricultural sector has been a problem in the province, in and around Can Tho City in particular.[23] Although precise unemployment figures are not available, many graduates from Can Tho University commonly have difficulty finding jobs. The university is mainly an agricultural school, and most students seek jobs in food processing or other industries related to their educational backgrounds, but there are not many positions available for them. Tran Thi Van Anh and Nguyen Manh Huan describe the employment situation and education in rural Vietnam: "Students' learning motivation to learn has dropped markedly because there are too few employment opportunities" (1995, p. 213). My research does not suggest that the small number of jobs outside of agriculture has actually reduced the desire for education in Long Tuyen Village, but job opportunities certainly affect education, because getting a job has become one of the main aims of school education.

CONCLUSION

Education, in the family and at school, is often considered crucial both for society and the individual in contemporary Vietnam. Family and school education is expected to play a big role for the future of the whole nation. On the one hand, the importance of family and family education have been socially recognized and stressed, now that the collectives of the socialist era have dissolved and the family has once again have the role of socializing the young. The development of the whole society is often thought to depend on the education of children by each family. People regard one of the main aims of education at home and school to socialize children to be good citizens of the society and the nation.

On the other hand, with uncertainties in their life, school education has acquired specific meaning for families in the rural Mekong Delta, too. Some farmers' families in Long Tuyen and other villages recognize the significance of education for their children's own future. It is only through education that parents often think they can assure a stable future for their children. Some worry that the next generation will not be able to live on agriculture, while others think their children would have a better life if they could get jobs other than farming, and having a good education is considered the best and most crucial factor for succeeding in other occupations. Even if their children are going to follow them into farming, people consider education useful for acquiring the knowledge and ability necessary for coping with changes in agriculture.

However, securing a good school education and a stable future for their children is not always easy for families in villages like Long Tuyen. Given the cost of school fees and expenses, many parents are not sure whether they can afford their children's school education. For families who live on the subsistence level, or only a little above, it is not easy to spend extra money for education. Poorer families, such as those who do not own any land, find it is almost impossible to educate their children well. This results in an education gap between children of the rich and the poor as Tran Thi Van Anh and Nguyen Manh Huan (1995) describe. Children of rich families do not always have a better education because they may not like to study or may stop going to school early for other reasons, but there is a clear tendency for children from poorer families to have less education. While this may be less of a problem in elementary school, it becomes a serious issue in higher grades as school fees go up. Moreover, children are expected to help their parents in farming once they are old enough, and since they are important sources of labour income, it is harder for poorer families to send their teenage children to school.

Even if families manage to spare enough money and sacrifice to provide their children with higher education, the younger generation's future is not totally secured, since school certificates do not always assure good jobs and a stable life. Although it is usually necessary to have at least a high school diploma to be employed in the industrial sector, the certificate is often not sufficient for securing a job. However, even though a good education does not always assure the next generation's future, for the time being, farmers think it is certainly one crucial way to give young people more opportunities. Without school education, farmers' children have little choice but to follow their parents into farming, and if the future of farming is clouded, the children's future will be as well.

Education is one of the spheres where family cooperation and family sacrifice play out in the everyday lives of many farmers. Parents cannot expect their children to help much in agriculture if sons and daughters go to school for many years. Sometimes there are conflicts with other members of the family. However, to increase their children's opportunities, as well as the whole family's future prospects, parents think they need to make certain sacrifices in the present.

Notes

1. According to a historian Woodside (1971), in the nineteenth-century Vietnamese society, there was the influence of the Confucian examination system just like that in China. According to Hue-Tam Ho Tai (personal comment), however, Confucian education was not introduced to the Mekong Delta at that time. She argues that educational system of the area was first developed mainly under French colonialism. In contrast, Hy Van Luong (also in his personal comment) states that the nineteenth-century examination laureates includes numerous names from the Mekong Delta. More historical study would be necessary on this point. See Vu (1959) on the history of Vietnamese educational systems. For specific historical accounts on education in South Vietnam, see Kelly (1980; 1982) on the French colonial period, and Hoshall (1971), Lavergne (1955), Spragens (1971) and Hunter (1977) on the war time.
2. In Vietnam, the role of parents as teachers of their children is often stressed. The mother is particularly considered responsible for educating children well (Bui 1995). In traditional Vietnam until the twentieth century, women had no right to formal education, and they were educated in the family. Tai (1992) introduces "family education in verse" dating back to the fifteenth century and written by a scholar Nguyen Trai, which was filled with taboos. This, the author argues, particularly applied to women of the elite families, but also represented the expectation for women of all class.

In a Taiwanese context, Fung (1999) discusses the role of family in the education of morality, shame in particular.

3. How filial piety is practised in everyday life of the farmers is further examined in Owada-Shibuya (2003). Burr also argues that filial piety is a significant aspect of Vietnamese value, and it results in a set of behavior "which create an environment in which the good and morally bound child accept his or her position within the family for the greater good of the collective" (Burr 2014, p. 167).
4. Rydstrom's (2003) study on the family in North Vietnam suggests that there are clear and profound differences in moral upbringing of boys and girls. However, distinction between male and female children in their moral education is significantly smaller in the Mekong Delta, though it does not disappear completely.
5. People often complemented me that I was simple, that I dressed simple and lived simple. They particularly said that it was good that I, with much money (by their standards) and some social status, still lived a simple life.
6. Tran considers the family as not only the basic unit of society, but also a model for it. He states, "The family is not only the least unit, but the model for social and governmental organizations. Villages, unions and the government are all put in good order after the model of family, particularly that linked together by affection" (Tran Dinh Huou 1996, p. 80). Here, the moral and emotional attachments of family members are considered crucial for building a good society.
7. According to Hong Ha's argument, the renovation reform emerged from the family, which is the smallest component of society, and in the reform, it is crucial for the development of the country that the family regain not only its economic function but also its social role.
8. Individualism is often understood as brought into the society along with other Western ideas during French colonialism.
9. There is no accurate data on gender proportion of the students. However, I did not hear villagers say their daughters stopped schooling "because they were girls". Also, as I observed the students in class or in the schoolyard, I did not particularly notice a difference in the number of boys and girls.
10. Vietnam boasts a high literacy rate thanks to its educational system founded under the socialist government. A census claims that 80 per cent of the whole population was literate. See *Vietnam Living Standards Survey 1992–1993* (1994) and *Vietnam Population and Housing Census 2009* for the data on educational system of the nation.

11. On the national level, in the early 1990s, only 85 per cent of primary school-aged children were enrolled in elementary schools, and fewer than 50 per cent of pupils entering primary school completed it (Kinh 1991: cited from Jones 1999).
12. The national gross enrolment rate at lower secondary school in 1991 was about 47 per cent and at upper secondary school was 17 per cent (Jones 1999). There were 1,880 lower secondary schools in 1989–90, which included every village (Hac 1991: cited from Jones 1999).
13. Truong Thi Kim Chuyen et al. (1999) give a quantitative analysis on the national level of the rate at which students finish elementary school, and proceed to and continue through secondary school.
14. Accurate data are not available at the school or at the People's Committee on the number of students who go to high school in Can Tho City.
15. I did not observe a large gap between genders in terms of higher school education unlike what Goodkind (1995) suggests. I observed a larger gap between class, both in economic and political senses.
16. Peterson (1991) argues that in the Philippines, education of children is regarded important by the parents as it affects their welfare in the future, as well of the whole kin group. The villagers of Long Tuyen do not refer to the aspect of contribution to the family in the future when discussing children's education. However, jobs outside of family are often pursued for the sake of the whole family as investigated in the previous chapter, and education of the children is likely to help the whole family in the future.
17. National Unification Day is on 30 April, the day when Sai Gon fell to the North Vietnamese force and the war ended in 1975.
18. Not all families of the village have a pro-Communist background. However, how these families feel about socialism's influence on education is not known. I did not encounter people complain about school education particularly in this respect.
19. Belanger and Liu argue that the introduction of school fees have had a particular impact on school enrolment of daughters, which is not particularly visible in the rural Mekong Delta. See also Nguyen Duy Quy and Sloper (1995) for the effect of the economic reform on education. Ikels (1996) discusses a similar situation in the Chinese educational system in the post-Mao era.
20. Kim's (1977) study in Korea examines the effect of the mother's education on decision-making concerning child rearing.
21. Pham Minh Hac (1998) gives a national statistic which shows that the percentage of class-repeating pupils and drop-outs in secondary schools increased after 1986, and then declined dramatically after 1991, although he does not give any reason for the trend.

22. The 2009 Vietnam Population and Housing Census also shows a difference in rates of people who attend secondary school between urban and rural areas. While there does not exist a discrepancy in attendance rate in primary school (urban 101.6 per cent, rural 103.3 per cent), those in secondary and tertiary school drop significantly in rural areas (Lower secondary: urban 93.8 per cent, rural 88.2 per cent; Upper secondary: urban 76.5 per cent, 60.3 per cent; Tertary: urban 54.0 per cent, Rural 11.1 per cent). For statistical data and information on educational attainment in Vietnam, see also *Education in Vietnam: An Analysis of Key Indicators* (2011).
23. Industrialization in the country since the economic reform has more concentrated in areas around Ho Chi Minh City and the Red River Delta. The country as a whole has recorded a rapid economic growth, but during the 1990s and the early 2000s the Mekong Delta was not as industrialized as some people had expected. Many foreign investors that I knew of personally left the region, too. However, the area has been more industrialized during the 2000s.

7

FEELING POOR

POVERTY

The villagers of Long Tuyen Village constantly mention "poverty" as the main problem in their life. When I first met them and explained that I wanted to learn about their life, the first comments I received were, "Vietnam is poor, because it is a developing country", "in Vietnam, farmers are poor", and "our life is difficult because we are poor". Later on, after I had spent a few months in the village, the villagers would ask me, "Have you found out why Vietnam is poor?" or "do you know how the farmers could be helped so that we are not poor any longer?" Leshkowich states that the female market traders in Ho Chi Minh "consciously perpetuate negative stereotypes" about petty traders for their own benefit (Leshkowich 2000, p. 8). It is possible that the farmers stressed their "poor" life in to me because I was a foreigner from a rich country and they expected me to help them. However, my research suggests that the farmers' use of the word is not only for taking advantage of "being poor". Poverty constitutes a part of their perception of the reality that they see in their actual life, and it also forms their identity.

Are the farmers actually poor? It can be said that the villagers of Binh Thuong B Hamlet are poor in a general sense. About one third of all houses do not have electricity.[1] Only a few have water pumps, and the rest use muddy river water for drinking and cooking, as well as for other daily purposes. Many houses are made of water coconut leaves, and many have dirt floors. The villagers do not regularly eat meat which they have to buy in the market, and they often eat only fish from the river, vegetables from their garden, and rice from their field. However, to say whether the villagers are poor in any objective sense is a difficult task beyond the scope of my work.[2] Rather, what is important is the strong "feeling" of poverty among the farmers. Why is it so widespread and where does it come from?

Poverty is often relative or subjective, and I argue that the villagers feel poor for several reasons. First, they do not have enough money to buy things they consider necessities. Second, the uncertainty of income and market prices make people worry about their present and future financial well-being. Third, farmers feel that government policies on taxation and development are not adequate for helping them achieve more financial security. Fourth, people make comparisons between rural and urban life. Fifth, farmers also compare their present situation to their past life. Finally, farmers' perception of local as well as national politics also contributes to their feeling of poverty.

Interestingly, all villagers do not necessarily share this feeling. There is a conflict between "the rich" and "the poor" which further increases many villagers' sense that they are poor.

"Het Tien"

Villagers often say they have "run out of money (*het tien*)". When they use this phrase, they express their feeling that something is too expensive for them to buy. For example, some say they cannot buy enough food because it is too expensive and they ran out of money, *het tien*. (Whether the villagers think that food is expensive or not varies. Some farmers say food is too expensive and they cannot buy enough, while others think the price of food is reasonable and they can afford it.) Electricity is one thing that most people find expensive. Electricity in the village is supplied privately and according to the villagers and some people from the city, it is almost three times as expensive as that supplied publicly in the city. Long Tuyen Village has had electricity since 1993, when the villagers contributed money to building the wire system. Those who could not contribute have no access to electricity. They say that they do not have electricity because they "ran out of money".

Villagers also often complain about how expensive house repair is. As mentioned above, many houses are made of water coconut leaves, which need to be re-thatched every few years. The thatch is made of natural leaves, but it often takes professional carpenters to prepare them and thatch the whole house, although some families manage to do the work by themselves. The cost of re-thatching an entire house varies depending on the quality of the leaves and the way they thatch, but it is a burden for many families. I visited houses where the wind blows in through holes in the walls and rain leaks in through the roof. Often people patch holes and cracks with thin plastic shopping bags or plastic sheets that are used in agricultural tasks. Some houses look quite torn down, but the owners cannot afford to repair them. Besides the walls and the roof, the floor is another part of a house that is considered to signal the wealth of the owner. For example, houses with dirt floors are thought to be poor. Those with so-called Chinese tiles (red or yellow tiles made of bricks) used to be a symbol of wealth until a few years earlier. However, the villagers say that the Chinese tiles are no longer the best. Many newly rebuilt houses have more shiny, colourful ceramic tiles on the floor which have now become the new symbol of wealth. In Long Tuyen Village, they are becoming more popular, and people who are renovating their houses like to choose them as long as they can afford.

The house as a whole is also an indicator of wealth and status. In order to renovate or rebuild their houses, people usually save money for many years. Therefore, it is not simply that those with new and large houses are wealthier than others, because a family with a small, old house may in a few years build a large one with the savings accumulated over many years. The new houses built in the past couple of years are not thatched with coconut leaves, but made of bricks and cement with zinc roofs. The front facades of these houses are often painted white or sometimes in light colors such as blue, pink or yellow, which makes them look more luxurious compared to the thatched houses. My host family had built such a house six months before I arrived in the village. According to Uncle Bay, they rebuilt the house because their former house was damaged by a falling coconut tree. It took two months to build the house and cost one hundred million Vietnamese dongs (equivalent of seven thousand US dollars).[3] Uncle Bay used the money he had saved from the income from his garden. He says, "Before, when we started the fruit garden, the price of fruit that we sold was very high, so we could save money. We started at the right moment." They also wanted to transform the front yard, which is made of dirt now. At that time, their neighbour was covering his front yard with cement blocks, and the father wanted to do the same. However, he says, "we could have paved the yard, if the last two years had had good fruit seasons, but we are not able to, because we did not make enough money from our fruit orchards."

In Binh Thuong B Hamlet, at the time of my research, there were new houses made of bricks and cement, but it is hard to estimate the exact number because some houses are only partly renovated and the old sections stand next to the new ones. For example, Fourth Sister's family lived in a thatched house when I first arrived. A couple of months later, when I visited her house just before the Lunar New Year, I was surprised to see the brick front façade painted in brilliant white. However, as I entered the house, I noticed that the house was only partially renovated and, at the back, the sidewalls were still the old ones of thatch and unpainted plywood. Fourth Sister says, "we wanted to renovate the whole house, but we ran out of money. We were counting on the income from farming this year. But the sales were not good this year, and we did not make much money." In fact, it is quite common to see such houses. Often, people renovate before the Lunar New Year, so that they can greet the New Year in a new house. Therefore, farmers start renovating their houses before the last harvest of the year, counting on the income they will get from their last sales. However, the final harvest may turn out to be poor or the sales price may be lower than expected, and they may have to give up renovating the whole house. At other times, farmers may decide to start renovation with whatever money they have, knowing that they can rebuild only part of the house, leaving the rest for a time when they can afford it.

UNCERTAINTY

It is not only a lack of sufficient income or "running out of money" but also the uncertainty of income and expense that gives farmers the feeling of poverty. As we saw in the chapter on agriculture, productivity depends on many unpredictable factors such as the weather, tree diseases, the crop, and the market. Therefore, farm income fluctuates from year to year and it is difficult for farmers to predict their earnings, unlike wages from other occupations. Not much information is available on exactly how fruit and other agricultural product prices were set in this area in the past, and it is not easy to assess how stable they were under socialism, so I cannot compare the situation of the 1990s and the 2000s with the past. However, farmers see more rapid and drastic price fluctuations now than in the past. According to one farmer, "Prices have changed more after the open-market policy by the government. Because the price changes all the time, our life is unstable. If we had fixed prices, life would be more stable." What farmers find the most difficult to deal with is, contrary to the national economic growth, that prices of the products they sell have been falling rapidly over the past couple of years. Uncle Bay says growing fruit used to be a good business when he started more than ten years ago, but it has become difficult to earn much money from it. Another farmer turned his rice field into a fruit orchard only three years earlier because he thought other people were successfully raising fruit, but regrets that his business has not been going well since then. The farmers think that the price decline has been due to more severe competition. "There are more farmers who grow fruit now, so there is more competition. Because many farmers go to sell the same product, the price goes down", they say.

In addition to the more severe competition among farmers, farmers see the effects of the global market as a big threat. The village chairman of Long Tuyen says, "A big problem in the village right now is the outside market. There are apples and oranges imported from foreign countries such as Thailand and China. Because of them, it has been difficult for the farmers to sell their fruit at good prices. Particularly in the last two years, the income of the villagers decreased by about thirty percent. This is the biggest problem of the village." According to the villagers, the importing of fruit from abroad has accelerated in the past few years, hitting the local markets. One farmer says, "because of the fruit imports, the price of our product changes. And we do not know what fruit we should choose to plant." Another one says, "The price of fruit is low this year. It has been fluctuating all the time, and we farmers cannot negotiate the price, because the wholesaler, who buys our fruit, decides it. The market determines it. When fruit is imported from other countries, it is difficult for us because the price of our product becomes set low." Products from Thailand seem to directly and seriously impact the sales of local fruit, because many Thai varieties are the same as those in the Mekong Delta and they compete with the local products.[4] In particular, the importing of oranges has seriously affected Long Tuyen farmers, since that fruit is a major commercial product of many village farms. To make matters worse, orange orchards in the village have been suffering from a widespread disease, which has reduced the quality of oranges. When crop quality suffers, competing in the global market becomes tougher.

Some farmers try to protect themselves from price fluctuations and the unpredictability of their income. For instance, one farmer describes his strategy as follows: "We pay attention to the price at the market, and decide when to sell our products. We save our products until the time is good." However, this farmer is supposedly rather well off, because he does not have to sell his products right away for money and can wait to sell them in the future. Many other farmers need to sell their products as soon as they are harvested for immediate cash income to cover their daily needs. They feel totally powerless in the face of price fluctuations. Another farmer expresses his feeling this way: "The price of lemons this year is about ten to fifteen thousand Vietnamese dongs. The price changes every year, and this year it is very low. But we do not know why. The wholesalers at Cai Rang market do not buy all of our fruits, so we farmers have to sell the rest at a lower price to other buyers. The government, when they sell fruit, they sell at a high price, but when they buy, the price is low." As this farmer's comment demonstrates, sometimes villagers do not know who buys and sells their products, whether private merchants or the state, and it is not always clear to them how the system works and product prices are decided. They are also unable to assess the quality of their products in comparison with other domestic and foreign products, and hence feel more confused about the price fluctuations. Sometimes, farmers feel that their yearly crop is good, but find the selling price much lower than they expect.

Therefore behind the feeling of poverty among farmers lie not only the unpredictability of income, but also the feeling of having no control over their earnings. Farmers feel that their income is controlled by someone else, such as the buyers (both private and governmental) of their products, and more generally, by the market. Because market competition is severe, they feel that there is less space for them to decide or negotiate the price of the products they sell. When farmers go to sell their products, they do in fact negotiate. I described in an earlier chapter how Third Sister-in-Law and Fourth Sister sold their lemons to a wholesale merchant. Thus, prices are not entirely decided and fixed by buyers, and there is some room for negotiation. However, that room is limited and farmers often have to compromise. The two sisters had to either sell at the unsatisfactory price offered by the buyer or not sell at all, so they decided to compromise and sell at a lower price than they wished. After the negotiations with buyers, farmers are often left with the feeling that they have less power over the price of their own products than the buyers, and they are pressed by the need to sell their products, even if they are not satisfied with the price. This powerlessness is one factor that makes farmers feel they are unable to control their income.

TAXATION AND GOVERNMENTAL LOANS

Besides fluctuating and falling market prices, many farmers also constantly blame taxation for their poverty and feeling of uncertainty. One early evening, when we were having dinner and talking, Youngest Brother, who was always eager to help me understand the lives of Vietnamese farmers, argued: "Vietnamese farmers are poor, because we have to pay a lot of taxes (*thue*)." According to the brother, there are four kinds of taxes that farmers of Long Tuyen Village have to pay: land (*dat*) tax, agricultural production (*nong nghiep*) tax, house (*nha*) tax, and national defense (*quoc phong*) tax. And the taxes keep changing and increasing.

He stresses that high taxes have been a big burden for farmers. For example, he explains, "in the rural area in Vietnam, farmers pay tax on their rice fields. It is one thousand and five hundred dongs per kilogram of rice we harvest. But when we sell the rice, we only receive one thousand and four hundred dongs per kilogram. So we pay more tax than the money we make by growing rice." "The government suggests that rice be bought at one thousand and eight hundred dongs per kilogram, but it is only a suggestion and they do not control the price. In reality, rice is sold at a much lower price." Farmers of the Mekong Delta generally sell the rice they harvest to private rice mills, and not to the government. The government advises mill owners on the price they should pay farmers for rice, but does not enforce these recommendations, so the mill owners can pay what they like. Therefore, Youngest Brother stresses, farmers end up losing money by growing and selling rice.[5] In fact, many other farmers consider taxation one of their main expenses, and mention that they have converted rice fields into fruit orchards because growing rice does not bring in income to their households. One farmer expresses his anger: "The government puts taxes on everything, even on these canals in front of our house. Each household has to pay tax for some meters of the canal in front of them."

Taxes are collected by each village, and there are tax collectors in the People's Committee of each village. Villagers are normally supposed to pay taxes at the tax counter of the Committee office in the centre of the village, but the collectors also visit each house to collect taxes from those who live far away and those who have not paid. I interviewed one tax collector of Long Tuyen Village, who reported that about 80 per cent of the residents of the village pay the tax regularly. Those who do not pay often do not have enough cash. The collector continues, "so I visit each house and collect taxes that they have not paid whenever they have money ready for the payment." If someone cannot pay the tax for a long time, the government will take away his land, and when he pays the tax that he owes to the government, they will return it. There are cases in which people who cannot afford the rising taxes lose their land forever.

Villagers are not only unsatisfied with the government for high taxation. They also often mention that the government does not help the poor farmers feel more financially secure. One villager comments, "In Vietnam, farmers are poor, because we cannot borrow money from the national government. You can borrow money from the state bank if you have a large piece of land or a big house, so that when you cannot repay the debt to the bank, they can take the land or the house. But in Vietnam, most farmers don't have big land plots or big houses." Many other villagers say that the procedure is too complicated, so it is too difficult for the farmers, most of whom have not had high education, to get a governmental loan. I am not claiming that the government does not try to help the farmers. In fact I knew a government bank officer in Can Tho City, who often visited the villages in the province to finance local development projects and lend money to the farmers. However, farmers, especially those without much land, feel they are not able to borrow as much money from the government as they would like, and this contributes to the sense of poverty and insecurity shared by many Long Tuyen Village farmers.

Farmers remember one economic programme run by the government in the past as successful and helpful: the Poverty Elimination Programme, launched in 1991. The government lent money to farmers, who then had two years to repay their debts. Many people consider it as a good programme and they used it to purchase what they needed to improve their farms and houses. However, they recall, some people used all the money for gambling and pleasure and could not repay their debts, so the programme was terminated. After that, the government has not extended credit to farmers without a mortgage, and there is no programme like the Poverty Elimination Programme in the village. From what people argue about this programme, we can see that on the one hand many farmers expect the government to help them escape poverty and improve their economic situation. However, on the other hand, they acknowledge that it is also the responsibility of farmers themselves not to waste government money. One villager comments, "if you use your money properly, your life is okay. Many families who are poor waste money on gambling."

POORER THAN OTHERS

Another key issue that should be considered as a source of the feeling of poverty is comparison. The farmers feel that they are poor because they think they are poorer than other people in the nation or the world. The villagers constantly say, "In Vietnam, farmers are poor." When they utter this phrase, they are often comparing themselves with people who are not farmers. As farmers, they think they belong to a low, or the lowest, social class.

It may be common in other societies as well that farmers find themselves poorer than most people, and hence live with a feeling of poverty. The villagers of Long Tuyen fit this pattern. They often compare their lives with people living in urban areas, and consider life better there. In villagers' mind urban life is better than rural because there are better facilities in the cities, and the standard of living is higher. Moreover, people can have easier jobs than farming in urban areas. Farmers think that agricultural labour is harder because it is not mechanized and every task has to be done manually. Unlike urban workers, they have to work all day and every day without a break. In addition, some parents think the city is better for their children's education. Some families moved to villages closer to Can Tho City so they could provide their children with better educational opportunities in town. Better access to other services such as medical care is also considered an advantage of urban life.

While many Long Tuyen villagers seldom go to Can Tho City, some travel there regularly, usually for work or other business. Most adult villagers have been to Can Tho City at least a few times, and have seen what it looks like. When they go there they realize that many people in the city are wearing better clothes and riding newer bicycles than their secondhand ones, or new motorcycles that they cannot afford. (Not many villagers own motorcycles, and when they do, they are usually used ones of fifty or seventy cc. In the city, you find newer and larger motorcycles of one hundred cc.[6]) If villagers go to the market in the city, they see a variety of products that are more expensive than most things sold in the village and many that are beyond their reach, such as a new TV made in Korea. The cement houses in the city look nicer than their grass-made ones. For the income farmers make from agriculture, many things in the city may seem luxurious and out of reach.

Residents of Can Tho City are not the only people that Long Tuyen villagers compare themselves with. They also have some idea of life in the larger cities of the country such as the capital Hanoi and Ho Chi Minh City, the central city in southern Vietnam. Although not many have visited these larger cities, a few have lived there and can compare their village life to their past experiences in the city. A fifty-one-year-old woman introduced earlier, lived in Ho Chi Minh City between 1953 and the end of the war in 1975. She recalls that when she first came back to live in the village she found it boring and wanted to leave. She gradually got used to the rural life, but after her three children get married, she wants to return to the city to spend the rest of her life. Another forty-six-year-old woman, who is from Ho Chi Minh City and moved to her husband's native village upon marriage, does not like living there because, she says, the standard of living is low. She complains, "Life is hard with income coming only from the garden. If we had more money, life would be better." She thinks she has very different ideas from other villagers, a distinction she values, and she wants to start a tourist business in the area. Another woman, fifty years old, lived in the cities of Vung Tau, Ho Chi Minh City, and Da Nang, because her late husband had taught in public schools there. She returned to the village when her husband died. She finds the farmer's life difficult, particularly because she has little experience with farming. Although these women's views about urban life may be nostalgic in some ways, they reveal how villagers compare their life to life in an urban setting.

Some parents have children who work in the city through whom they learn about urban life. A mother whose daughter works in a factory in Ho Chi Minh City thinks life is better there because it is easier to find good jobs. Her daughter went there because she could not find a good job in the province. She worked in a restaurant in Can Tho City, but her salary was not good, and her friend introduced her to the factory job in Ho Chi Minh City. The mother went to the city when her daughter had an accident, and found that the cost of living was higher there than in the village. However, she thinks it is better for the daughter to live in the city because of better employment opportunities.

Aside from their own experiences and trips, villagers also learn about urban life through TV programmes and news. The concept of many of the villagers, particularly those who have seldom been to the cities, about urban life springs from their imaginations, and is based on what they have seen on TV. Life in big cities may not be as good as the villagers imagine, but on TV they see a highly developed, modern space with a more comfortable life. A few high-rise buildings have been built in the central part of cities, giving them a "modern" (or "*moden*" in Vietnamese) look. Although only a small part of Hanoi or Ho Chi Minh City has this special look, high-rise buildings are often portrayed as symbols of the big cities on the TV news, and they are broadcast throughout the country, including the rural village of Long Tuyen.

Television images not only give villagers the impression that people in large cities are wealthier. But TV also sends the message that "Development (*phat trien*)" is one of the central slogans of the nation.[7] As Beresford and Tran (2004) argues, Vietnam is undergoing "double transition": one from central planning to free market system and the other from under-development to development. There is a strong feeling shared by citizens that the more developed the country becomes, the better and wealthier their lives will be. The concept of "development" is often connected to what is considered "modern". Therefore, many people in rural areas may see the modern buildings of big cities as symbols of development, and hence, greater wealth.[8]

As development and wealth are often linked, the underdevelopment of agriculture is also seen as the basis for widespread poverty. As Youngest Brother expressed his view to me, "Vietnamese farmers are poor, because the rural area is not developed. Everything is done manually. We have little technology unlike farmers of developed countries such as Japan." Gupta (1995) argues that in the post-colonial world, underdevelopment has become a form of identity. This also applies to the villagers of Long Tuyen, who contrast themselves with people of more developed societies. TV often broadcasts agricultural news, and describes how development projects are run in this sector. It is at least partly from these programmes that farmers get the idea that the agricultural sector urgently needs development. Some farmers know how agriculture can be developed with modern technology and new knowledge. However, they are aware that such projects are costly, and they cannot afford them by themselves. They feel they are stuck: because their life is underdeveloped, they are poor; and because they are poor, their life cannot be developed. I agree with Taylor (2001) that the villagers feel that their present life is in decline, which they contrast with the urban fortunes and urban dwellers who can enjoy the "modernity".

As Youngest Brother's comment on Japan suggests, Long Tuyen villagers place themselves not only in a national context, but also within the global space. The large metropolitan cities of Vietnam are not the only images portrayed on TV as symbols of development and wealth. On TV, farmers can also observe life in other countries including the so-called developed ones. Farmers acknowledge that many of the development projects in their country are run not only by their own government, but also with the foreign assistance of developed countries. When I met villagers for the first time, some of the questions I received from them again and again were: "Can Japan help Vietnamese farmers develop our technology?" or "Do you know any Japanese aid agency that can help the development projects of Long Tuyen Village?" When I left the village several months later to return to my country, Youngest Brother brought me a plan for the village to build two small bridges, and asked me if I could find a Japanese organization that would financially support the project.

In fact, in their conversations with me, the villagers often used Japan as a country of reference, sometimes showing their admiration. Many villagers think that Japan is one of the most developed countries in Asia, as well as the world, and has a very high standard of living. Among the farmers, Japan is known for its high technology, and people often teased me saying the few Japanese brand names they knew, such as "Seiko", "Toyota", and "Sony". As a highly developed country with cutting edge technology, Japan is also thought to be a rich country, and the villagers contrast it with Vietnam. Fifth Sister once asked me, "because you are from a rich country, do you find it difficult to live in a poor village like ours?" Her comment suggests that her perception of her own country is constructed at least partly in comparison to the image of a richer country, and she assumed I compared the poor village life to the wealthy life I must have had in Japan.

Much of the villagers' interest in Japan centred on how rich Japan really was. In the evenings when family members got together and enjoyed tea, they would ask me what my salary was in Japan, how much my husband's was, and my father's and so on. Because the salary of a Japanese worker is hundreds of times the monthly income of the farmers in Long Tuyen Village, every Japanese would be a millionaire by their standard.[9] On one occasion, Third Brother came to me and asked, "I heard that if a Vietnamese goes to Japan and works there, he can earn a salary of 3000 US dollars every month, but I do not think it is true. Is it true?" When I answered that it may be true, he said in astonishment, "If someone works in Japan and brings the money back to Vietnam, he can be very rich here." Hearing this, Fifth Daughter then said, jokingly, "I want to go to Japan to work. You will help me, won't you?" When I asked her if her husband would go with her, she said with a serious look on her face, "No, of course not! I will go alone. I will go by myself, like you coming to Vietnam alone, and send money to my husband!"

After asking questions about salary, they would go on to ask me how much we paid for housing in Japan. Then they would ask how much things cost in Japan such as, "how much is one kilo of beef in Japan?" and "how much is a TV?" It always seemed to be amusing for my host family to find out how expensive things were in Japan. One night Eighth Sister-in-Law pointed to the shirt and pair of pants she was wearing and asked me how much I would pay for them in Japan. When I answered that a pair like that would be nearly one hundred US dollars (when talking with me about a large amount of money people usually used US dollars as a currency unit), she calculated what this would be in Vietnamese dongs with the help of Youngest Brother. She was shocked and said, "You can buy this for five dollars in Vietnam. I am a tailor, so why don't you take the clothes I sew and sell them in Japan?"

Hearing how expensive everything was in Japan, my host family was amazed at how the Japanese could live. In particular, they were often puzzled how Japanese farmers could live in such an expensive country. They were greatly concerned and curious about whether farmers were also poor in Japan. They believe Japanese farmers are richer than themselves because agriculture is more developed and farmers have better technology and access to machines. However, they are eager to know if farmers are poorer than other people in Japan, or if farmers are as rich as any other Japanese, in contrast to Vietnamese farmers who consider themselves the poorest people in their country.

THE RICH AND THE POOR

It is not only with urban residents and people in other countries that the villagers contrast themselves with. There is comparison within villages, too. When talking about village life and about other villagers, it is common for people to categorize villagers by wealth, and make a clear distinction between the rich and the poor. For example, my host family, although they have one of the newest houses in the hamlet, consider themselves poor, and constantly contrast themselves with those they consider rich. To them, the rich are people with relatives in foreign countries, like their neighbour who has a daughter in the United States. Youngest Brother explains to me that if you have relatives in the United States you can be rich, because one US dollar is a lot of money in Vietnam. Then he goes on to say, "From the town of Binh Thuy to Long Tuyen Village, when you see big houses on the road, most of them have overseas relatives. Some of them are also businessmen and sometimes, though rarely, they are families who inherited a large land from their parents." It is a widely held belief that some people in Long Tuyen are richer than others because they have families and relatives in foreign countries.

Long Tuyen Village was an area where fighting was severe during the war with the US, and many villagers fought for the old government (*che do cu*), while others supported the new government (*che do moi*). Some of the people who helped the old regime fled the country after the end of the war, fearing that they might be persecuted by the new leaders whom they fought during the war. Most of these people who fled from Long Tuyen Village now live in the United States or Australia. These emigrants, after having settled in the new country, send money back to their family and relatives in the village. Due to the currency rate and difference in living standards a small sum of money in their adopted counties may go far in Vietnam, particularly in rural areas like Long Tuyen Village.

Curious about the existence of these "rich people" that the farmers talk about, I asked Uncle Bay how many "rich" families there were in Binh Thuong B Hamlet. After thinking for a while and counting one by one, he concluded that there were twelve families. He thinks these "rich families" are different from ordinary villagers because "they are 'fictional' farmers". "They have farms, but their children live overseas, and they can live on the money their children send from abroad, so they do farming only for fun, and not for living." "Although", he says, "some of these families are still poor, because they waste their money in gambling."

The daughter of Uncle Bay's neighbour followed her husband to California, where he fled after the war. The parents recall that the daughter left for California in the mid-1980s. Although she came back only once about five years after she left the country, she talks to them by phone so the couple is in close contact with their daughter, who also regularly sends money back home. Although it was not clear from my conversations with the parents how much money she sends on average as the amount varies greatly each time, I saw that they owned things other villagers did not. For instance, their house is the only one in the hamlet to my host family's knowledge that has a telephone, which most villagers cannot afford. During my stay in the village, they were repairing the front yard of their house, and covering it with cement blocks. At that time, my host family also wished to renovate the front yard, but did not have the money to do so. One afternoon, watching the neighbour couple working on the yard, Youngest Brother told me, "they are wealthy enough to repair their yard because they had a family member in a foreign country."

In fact, villagers whose family members live overseas do often have a better life, or at least have more security, than many of their neighbours. For instance, a sixty-three-year-old farmer explains why life is not difficult for his family. During the war, he and his brothers fought for the old government in Ca Mau Province, the southernmost province of Vietnam, from 1968 until the end of the war in 1975. His three brothers who left the country after the war now live in the United States. With overseas relatives, his life is easier than his neighbours. The farmer says, "in case of financial difficulty, my daughter will write a letter to my brothers, and they will send money to us." The farmer's house is not one of the newly built luxurious-looking cement ones that are emerging in the village, but a wooden one, which may not at first glance show his wealth. However, when one looks more closely, one can tell that he is relatively well off, because the house is large, and the front yard is decorated with many bonsai plants, which are known to be expensive and generally considered a symbol of wealth in rural Southern Vietnam. I visited this house with my assistant from Can Tho City, and he said, "you see, they have a lot of bonsai, and that means they are very rich."[10]

While Youngest Brother believes their neighbours are rich, he considers his own family poor. He says, "In the past, my family was very poor, and life was very difficult. Now, some of the children (meaning he, his brothers and sisters) have good jobs, so life is better, but we are still poor." Although the house of my host family is one of the newest in the hamlet, and two children have stable jobs in the local government (though salaries in public sectors are not very high), the members of my host family do not consider themselves rich. To them, the rich are other people.

Those who see themselves as poor do not always have a peaceful relationship with those they consider rich. Many of these farmers often complain about rich people in the village. For example, when we were talking about these rich families, I asked one farmer if other villagers could borrow money from them. He answered, "They lend money at a very high interest. If you borrow money in the morning and return in the afternoon, it is all right. But after one day, you have to pay interests. For example, if you borrow four hundred thousand dongs, you have to pay an interest of thirty thousand dongs after one month." I do not know the exact rate of interest, villagers claim they have to pay nearly 10 per cent per month. The public bank also lends money to farmers, but as mentioned earlier, the procedure of borrowing is complicated, and not many farmers have houses or land to mortgage, so many families end up borrowing from private lenders at high interest.[11]

In fact, quite a few villagers seem to have borrowed money from these private moneylenders. One of our neighbours borrowed but could not repay the debt, so she has given her land to the lender. Now she cannot make enough money to get the land back, and it is a source of constant anxiety for her. Another woman regrets that they borrowed money from a moneylender at a high interest rate because she also cannot repay it and now she worries about money a great deal. She maintains that her mentally ill son damages other people's houses and gardens, and her family has to compensate. To make these payments they have had to borrow money. However, they are not able to repay the debt. The mother says their life is getting harder and harder and she worries a lot, and she starts to cry as she explains their difficult situation to me.

Farmers also complain that "rich" villagers do not help the poor. They think the wealthy are only interested in making more money and taking more from those who have less. Uncle Bay says, "the rich get richer, and the poor get poorer. It is a big problem in the village that the difference between those who have money and those who don't is becoming bigger and bigger." Uncle Bay complains that "the poor" want "the rich" to help them with money, but the latter seldom do so, and this has caused a division between members of the same village and hamlet. He says, "people's psychology changes when they become rich". With money, they no longer think about others as they used to, and they become interested only in money and keeping it only for themselves. Many other villagers share Uncle Bay's dissatisfaction.[12]

The conflict that villagers see between those who have access to outside money and those who do not is not only a matter of economy, but also of politics. What lie behind some farmers' resentment of "the rich" is not only their financial insecurity and feeling of poverty, but also the feeling that injustice and inequality are growing in society. Those who resent the wealthy are angry not only with the rich per se, but also at a social system that seems to privilege those who have connections with overseas families and relatives. A crucial issue is that most of those who have such overseas connections fought for the old regime (South Vietnamese government) during the war, while those who consider themselves to be the poor supported the current government. One villager expresses his discontent: "The people fled the country, because they supported or worked for the old government during the war. They had to leave the country to avoid the new government. But now, they behave like kings." It has been reported in newspapers and other media that the money sent into Vietnam from relatives abroad constitutes a large part of the country's income in foreign currency. The government encourages the overseas Vietnamese community to "help" their country by sending money and other resources from the foreign countries where they reside.[13] In some villagers' eyes those with relatives abroad seem to be encouraged to become richer while they are left with nothing.

These farmers feel that they are underprivileged in the social system, which they consider unjust. A farmer elaborates: "We always hear in this country that farmers are the foundation of the whole country and farmers are important, but in reality, people only take money from the farmers. They do not think of the farmers, and they only exploit us. It is not fair." The farmer goes on to say, "If a foreign company comes to Vietnam, they pay a tax only once, and after that they return to their country, they can keep their money, and nothing remains in Vietnam. But we Vietnamese farmers have to give our money all the time and we cannot keep it."

Farmers also express their dissatisfaction with development projects in the region. They feel that they will not be able to enjoy the effects of local developmental programmes and they will be left out because many projects are not in agriculture and benefit only those already wealthy. Some projects such as construction of hospitals or factories, they fear, will take away their land and only bring job opportunities that they are not qualified for.

PAST AND PRESENT

Time also plays a role in how villagers evaluate their life and compare it with the lives of others. Farmers of Long Tuyen Village commonly refer to the "past" when they try to explain everyday life. However, it is not always very clear what "past" they are referring to. Sometimes the "present" is contrasted with the years of the war, sometimes with the time of collectivization, and sometimes with the post-reform period. In this section, I try to examine how the farmers look at their present life, and compare it to the "past".

First of all, some villagers, particularly aged ones, compare their present life with their life during the war before 1975. In their view, post-war life, both during socialism and after the reform, is a single phase of their experience. For some, life after the war has been more difficult than during the war. Uncle Bay says, "Life is very difficult now. It is harder than during the war. During the war, it was dangerous, and there were chances that you could get killed, but life was easier. You could earn enough from your farm. Now we cannot make enough money from farming." (Because Uncle Bay and Aunt Tam had to abandon their farm and evacuate the village for some years when fighting was severe, the time the father refers to as the war may not include these years of exile.) As mentioned earlier, Uncle Bay is often nostalgic about his war experiences, which he contrasts with his present life that he finds more difficult. Another villager joins Uncle Bay, "Life has changed much since twenty years ago. It was easier in the past, because people could make enough money to support their family and parents. Now it is difficult to support parents." Some villagers, on the other hand, think life is better after 1975. One farmer says, "after -75, things are settled, and our garden income is more stable".

There are villagers who look at their situation as a consequence of the war and its end that brought socialism to the region. One old man says, "I had to follow a special course after the war, because I worked as a policeman of the old government. In 1980, I became a *xe loi* (motorbike cyclo) driver. We have only one thousand square meters of land. Life has been very difficult for us since the war ended in 1975." A primary school principal of another village thinks teachers' lives also became more difficult after the school system was socialized. According to him, "Before 1975, income from teaching was good, and it was enough to support a family. But after 1975, income is too low." A former nurse also explains that she left the job after 1975 because her salary became very low. For these villagers, the end of the war was the incident that brought a major change to their lives, and has had lasting repercussions to this day. (Vietnam remains a socialist country. The economic reform structurally transformed only a part of the economic system, and many sectors of society, including education and health, retain the socialist ideology and system.)

Villagers have also experienced certain changes in life particularly because of the *doi moi* reform. These have been positive for some, but negative for others. Many villagers complain that living expenses have increased after the reform, and one Long Tuyen villager complains, "we need more and more money everyday. Everything is more expensive: food, fertilizer, pesticide, house and other things." As we have seen in a previous section, the rise in cost of living has caused a feeling of poverty among the farmers. Some, however, see the change in a more positive light. As one widowed mother says, "it is easier to get jobs after the reform, and life is better now. We have better media and facilities. In the past, children had to help me in the garden and to catch fish in the river. That was the only way for us to live. Life was hard then." Another father says, "Life has been better since 1990. We now have electricity and thanks to it, I can improve my children's skills in agriculture and other tasks."

We see there are both positive and negative perceptions of the "past versus the present" among the villagers. In addition, the time frame they have in mind also varies. Sometimes change is experienced in the long term; at other times, more short-term changes affect perception of the present. For example, when I visited villages in the first phase of my research, I heard many villagers say they felt their life was improving, although gradually. However, when I returned to the area nearly two years later, people were very pessimistic about their present life, and even more so about their future. One reason was that over the two years, the orange orchards of the village suffered from a disease, and the price of their fruit products fell, significantly lowering the farmers' income. These short-term changes also contributed to the farmers' negative perception of the present. For example, one woman says, shedding tears, "right now, life is harder than in the past, because of the bad harvest in recent years. Ten years ago, life was better. Life was better before 1975." It is possible to argue that the bad experiences of the past several years have made her pessimistic about the present and nostalgic about the past. This case illustrates how past and present interact with each other constantly in peoples' perceptions, affecting their views of both.

Lastly, perceptions of the past and present also depend on individual experiences and life cycle. Some farmers think their life is harder than in the past because they have aged. Others think that their children have a better life because they are now married. A widow says life has grown harder and harder since her husband died two years ago. People's views of their life depend to a great extent not only on social transformations over time, but on changes in personal life as well.

POWER OF THE LOCAL GOVERNMENT

Although farmers are not always satisfied with local and national policies and sense of community is not strong in the village, they also pay high respect to the local government and acknowledge the power it has over their lives. One incident opened my eyes to the respect villagers pay to the local authorities. When I got permission to stay in Long Tuyen Village, I knew the village government was responsible to make sure my stay and research went well and did not cause any trouble in the village. However, I did not realize how involved they actually were. When I visited the village for the first time with people from Can Tho University, I was introduced to my host family, but not to the village officers. I thought their involvement would be rather formal and administrative and that they were not really interested in my stay and my activities.

So I was a little surprised when my host family told me that they took one of two packages of Japanese cookies I gave them to the People's Committee office in the village and gave it to the chairman. Until then, although I gave some gift to my host family from time to time, I had never given anything as a souvenir to the People's Committee because I just did not find it necessary. In fact, I had not yet met anyone from the Committee. However, my host family's gift to the Committee made me realize for the first time that the Committee had been involved in my stay more than I had thought.

Uncle Bay then said, "Because we gave your cookies to the government, someone from the committee will come to visit you this Friday, so do not be surprised." I am not sure if my host family invited the committee members, or it was customary for them to visit me. Anyway, at that time, I was happy to be able to meet the local officers for the first time, and expected a casual conversation over tea much like my visits to the neighbours' houses for interviews. But on Friday morning something quite different happened: many members of the family came to help Aunt Tam with cooking. Fifth Brother-in-Law, Fourth Sister, Fourth Sister-in-Law, the daughter of Third Brother, Third Sister-in-Law, and Third Brother came and started to butcher ducks and wash vegetables from early in the morning. Then at lunchtime, Fifth Sister came from work at the People's Committee, and Youngest Brother came home from work at the security office in the city, which had never happened before during my stay. I could see that something very special was going to happen in the house. At eleven, the usual time for lunch, eight people came from the Committee, five men and three women, including the chairman, which surprised me as I was expecting only one or two people.

We had a real feast that afternoon. The first week I stayed with my host family, they cooked a lot of special food for me. For the Lunar New Year and death anniversaries, they cooked special cuisine too. But the lunch for the committee was the most lavish I had experienced in the house: pieces of large broiled snakehead fish for spring rolls, hot pots of duck stew (I did not even know that they owned the special hot pots for the dish), chicken soup and fried pancake, a specialty of the Mekong Delta, all at the same time. And they prepared apples for dessert. Farmers in the area seldom buy fruit because they only eat bad fruit from their own garden after selling good ones. Apples are a luxury for them because they have to buy them, and they are very expensive because they are imported from abroad, mostly from China (when I brought some apples to my friend in Can Tho City, she said "you should not buy such expensive fruit."). The members of the committee ate and drank until two in the afternoon (the chairman left at twelve thirty and the women left at one) when the last person left. I could see quite clearly that the lunch had taken a lot of work and had cost my host family a lot.

MORAL ECONOMY OR POLITICAL ECONOMY?

How does one account for the economic and political behaviour of Long Tuyen villagers? Peasant economic and political behaviour has often been understood in the framework of two competing paradigms: the moral economy approach and the political economy approach. The contrast between the two positions shows a theoretical debate of society vs. individual: whether the society presides over individual interests or individual interests are more important than the society as a whole. In the moral economists' view, the most crucial factor that determines the village ethic in subsistence economy is that it assures the subsistence of all village members, and for this purpose, village society is structured according to the norms of dependence (Scott 1976). While moral economists look at subsistent peasant villages as socially autonomous corporate groups, political economists, by contrast, focus on the individual and see village society as a sphere of conflicting individual interests. Popkin (1979, p. 4) argues that "the exchanges between peasants are shaped and limited by conflicts between individual and group benefits", instead of reciprocity and the norm of dependency as moral economists suggest.

However, I argue that neither of the two models is sufficient to understand the economic behaviour of the farmers in the contemporary rural Mekong Delta in Vietnam.[14] Of course, farmers of the Delta cultivate the land to sell their products, hence, they are not subsistence farmers and Scott's model cannot be applied to them automatically. However, I do not think political economy fully explains the economic behaviour of the farmers in the delta fully. One major problem with both models I find is that they assume the framework of "society vs. individual" exists in every society, and the systems work at all levels of the villagers' economic and social lives. My findings suggest instead that there is a need to look at different levels, or spheres, of the villagers' economic behaviours because a different logic may apply to different levels or in different spheres of one society, coexisting in one social space as a whole. [15] Brocheux (1983) and Cheal (1989) also argue that peasant behaviour is a more complex mixture of two models of moral economy and political economy, which are not necessarily mutually exclusive and may exist within one society. In the case of the villages of this study, however, while both models are found, they do not coexist in all levels of the society. Instead, each model explains two different social spheres: family life and village society.

We have seen that moral economy is more prominent than political economy in their family lives. Many villagers are much more concerned with the welfare of the family than of the self, and one is often expected to sacrifice his/her own self for the sake of the financial well-being of the whole family. In agriculture, members of a family, occasionally including married ones, cooperate in the daily economic activities, share daily information and knowledge on agriculture, help each other with selling the produce, and work together on their parents' land. It is a primary concern of the members to secure income cooperatively in agricultural activities for their own households and also for their extended families. Income from jobs outside of family farming is also spent for the whole family rather than for the earners themselves. If they are not married they generally share the money they make with their parents and siblings, and if married the money is spent for their own households and their young children. Education is also offered to the children cooperatively within a family, too. Sometimes, parents sacrifice themselves for their children's education, because it will secure the future of the whole family. In all these ways, family cooperation is important. Individualism is therefore not prominent within the family.

However, on the village level, political economy explains better the economic and political life of the villagers. Different families do not cooperate much in agricultural activities. They do not like to share information and knowledge with other villagers. They seldom work together on the production and sales of products, and other village activities. There is little sense of community in the villages. As mentioned earlier, the villagers confess they usually do not trust others and prefer to rely on their own knowledge and capacity instead of depending on other villagers. The norm of dependency is therefore little observed in this society. In contrast to the village life that moral economists illustrate, the security of all villagers is not the concern of most, unless they are officially in positions such as village committee chairman. Families are often in competition with one another, and some are successful in accumulating wealth, which has provoked the jealousy of others and caused conflicts among village members.

Thus, both moral economy and political economy exist in the villagers' economic activities. The important thing to note, however, is that moral economy vs. political economy in this situation is not the question of "society vs. individual", but that of "society vs. family". The problem I find in Popkin's argument is that he is not aware of the importance of the family as the basic economic unit. In his discussion on Vietnamese peasants, Popkin, stresses the importance of self, but his argument on self and family is confusing. While he often uses the concepts of "self" as "individual", he sometimes refers to the "family" as a unit that seeks its own interest, too, and he is not explicit about the difference between the two. For example, he states, "a peasant is primarily concerned with the welfare and security of self and family" (Popkin 1979, p. 31).

My research suggests that there is a need to be aware of the difference between self and family. The "individual unit" in villages in the rural Mekong Delta is the family and not self. It is the family and not each person that seeks its own interest in the villages. Each family forms one interest group, but there is less sense of individualism found in each family member. In this sense I follow Peletz (1983) in his criticism on Popkin's argument that it presumes the concepts of self and personhood exist in all societies.

It is arguable that kin and relatives outside of the extended family inhabit a status somewhere between family and village society, given that they do not cooperate much in daily activities, but nevertheless share a certain group membership that is manifested in rituals, such as death anniversaries of ancestors. Ties are less strong between affinal relatives and many of the serious problems I know between relatives were between affinal ones (that often originated in conflicts between daughters-in-law and mothers-in-law). Perhaps kins outside of extended family function in both moral and political economies depending on the situation. In this sense, as Bailey (1991) argues, moral economy and political economy may exist not as a dichotomy but as a continuum within the society. However, in the case of the villages in the rural Mekong Delta, there exists quite a sharp contrast between within family and outside society, with a relatively narrow blurred boundary between the two.

CONCLUSION

The economy and politics of Long Tuyen villagers are closely interrelated. What dominates villagers' economic life is a feeling of poverty. Behind this feeling lie various uncertainties in their life. This feeling is also responsible for the local village politics, as manifested in conflicts between the rich and poor and the many villagers' dissatisfaction with the social system. Their perceptions of village economy and political life reveal the difficulty they see in their present life, which fluctuates under the effects of the larger social sphere. In this uncertain environment family members have to cooperate to secure their life. At the same time, families are in severe competition with one another to survive in the changing social world.

In investigating the farmers' economic and political life in Long Tuyen Village, it is important to isolate two spheres of their daily activities: that of the family and that of the outside society. By examining how economic and political theories function at these two levels, one can better understand Vietnamese farmers' daily struggles in the midst of social uncertainties. As I have illustrated in this and previous chapters, villagers perceive a distinction between family and outside society, although the boundary between the two is sometimes blurred and flexible. However, the boundary is narrow, and beyond the scope of the family, the villagers' economic and political activities present quite different pictures.

Uncertainties bring not only dissatisfaction with the economic condition and social system, but also worries about the future. Faced with an uncertain society and life, farmers often express their anxiety about the years to come. We saw in this chapter how villagers interpret their present life in comparison with their past experiences. At the same time, their present experiences often shape their views on the future, to which I turn in the concluding part of this book.

Notes

1. Electricity has been introduced to more houses during the 2000s.
2. The issue of poverty in rural areas has also been a focus of studies by Vietnamese social scientists (e.g. Nguyen Thi Hang 1997).

3. The currency rate at the time of research was 1USD = 14,000VND.
4. South Vietnam has been considered incorporated into the world market since French colonialism. However, many Long Tuyen villagers look at the problem of imported fruit as rather recent, starting several years earlier.
5. In reality, the government does not set higher tax than the selling price. Agricultural taxes is set by the government in kilogrammes of paddy. Many local governments prefer to collect taxes in cash and when the paddy tax is converted into cash, the amount becomes higher than market prices (personal comment from Hy Van Luong). However, from the farmers' viewpoints, they think they are required to pay more tax than what they earn, hence they are losing money.
6. The number of motorcycles in the village have increased since then.
7. All TV stations in Vietnam are public, owned by the state, and there are no private broadcast companies.
8. In the 1990s, rural development became a focus of studies by Vietnamese social scientists (e.g. Le Thi Ngoc Thanh 1995; Pham Xuan Nam 1997; To Duy Hop 1999).
9. In 1999, the GNP of Long Tuyen Village was US$200 (per capita). A yearly income of a Japanese worker would have been more than one hundred times as much as that of a Long Tuyen villager.
10. Discussing money in Ho Chi Minh City, Truitt (2013) argues that US dollars have not only monetary values, but also symbolic values such as security, which also applies to the residents of Long Tuyen Village.
11. A credit association called *hui* is widely known to exist in many parts of southern Vietnam, but no one in the hamlet I asked about it knew its existence in the hamlet either in the past or present.
12. In Vietnam, the increasing inequality among the population has been recognized by the Communist government as a serious social problem occurring under the reform. The Mekong Delta in particular has been considered one of the places where largest inequality is found. Furuta (1996) attributes this to a more rapid shift toward a market-oriented economy in the Delta.
13. During the Lunar New Year in particular, when a lot of overseas Vietnamese return, the government encourages them to contribute to the country. This message was broadcast in Long Tuyen Village, too, on the TV news.
14. While many scholars consider the debate an important one that focused attention on peasant individual and collective choice (Feeny 1983), some have also criticized both approaches as inadequate and often too simplistic

to explain peasant societies that they study (Ireson 1992; Evans 1988; Parker 1988).

15. Some (e.g. Moise 1982) discuss that while moral economy applies to subsistence economy, political economy functions in a different type of peasant society. However, I would argue that they can be found at different levels of the same society as well.

8

SOCIAL CHANGE AND THE FAMILY IN THE RURAL MEKONG DELTA

One day Aunt Tam came home with a worried expression on her face. Her right eye hurt, and she had gone to see a doctor at a hospital in the nearby town of Binh Thuy, where she was told she had an eye disease and would have to undergo an operation the following week. The news spread quickly to her children, and that evening, members of the family, Fourth Sister and her husband, Fifth Sister and her husband, Eighth Brother and his wife, and Second Brother, came to the house to see her. Fourth Sister, Fifth Sister, and Second Brother lived in the same hamlet not too far from their mother's house and frequently visited her, but Eighth Brother lived near the town and came to visit the parents only once in a while, so his arrival that evening meant something important was happening. It was rare for so many members to assemble in the house, also signalling the significance of the mother's illness for the whole family. As Aunt Tam lay down on her wooden bed, the children asked how she felt and consoled her. A great concern for all the family members was not only Aunt Tam's condition, but also how to finance the operation, which would cost the family a lot. The children, while they discussed the matter, seemed unsure about what they could do.

Next morning, Aunt Tam, who usually got up earliest of all to work in the kitchen and greet other family members with a smile, stayed in bed. She was still discussing with Youngest Brother how they could collect the necessary money. When she got up a couple of hours later than usual, she started to gather and count the money they had in the house, including what they had made from the small tobacco shop they ran at home. Most of the bills she was counting were 200 dong (about 2 cents), 500 dong (5 cents) and 1,000 dong (10 cents) bills that obviously did not add up to a lot. At that time, I did not know how much the operation would cost, but I could easily see that the money she was counting would not be sufficient. Several weeks later, Aunt Tam had not yet undergone the operation, but she went to see the doctor regularly, and was getting medicine. Uncle Bay complained, "Medicine is so expensive. Aunt got medicine for seven days, and it cost as much as one hundred and seventy thousand dongs."

One month later, Aunt Tam had still not had the operation, and Uncle Bay said, "Because the mother has an eye disease, life is difficult for our family. Medicine costs more than eleven thousand dongs per day. And we have to pay the doctor for an operation. It costs one million and nine hundred thousand dongs. In Vietnam, if you don't have money, you will die." In fact, medical costs have been one of the biggest financial burdens for many families, and many villagers agree with the father's statement. One farmer said to me, "Those who are poor are sick, and those who are sick are poor." Illness can often threaten the financial well-being of a family. I met a number of sick people who could not receive necessary medical treatment, because it was too expensive. Another farmer told me she suffers from a stomach problem and had an operation last year, but now she feels sick again, and has severe pain. Once she fainted in the field while she was working and had to be carried home, and now she cannot work on the farm because of the pain. She thinks she has to go to the general hospital in Can Tho City and have another operation. However, she does not dare to go because her family has spent all the money they had for her operation last year, and they cannot afford another one. Her family describes the difficult situation: "We are very much worried about her health. But hospital fees are too expensive for farmers. Last year, the hospital reduced the fee for us because we were poor, but the larger hospital in Can Tho City does not give discounts, and it is too expensive for us."

As we can see from these experiences, Vietnamese farmers can face life-threatening situations because they cannot afford necessary medical treatment. In one family the father fell ill and died a few years ago. The mother says life had been much better before her husband got sick because he could work and help her, and moreover, they did not have to pay for medicine. After he fell ill, they had to sell all their furniture to pay medical expenses. In fact, little furniture is left in her house — only a wooden bed for her and her son, a small cupboard and a couple of chairs. Another family is considering selling their land, because the mother has been sick for four years and this has cost them so much that they no longer have any money.

When I left the village two months after Aunt Tam first went to see the doctor, she had not yet undergone an operation. A few months after I returned to Tokyo, I received a letter from Youngest Brother. He explained that they would need four hundred US dollars for his mother to have an operation, and asked for my help. Though I did not know the exact figure of the family's annual income, the village survey data states that the average annual GNP was two hundred US dollars in 1999. Considering that the income of my host family was probably close to the average, it is not hard to see how difficult it was for them to afford the operation. At the time of the mother's illness, there was no medical insurance in Vietnam, neither public nor private, so the family had to depend on their own savings, whose value I was not aware of. (People often keep their savings not only in cash, but also in gold.)[1]

Thinking this was one way that I could show my gratitude for their kind hospitality and their assistance during my stay, I took one hundred US dollars out of my savings, added another one hundred dollars from my husband, who was also grateful to them for taking care of me, and sent the money to Youngest Brother.[2] A couple of months later, I received letters from Youngest Brother and from Fifth Sister, who had become a good friend of mine, saying that their mother had had a successful operation and they wanted to thank me. Since sending international mail from Vietnam is expensive, given a farmer's standard of living,[3] I was not expecting to hear from them so soon, so the fact of their letters told me how concerned they had been about Aunt Tam's illness. To this day, however, I do not know where they got the remaining two hundred US dollars. They may have had enough savings, sold a part of their property, or borrowed money from moneylenders.

Most villages, including Long Tuyen, have medical clinics. Given the living standard of rural Vietnam, the presence of a medical facility in each village suggests good access to medical care. However, these village clinics or traditional medical doctors do not treat patients with serious illness. Many farmers who are gravely ill must go to hospitals in nearby towns or Can Tho City. Because of rising medical costs, families with sick members live in constant anxiety about the health of the sick person and also the burdensome cost of medical treatment. Those who are healthy also worry about getting sick someday, which will most likely result in great financial difficulties. Falling ill is a constant fear and bad health is a constant worry for many of the villagers, bringing uncertainty into their lives.

UNCERTAINTY: PRESENT AND FUTURE

Aunt Tam's medical problems as well as those of other villagers illustrate another aspect of uncertainty the residents of the rural Mekong Delta live with every day. Increase in the medical cost has not only been regarded as one of most serious social problems in Vietnam, but is also related to other social and economic situations that the farmers live in. Along with health, as we have seen, a number of other factors contribute to their anxiety. Agricultural production, land ownership, children's education, jobs outside of agriculture, national policies and the world market all affect their lives in unpredictable ways.

Present uncertainties also make farmers of the rural Mekong Delta anxious about the future because they do not know how life changes the short term and how they will live in years to come. They worry that the future of agriculture is not certain, not only because the weather is unpredictable and the quality and quantity of products unknown, but also because prices, taxes, and governmental policies can change abruptly. They say, "It is hard for us to live. We do not know what will happen next, and we only wait and wait." This feeds their worry about being left behind in this new era, and pushed down into weaker and weaker social positions.

An uncertain future is a source of anxiety for older people, too. Uncle Bay and Aunt Tam express their concern: "we are already old, and we cannot work on the farm as much as we used to. We worry if our children can take care of us when we are older, because everybody has a difficult life and has his or her own family to take care of. We hope that our youngest son will marry an ordinary girl from the village and take care of us, but we are concerned that he will marry someone from the city, where he works." The father continues, "I am very old and weak now, so I can't work very much. I can only water the pigs and do some light work on the farm. If I did not have savings, I would have died already, because I cannot work much now. I do not want to borrow money, because I do not know if I can repay the debt." Uncle Bay often complains that he is weak and not healthy. Some days he would spend the whole afternoon lying on a hammock in the front yard without going to the field, and he would tell me how unhealthy and sick he felt. His body and stomach often hurt, and he took medicines regularly.[4] Especially because some of their children have left the village to work outside of family farming, Uncle Bay and Aunt Tam wonder if any of their children will be able to support them when they are old.[5] With rapid urbanization and industrialization taking place in areas around Can Tho City, their concern is more widely shared by old parents. They fear that they may not be able to sustain daily life and may just have to "wait to die", particularly if they cannot expect their children to support them in old age, which was the custom in the past.

Youngest Brother, however, is aware of his parents' concerns. He acknowledges that they are already old and it is getting difficult for them to support themselves. He thinks it is difficult for older people to stay healthy when old. When I was talking with Youngest Brother about my own family and told him that my grandfather was ninety-two years old and my grandmother was eighty-three and that they were both healthy, he commented, "In Japan, life is more comfortable, so maybe people can live longer and healthier than in Vietnam. In Vietnam, like my parents, people have to work hard when they are old, so they become weak. But in Japan, maybe it is different." Fifth Sister also comments on Uncle Bay's and Aunt Tam's difficult life: "My father and mother have had to work all their life, and they still have to work hard even though they are already old. In Vietnam, you have to work all your life to survive, but it is difficult for old people like my parents." Youngest Brother acknowledges that as the youngest son of the family, he will have to support his parents. Although he likes living in the city where he works, he plans to stay in the village after he gets married so that he can take care of them. (At the time of my research Youngest Brother was not married yet, but family members often got together and discussed his marriage, which was a family matter.) However, the brother questions how he can actually support his parents with his modest salary, when the cost of living and medical treatment in particular has become so high.

With the present situation so difficult, and with life uncertain in so many ways, not only the old but many adult villagers are also anxious about the future. There are a few younger people, like the second son of Second Brother who is a high school student, who express some hope. The son likes studying and he says he wants to be a businessman, though he does not think it will be easy for him to become one. However, in contrast to this high school student, other villagers share a strong feeling of fatalism, and do not even think about their futures. One woman lives an impoverished life because she does not have any land. She takes care of the land of her sister who lives in the city, and receives only a portion of the income from the farm. She says she accepts this life because she thinks it is her fate. Another woman says although she is not satisfied with her life, she has to accept it as her destiny. Her life is difficult financially, and agricultural production is not going well, but there is little she can do about it. She explains, "everyone wants to have more money, but it is our destiny, and we have to accept it." Another female farmer claims she does not even care if she is happy or not now, or if she will be happy or not in the future: "this is life, and every day is the same. I do not think life will be much better."

In the rural Mekong Delta, farmers live in a state of anxiety because of the unpredictable nature of the present life and the uncertain future. Farmers have little means for coping with these uncertainties, and the sense that they have no control over their lives contributes to a general feeling of poverty. In such a situation, one of the few ways villagers can sustain life and cope with the uncertainties of daily life and society in general is through the support of the family.

THE ROLE OF THE FAMILY

Some observers have argued that the Vietnamese family is deteriorating since the economic reform started in 1986 (Hiebert 1996). However, the results of my research in the rural Mekong Delta in the late 1990s and the early 2000s suggest that this assertion may not apply to the family in the area. My findings show instead that family ties are strong and that the family retains an important role in everyday life in a new, less predictable environment. In this book, I have looked at the family's significance and role in everyday life by examining how families experience and cope with these conditions. I conclude that the family still played a crucial role in farmers' lives in the rural Mekong Delta in a time of natural and social uncertainties.

Uncle Bay comments, "Right now our family is still poor, but life is all right if we work hard together. Those families who are lazy are poor and have difficulty. If you try hard, you can have a better life." He also says, "I try to be optimistic so that my children will not have to worry. If I am pessimistic, my children will be worried." Two seemingly contradictory feelings coexist in the father's mind: on the one hand, he worries about his old age, but on the other hand, he tries to be optimistic about his life and his children's future. Also, although Uncle Bay complains about his bad health and poverty, he claims he is happy with his present life because all his children are grown up and have decent lives. In fact, he feels he may be the happiest ever right now because all of his children are well and they visit and help him regularly. His perception of his present life as well as the future shows how important a role the family may play in bringing assurance and stability of life to farmers both economically and psychologically.

The family in the Mekong Delta is directly exposed to the influence of society. A few studies have pointed out that the Vietnamese family was traditionally not only the basic unit of society, but also an entire world around which most members' lives revolved (e.g. Jamieson 1986*b*). My own research in a farming village corroborates this observation. There each household of nuclear families forms a relatively independent unit separate from neighbouring families except those of children and parents, and a large part of everyday life is conducted there. Within a family, members are closely tied together, and the family functions as a highly cooperative unit. Other relatives, in contrast, demonstrate much weaker ties except during rituals, and they do not often cooperate with each other on a daily basis. Outside of the nuclear and extended families (of children and parents), there is only a weak sense of community on the hamlet or village level but in an administrative sense.

As a highly independent unit, the family not only feels the direct impact of social conditions but also often has to cope with them by itself without many intervening layers of assistance. Therefore, it is the crucial sphere in which people deal with the uncertainties of life. Faced with difficulties and problems in their agricultural activities — such as fluctuations in the price of rice and the sale of fruit, or land shortages — which make it difficult for farmers to secure sufficient household income, the family is often the farmers' last resort for assistance. Many families try to sustain themselves by cooperating in production and sales.

Members work together in agricultural activities as well as sales of products, even though income is divided among households. Children help secure the financial well-being of their parents not only by providing them with money or food but also by working together on the family land that their parents own. Children toil on their parents' land not only because they are obliged to, but also because they consider the land as the family property and that it is their responsibility to maintain it. In this way the land, their property, is kept in the family. The shortage of land, due to overpopulation and development, is a serious problem in Long Tuyen Village, and if people lose the land they now own it is unlikely that they will be able to acquire more later. When the parents pass away they will divide their land among their children, and it will remain a valuable asset for the next generation. Family members also help each other by sharing knowledge and information. It is common for family members to advise each other on agriculture and other economic activities in everyday conversation, which helps them acquire more skill to survive difficult conditions, even if they may not regularly work together on the farm.

The family is also the main source of information and support in the midst of the unpredictable local and world market. Sisters and sisters-in-law get together to cooperate in selling products their parents and brothers have harvested. Other members always advise them on the market price and the state of market sales. Often, after coming back from the market, the sisters share information with others, discussing when and how they will sell their next products. In fact, a constant topic of conversation in a family is how the market sales went that day, how much the prices changed, and how much they earned or lost through sales. With all market news gathered this way, siblings as well as parents discuss and decide on their next strategy for selling their products at the highest possible price.

Aware of the problems that threaten their agricultural activities, some families recognize the importance of education in enabling their children to have a more secure life. Family plays a large role in children's education: it requires not only the effort of the students themselves, but also commitment and sacrifice by other family members, parents in particular, for children to attend school. This is especially true of the higher education needed for getting jobs outside of farming as sending the children to school means a loss of income-earning labour for family farming. Rising school fees often burden many families, too. For these reasons it is not uncommon to see parents weary of sending to children to schools, and many students dropping out at an early stage such as during primary school. However, some parents are determined to sacrifice their own life for the sake of their children, by providing them with a good education for a better life and a more promising future.

In acquiring jobs, family plays a role, too. It is often through other family members that people find jobs. For instance, two or three members of one family, usually siblings, work in the same factory because they introduce each other to jobs. Parents' connections sometimes also help children get jobs. Jobs held by its members are a family matter, because they have financial significance for the whole family. Younger generations, both sons and daughters, work to support their family financially. The primary goal of their working outside of family agriculture is to bring enough money into their households to make life secure. The unmarried usually give their salaries to their parents who then spend it on the family. Married people, by contrast, often use their income to support their own spouses and children. Working outside of the family rarely makes its members more independent. Instead, it gives them an important role as wage earners for the whole family.

With health care also, support and cooperation among family members are crucial. When someone, a parent in particular, becomes sick, all members pool their money to pay for necessary medical treatment. It is considered the entire family's responsibility to contribute to taking care of the sick. Supporting the elderly is particularly an important responsibility of younger members. Children, on their part, try to make sure that they can take care of their parents in the future.

We have also seen that the money overseas family members send back to family members in the village is significant for their well-being. Many wealthier families in the village of Long Tuyen have relatives in foreign countries such as the United States or Australia. The wealth some villagers acquire from siblings and children overseas sometimes causes conflicts between neighbours, as well as within the hamlet and village because money is usually kept within the family, and they do not generally share the remittance with other people in the village. In this sense, the family is also crucial for asset acquisition, management and ownership protection.

FAMILY AND SOCIETY IN THE MEKONG DELTA

In this book I have examined the struggles of the farmers in the rural Mekong Delta under the social conditions from the late 1990s to the beginning of the 2000s, and the role family plays in them. As the society that the residents live in transforms over the years, the family remains the basic social unit for the people, and this finding has corroborated in many ways the significance of the family asserted by other studies on the Vietnamese family. It also gives some interesting points to examine applicability of the results of other studies to understanding the family in East and Southeast Asia.

There is a boundary that distinguishes the family from the larger society in the rural Mekong Delta. Unlike Japanese society, as illustrated by Kondo, where the concept of family often penetrates other social relations such as one's colleagues at work, in the rural Mekong Delta, this sense of belonging rarely extends beyond the family.[6] Compared with company workers in downtown Tokyo, the members of Long Tuyen Village spend much less time outside of their family, and most of their daily life takes place within the family, with social life revolving around it.

However, this does not imply that the "Vietnamese family" is a static construct with the same importance for people in every context. On the contrary, I emphasize that the family has acquired a meaning and role specific to a given social context. It shares some similarities with the Chinese family in the post-Mao era which is gaining importance as the welfare covered by the state diminishes, although the Mekong Delta region has never experienced socialism on a daily basis to the extent that China has, and the role of the Vietnamese family may not extend to larger kinship as in China. The social conditions that the family in the rural Mekong Delta experience come not only from the village, but also from the national and global factors. Various socio-economic factors bring uncertainties to the lives of Long Tuyen villagers. Because many of these situations originate outside the local village, the factors affect villagers in sudden and unpredictable ways. Like the Rungus, a highland minority people of Malaysia, the farmers of the Delta struggle for control over their lives in the face of social and economic factors that are in fact beyond their control.

However, the family is not only passively affected by the outside world. It takes an active role in opposing the pressure of external forces, even though it may have only limited power. The family is the channel through which people act on the larger society. Such relationships continuously reshape the role and meaning of the family. Because of weak communal relationships at the hamlet and village level, and the few social units that connect the family to the larger society, the family often has to actively respond to the impact of societal events and changes.[7] The villagers of Long Tuyen, like the Thai villagers, approach agricultural and non-agricultural problems strategically. For instance, the family carefully plans its agricultural activities. At the same time, many family members, the young in particular, find jobs outside of family farming to bring more secure income into the household.

As we have seen in the chapters on agriculture, education and employment, struggles with uncertainties influence and shape family relationships and family morality in many ways. Although I did not closely examine changes in family relationships over time, my research provides evidence for the continuing significance of the vertical relationship between family members. The result is closer to that of a study in North Vietnam where the ties between parents and children remain important unlike other societies where conjugal ties have become stronger and have replaced vertical ties between parents and children. Parents are often the children's last and only resort in a time of volatile economic conditions, changes in agricultural production, education, and other employment.

It is not only parents that help their children, but it is children, too, that support their parents. It is generally considered the children's obligation to help their parents. The support of children is even more important as life is increasingly clouded by uncertainties. Children are of crucial significance for parents' present well-being as well as their future comfort. As some studies in Thailand illustrate, the notion that children are responsible for taking care of the elderly remains very strong in the rural Mekong Delta and the system of caretaking for the elderly still operates, although, at the same time, some old parents worry that they may not be able to depend on their children in years to come.

Given the unpredictability of the present life, and anxiety about the future, the family is an important resource, financially, socially and psychologically, for the villagers of Long Tuyen and other villages in the Mekong Delta. Most farmers have nowhere else to turn to when life is difficult or when the future proves insecure. Most villagers have to depend on the family, and family members cooperate closely to survive in difficult social conditions. The family of the rural Mekong Delta is a strong and important unit of society and it plays a crucial role in people's everyday lives.

LATE-SOCIALISM AND GLOBAL ERA

It is not easy to determine whether the social conditions of the rural Mekong Delta belong to post-socialism, late socialism, or global capitalism. Moreover, assessing them in a historical context, particularly in relation to socialism poses a challenge. The political history that the area went through from the latter half of the nineteenth century is rather complex, perhaps more complex than northern Vietnam. First, we need to pay attention to French colonialism and also the existence of American troops prior to the end of the war in 1975. The western colonialism is known to have already introduced modern style capitalist economy to the area, and under the American influence market economy flourished in large cities in South Vietnam such as Saigon (present day Ho Chi Minh City), though it may not exactly apply to the rural Mekong Delta. Moreover, as I have stressed in a number of places, the Mekong Delta area did not experience profound penetration of socialism even after the end of the war. The difficulty also lies in the lack of information and literature on the social history of the rural Mekong Delta. There is little information available on the society prior to French colonization, making it hard to know what "traditional society and family" means in this area, and little is known about the society during and after the war, too. The society presents a mixture of many elements of all three of post-socialism, late socialism, and global capitalism as well as other traditions, such as pre-capitalist conditions.

For this reason, it proves problematic to examine the social conditions of the rural Mekong Delta at the end of the twentieth century simply in two political as well as economic frameworks: one of post- or late socialism and the other of globalization. For example, how can we account for that in the family in the Delta, while vertical bond between parents and children remain strong, horizontal bond between married couple is also tight and important? It could be argued that the family of the Delta is in transition from the "traditional" Confucian family to "modern" nuclear family as some studies on North Vietnam and China argue.[8] It is, however, also possible to discuss the possibility of strong conjugal relationship in this area even in pre-modern era considering its origin as a fluid migrant community and its proximity to Southeast Asia at the same time as to East Asia. Or, the tendency may have been effects of western culture brought about by the French and the Americans. However, these arguments still remain only speculations. In order to assess the transformation of the family in the rural Mekong Delta in a comparative framework of post- or late socialism, more research would be necessary.

Another framework to possibly situate this study in is that of globalization. Watson (1997), in a study of one global industry, McDonalds, stresses the importance of looking at the complexity of global products and the cultures they carry, and how they become localized in each specific context. He states, "The process of localization is a two-way street: It implies changes in the local culture as well as modifications in the company's standard operating procedures" (ibid., p. 37). McDonald's has not been introduced to Can Tho City or Long Tuyen Village. However, the villagers in the rural Mekong Delta now experience the effects of global market through the competition of their own products with those imported from neighbouring countries. Although the economy of the Delta had been incorporated into the world market during French colonization, it is more likely to have been export-oriented rather than the two-way process that we see today. It is interesting to see if and how the farmers of Long Tuyen Villages as well as other villages in the Delta may "localize" the imported products as they are keenly aware of the effects of international products.

Another form of global culture, consumerism, is observed by Yan (2000; 2009) in China, where imported material goods and cultural products such as Japanese colour television sets, refrigerators, other household appliances, cosmetics, soft drinks, toothpaste and laundry detergent are consumed. There are other forms of imported cultural products, such as pop music, Hollywood movies and World Cup soccer games. Many farmers of Long Tuyen Village have not really been introduced to the culture of mass consumption, especially that of foreign goods, yet, and the foreign products are beyond their reach as they are too expensive for them. However, there are signs that they are entering the age of consumption of global goods. For instance, most houses with electricity now own TVs. People are aware of such brand names as Sony and Panasonic. Once they gain enough money, there is tendency to start to buy more expensive appliances. With TVs, as I have discussed earlier, farmers are exposed to the culture of the outside world, not only of larger cities in the country but also of more "developed" nations. The images and messages carried by mass media, though controlled by the state in the case of Vietnam, trigger taste for foreign goods and culture among the villagers. It is not easy to speculate if they will generate cultural conflict with local norms and ideas, and raise nationalistic concerns in the rural Mekong Delta as Yan points out in his study on China. However, these issues are interesting to keep in mind as we continue to investigate the effects of global culture on the local everyday life of the farmers of the Delta.

AFTERWARDS

I returned to Long Tuyen Village in September 2014. Over the years since the research for the most part of this book was carried out, some major changes occurred in the family I stayed with. The biggest change and the saddest thing is that Uncle Bay passed away and Second Brother has also died. On the other hand, the family has experienced some happy developments as well. Youngest Brother is now married and has two young daughters. Unlike his former wish to marry a woman from the city, the brother married someone from a neighbouring village, and in the house Aunt Tam, Youngest Brother, his wife and their daughters live together.

Youngest Brother is still working at the security office of Can Tho City, and with Uncle Bay now gone, no one from the family toils the land of the uncle and the aunt. Instead, they earn money by leasing the land, which is also a big change in their life. At the time of my visit, the family was in the process of renovating their house. They no longer cook with firewood, but now have a newly built kitchen with a gas bombes and cooking ranges. They have also added a bathroom to the house, where you can take shower, too. They no longer have to go outside for toilets or bathe in the river. In the house, I saw many new electrical appliances, such as a large TV and refrigerator. They have even installed an air conditioner in one of their bedrooms, which was almost unthinkable before. All these show the wealth they have acquired over the years. Responding to my question, Fifth Sister said, "Our life is now more stable."

However, I also noticed that family relationships have not changed much. Youngest Brother, following the tradition, stays in his natal house after marriage and takes care of his aging mother. As they prepared a meal for me, most of the children, and now grown-up grandchildren, of Uncle Bay and Aunt Tam gathered and helped one another with cooking. When sharing the meal, female and male members sat on different tables. Seeing all the new appliances, one may be tempted to rush to a conclusion that the brother is more interested in materials now. However, this can also be part of their family relationships that adult children spend money for the sake of their parents and to expand the inherited house. In fact the warm family atmosphere has remained the same.

I observed some new social relationships, too. Some of Youngest Brother's friends from work in the city joined the meal, which I did not see before. A new road has been built between Can Tho City centre and Long Tuyen and the village has become more easily accessible, which may explain the presence of the brother's friends. But it also shows the increased significance of friends and colleagues at work. When I returned to my hotel in the city, one of the friends rode me on the back of his motorbike, from which I learned how they help each other, too. I was expecting before that as the members work outside of family farming, the family ties might become weaker, but I observed instead that the family was being incorporated into the new social sphere. The boundary between the family and outside is now flexibly changing.

Notes

1. The Law on Health Insurance came into effect in 2009. In the decade since 2000, Vietnam aims at achieving universal health insurance by the year 2014 (Bonnet, Cichon, Galian, Mazelkaite and Schmitt 2012).
2. I had given some fifty US dollars while I stayed with the family, to cover the cost for Aunt Tam's medicine. At that time, I did not carry a lot of money with me to the village, so that was all I could give to them.

3. Sending one envelope to Japan cost about fourteen thousand Vietnamese dongs.
4. For discussions on the social systems for old age security, the pension system in particular, see Goodkind et al. (1998).
5. Ikels (1993) also argues that "intergenerational contract" (in which older people provide economic and other support to the younger generation so that they can gain support later in life) has been weakened in post-Mao China as the younger generation seek new opportunities to work and live in communities other than the ones in which they were raised.
6. Hy Van Luong comments (as a personal suggestion) that the Vietnamese also use family metaphors for other social relationships. While he is right to some extent, I argue what Kondo suggests is more than that. In the Japanese context, a workplace may become like a real family, which may sometimes even show stronger personal ties between members than actual families.
7. Edgar's (2004) view that "it is not the individual that acts reflexively; it is the family which mediates that impact of globalization, community resources and government action" is at least applicable in the case of the rural Mekong Delta.
8. In a study of the family and its changes in the Red River Delta in northern Vietnam in the last half century, Pham Van Bich (1997) discusses the effects of socialism on the family of the Delta. He states that the family has undergone significant changes such as larger freedom in marital partner choices. According to the author, the changes cannot be attributed to industrialization, as some other studies on family changes may suggest, due to the low level of industrialization in the area. Instead, Pham argues, they should be understood as state-driven changes by socialism. Similar argument can be found in some Chinese studies (Yan 1997).

BIBLIOGRAPHY

Abrami, Regina. "Just a Peasant: Economy and Legacy in Northern Vietnam". In *Post-Socialist Peasant?: Rural and Urban Construction of Identity in Eastern Europe, East Asia and the Former Soviet Union*, edited by P. Leonard and D. Kaneff. Houndmills: Palgrave, 2002.

Appell, George N. "Land Tenure and Development among the Rungus Dusun of Sabah, Malaysia". In *Modernization and the Emergence of a Landless Peasantry: Essays on the Integration of Peripheries to Socioeconomic Centers*, edited by G.N. Appell. Studies in Third World Societies Publication no. 33. Williamsburg, Virginia: Studies in Third World Societies, 1985.

Arnold, Fred and Eddie Kuo. "The Value of Daughters and Sons: A Comparative Study of the Gender Preferences of Parents". *Journal of Comparative Family Studies* 15 (1984): 299–318.

Bailey, Conner. "Class Differentiation and Erosion of a Moral Economy in Rural Malaysia". *Research in Economic Anthropology* 13 (1991): 119–42.

Ban Chi Dao Tong Dieu Tra Dan Son Trung Uong. *The 2009 Vietnam Population and Housing Census: Major Findings*. Hanoi: Central Population and Housing Census Steering Committee, 2010.

Belanger, Daniele. "Changement Familiaux au Vietnam depuis 1960". *Cahiers des Science Humaines 33* (1997).

———. "Regional Differences in Household Composition and Family Formation Patterns in Vietnam". Paper presented at Annual Meetings of the Association of Asian Studies, 1998.

Belanger, Daniele and Magali Barbieri. "Introduction: State, Families and the Making of Transitions in Vietnam". In *Reconfiguring Families in Contemporary Vietnam*, edited by M. Barbieri and D. Belager. Stanford: Stanford University Press, 2009.

Belanger, Daniele and Khuat Thu Hong. "Mot so bien doi trong hon nhan va gia dinh o Ha Noi" [Some changes in marriage and family in Ha Noi]. In *Nhung nghien cuu xa hoi hoc ve gia dinh Viet Nam* [Some Sociological studies of Vietnamese family]. Hanoi: Nha xuat ban khoa hoc xa hoi, 1996.

Belanger, Daniele and Jianye Liu. "Social Policy Reforms and Daughters' Schooling in Vietnam". *International Journal of Educational Development* 24, no. 1 (2004): 23–38.

Beresford, Melanie. "Household and Collective in Vietnamese Agriculture". *Journal of Contemporary Asia* 15, no. 1 (1985): 5–36.

———. "Issues in Economic Unification: Overcoming the Legacy of Separation". In *Postwar Vietnam: Dilemmas in Socialist Development*, edited by D.G. Marr and C.P. White. Ithaca: Southeast Asia Program, Cornell University, 1988.

———. "The Impact of Economic Reforms on the South". In Doi Moi*: Vietnam's Renovation Policy and Performance*, edited by D. Forbes, T.H. Hull, D.G. Marr, and B. Brogan. Political and Social Change Monograph. Canberra: Department of Political and Social Change, Research School of Pacific Studies, Australian National University, 1991.

Beresford, Melanie and Dang Phong. *Economic Transition in Vietnam: Trade and Aid in the Demise of a Centrally Planned Economy*. Cheltenham, UK; Northampton, MA, USA: Edward Elgar, 2001.

Beresford, Melanie and Adam Fforde. *A Methodology for Analyzing the Process of Economic Reform in Vietnam: A Case of Domestic Trade*. Australian-Vietnam Research Project, 1996.

Beresford, Melanie and Angie Ngoc Tran, eds. *Reaching for the Dream: Challenges of Sustainable Development in Vietnam*. Honolulu: University of Hawaii Press, 2004.

Biggs, David. *Quagmire: Nation-Building and Nature in the Mekong Delta*. Seattle: University of Washington Press, 2012.

Blanc-Szanton, M. Cristina. "Gender and Inter-generational Resource Allocation among Thai and Sino-Thai Households". In *Women and the Household in Asia*, edited by L. Dube and R. Palriwala. New Delhi; Newbury Park, Calif.: Sage Publications, 1990.

Bloch, Maurice and Jonathan Parry. "Introduction: Money and the Morality of Exchange". In *Money and the Morality of Exchange*, edited by J. Parry and M. Bloch. Cambridge: Cambridge University Press, 1989.

Bonnet, Florence, Michael Cichon, Carlos Galian, Gintare Mazelkaite, and Valerie Schmitt. *Analysis of the Viet Nam National Social Protection Strategy (2011–2020) in the Context of Social Protection Floor Objectives*. Geneva: International Labour Office, 2012.

Brenner, Suzanne. *The Domestication of Desire: Women, Wealth, and Modernity in Java*. Princeton: Princeton University Press, 1998.

Brettell, Caroline B. "Not that Lineage Stuff: Teaching Kinship into the Twenty-First Century". In *New Directions in Anthropological Kinship*, edited by L. Stone. Lanham, MD: Rowman & Littlefield Publishers, 2001.

Brocheux, Pierre. "Moral Economy or Political Economy? The Peasants are Always Rational". *Journal of Asian Studies* 42, no. 4 (1983): 791–803.

———. *The Mekong Delta: Ecology, Economy and Revolution, 1980–1960*. Madison: University of Wisconsin-Madison, Center for Southeast Asian Studies, 1995.

Bui Thi Mui. "Nguoi me, nha gia duc dau tien cua tre trong gia dinh" [Mother is the first teacher of the young in the faimly]. In *Hoi Thao Chuyen De: Phu Nu & Su Phat Trien*. Can Tho: Can Tho University, 1995.

Burr, Rachel. "The Complexity of Morality: Being a 'Good Child' in Vietnam?" *Journal of Moral Education* 4, no. 2 (2014): 156–68.

Caffrey, Rosalie A. "Family Care of the Elderly in Northeast Thailand: Changing Patterns". *Journal of Cross-cultural Gerontology* 7, no. 2 (1992): 105–16.

Canh Bang. *Can Tho xua va nay* [Can Tho Past and Present]. Can Tho, 1966.

Chan, Hoiman and Rance P.L. Lee. "Hong Kong Families: At the Crossroad of Modernism and Traditionalism". *Journal of Comparative Family Studies* 26 (1995): 83–99.

Chayanov, Aleksandr Vasil'erich. *The Theory of Peasant Economy*, edited by D. Torner, R.E.F. Smith, and B. Kerblay. Homewood, Ill.: Irwin, published for the American Economic Association, by R.D. Irwin, 1966.

Cheal, David. "Strategies of Resource Management in Household Economies: Moral Economy or Political Economy?" In *Household Economy: Reconsidering the Domestic Mode of Production*, edited by R.R. Wilk. Boulder: Westview Press, 1989.

Chi Cuc Thong Ke Kinh Te Tinh Can Tho. *Nien giam thong ke tinh Can Tho 1998* [Name list of statistics in Can Tho 1998]. Can Tho: Chi Cuc Thong Ke Tinh Can Tho, 1998.

Chou, Rita Jing-Ann. "Filial Piety by Contract? The Emergence, Implementation, and Implications of the 'Family Support Agreement' in China". *The Gelontologist* 51, no. 1 (2010): 3–16.

Cohen, Myron. "Agnatic Kinship in South Taiwan". *Ethnology* 8, no. 2 (1969): 167–82.

———. *House United, House Divided: The Chinese Family in Taiwan*. New York: Columbia University Press, 1976.

Craig, David. *Familiar Medicine: Everyday Health Knowledge and Practice in Today's Vietnam*. Honolulu: University of Hawaii Press, 2002.

Croll, Elisabeth J. "The Intergenerational Contract in the Changing Asian Family". *Oxford Development Studies* 34, no. 4 (2006): 473–91.

Dahm, Bernhard and Vincent J.H. Houben, eds. *Vietnamese Village in Transition: Background and Consequences of Reform Policies in Rural Vietnam*. Passau: Department of Southeast Asian Studies, Passau University, 1999.

Dang, Phong. *"Pha rao" trong kinh te vao dem truoc Doi Moi* ["Breaking of fence" in the night before Doi Moi]. Hanoi: Nha Xuat Ban Tri Thuc, 2009.

Dang Thanh Le. "The loai gia huan va chuc nang giao duc phu nu cua thiet che gia dinh truyen thong" [Family education and educational role of women in traditional family]. In *Nhung nghien cuu xa hoi hoc ve gia dinh Viet Nam*, edited by Tuong Lai. Hanoi: Nha Xuat Ban Khoa Hoc Xa Hoi, 1996.

Dao The Tuan. "The Peasant Household Economy and Social Change". In *Vietnam's Rural Transformation*, edited by B. Kerkvliet and D. Porter. Boulder: Westview Press, 1995.

Dapice, David. "Vietnam at the Starting Point: Just Another Successful Asian Economy?" In *The Challenge of Reform in Indochina*, edited by B. Ljunggren. Cambridge: Harvard Institute for International Development, 1993.

Davis, Deborah, and Steven Harrell. "Introduction: The Impact of Post-Mao Reforms on Family Life". *In Chinese Families in the Post-Mao Era*, edited by D. Davis and S. Harrell. Berkeley: University of California Press, 1993.

de Gentile-Duquesne, Pierre. *La Situation Jurisdique de la Femme Annamite*. Paris: Jouve, 1925.

de Vylder, Stefan. *Toward a Market Economy? Current State of Economic Reform in Vietnam*. Stockholm: Stockholm School of Economics, 1990.

Do Thai Dong. "Modifications of the Traditional Family in the South of Vietnam". In *Sociological Studies on the Vietnamese Family*, edited by R. Liljestrom. Hanoi: Social Sciences Publishing House, 1991.

Drummond, Lisa and Helle Rydstrom, eds. *Gender Practices in Contemporary Vietnam*. Honolulu: University of Hawaii Press, 2004.

Duiker, William. *Vietnam since the Fall of Saigon*. Athens: Ohio University Center for International Studies, 1989.

———. *Vietnam: Revolution in Transition*. Boulder: Westview Press, 1995*a*.

———. *Sacred War*. New York: McGrow-Hill, 1995*b*.

Ebihara, May. "Khmer Village Women in Cambodia: A Happy Balance". In *Many Sisters: Women in Cross-Cultural Perspective*, edited by C.J. Matthiasson. New York: Free Press, 1974.

———. "Residence Patterns in a Khmer Peasant Village". In *Annals of the New York Academy of Sciences* 293, no. 1 (1977): 51–68.

Edgar, Don. "Globalization and the Western Bias in Family Sociology". In *The Blackwell Companion to the Sociology of Families,* edited by J. Scott, J. Teas, and M. Richards. Malden, MA: Blackwell Publishing 2004.

Eisen, Arlene. *Women and Revolution in Viet Nam*. London: Zed Books, 1985.

Elliott, David. *NFL-DRV Strategy and the 1972 Spring Offensive*. Ithaca: International Relations of East Asia Project, Cornell University, 1974.

———. "Waiting for the East Wind: Revolution and Social Change in Modern Vietnam". In *Vietnam: Essays on History, Culture, and Society*. New York: Asia Society, 1985.

Evans, Grant. "'Rich Peasants' and Cooperatives in Socialist Laos". *Journal of Anthropological Research Albuquerque* 44, no. 3 (1988): 229–50.

Fahey, Stephanie. "Changing Labour Relations". In *Dilemmas of Development: Vietnam Update 1994,* edited by B. Kerkvliet. Canberra: Department of Political and Social Change, Research School of Pacific and Asian Studies, Australian National University, 1995.

Fall, Bernard B. "The Political-Religious Sects of Viet-Nam". *Pacific Affairs* 28, no. 3 (1955): 235–53.

Feeny, David. "Moral of the Rational Peasant? Competing Hypotheses of Collective Action". *Journal of Asian Studies* 42, no. 4 (1983): 769–89.

Fforde, Adam and Stefan de Vylder. *From Plan to Market*. Boulder: Westview Press, 1996.

Foster, Brian. "Socioeconomic Consequences of Stem Family Composition in a Thai Village". *Ethnology* 17, no. 2 (1978): 139–56.

———. "Family Structure and the Generation of Thai Social Exchange Networks". In *Households,* edited by R. McC. Netting, R.R. Wilk, and E.J. Arnolds. Berkeley: University of California Press, 1984.

———. "Socioeconomic Consequences of Stem Family Composition in a Thai Village". *Ethnology* 17 (1987): 139–56.

Fox, Robin. *Kinship and Marriage: An Anthropological Perspective*. New York: Penguin, 1967.

Fung, Heidi. "Becoming a Moral Child: The Socialization of Shame among Young Chinese Children". *Ethos* 27, no. 2 (1999): 180–209.

Furuta, Motoo. *Betonamu no sekaishi* [World history of Vietnam]. Tokyo: University of Tokyo Press, 1995.

———. *Betonamu no genzai* [Present-day Vietnam]. Tokyo: Kodansha, 1996.

Gaevffier, Rene. *Essai sur le Regime de la Terre en Indochina* [A study on the land policy in Indochina]. Lyon: Bosc Freres et Riou, 1928.

Gallup, John Luke. "The Economic Value of Children in Vietnam". Unpublished manuscript, 1997.

Geertz, Clifford. *Agricultural Involution: The Process of Ecological Change in Indonesia*. Berkeley: University of California Press, 1963.

General Statistics Office of Vietnam. *Vietnam Population and Housing Census 2009- Age-Sex Structure and Marital Status of the Population in Vietnam*. Hanoi: General Statistics Office of Vietnam, 2011*a*.

———. *Vietnam Population and Housing Census 2009 – Education in Vietnam: An Analysis of Key Indicators*. Hanoi: General Statistics Office of Vietnam, 2011*b*.

Gettleman, Marvin, ed. *Vietnam: History, Documents, and Opinions on a Major World Crisis*. Greenwich, CT: Fawcett Publications, 1965.

Goheen, Miriam. *Men Own the Fields, Women Own the Crops: Gender and Power in the Cameroon Grassfields*. Madison: University of Wisconsin Press, 1996.

Goode, William. *World Revolution and Family Patterns*. New York: Free Press of Glencoe, 1963.

Goodkind, Daniel. "Rising Gender Inequality in Vietnam since Reunification". *Pacific Affairs* 68 (1995): 342–59.

———. "State Agendas, Local Sentiments: Vietnamese Wedding Practices amidst Socialist Transformations". *Social Forces* 75, no. 2 (1996): 717–42.

———. "Vietnamese Double Marriage Squeeze". *International Migration Review* 31, no. 1 (1997): 108–27.

———. et al. "Reforming the Old Age Security System in Vietnam: Legacies, Transformations, and Future Challenges". Unpublished manuscript, 1998.

Grandstaff, Terry B. "Human Environment: Variation and Uncertainty". *Pacific Viewpoint* 33, no. 2 (1992): 135–44.

Grossheim, Martin. "The Impact of Reforms on the Agricultural Sector in Vietnam: The Land Issue". In *Vietnamese Village in Transition: Background and Consequences of Reform Policies in Rural Vietnam*, edited by B. Dahm and V.J.H. Houben. Passau: Department of Southeast Asian Studies, Passau University, 1999.

Grossheim, Martin and Kirsten W. Endres. "Images of Womanhood in Rural Vietnam and the Role of the Vietnamese Women's Union: A Microscopic Perspective". In *Vietnamese Village in Transition: Background and Consequences of Reform Policies in Rural Vietnam*, edited by B. Dahm and V.J. Houben. Passau: Department of Southeast Asian Studies, Passau University, 1999.

Gupta, Akhil. *Postcolonial Developments*. Durham: Duke University Press, 1995.

Haines, David. "Reflections of Kinship and Society under Vietnamese Le Dynasty". *Journal of Southeast Asian Studies* 15 (1984): 307–14.

Hainsworth, Geoffrey B. "Beyond Dualism? Village-Level Modernization and the Process of Integration into National Economies in Southeast Asia". In

Village-Level Modernization in Southeast Asia, edited by G.B. Hainsworth. Vancouver: University of British Columbia Press, 1982.

Harms, Eric. *Saigon's Edge: On the Margins of Ho Chi Minh City*. Minneapolis: University of Minnesota Press, 2011.

Harrell, Steven. "Geography, Demography, and Family Composition in Rural China: Some Evidence from the Pearl River Delta". In *Chinese Families in the Post-Mao Era*, edited by D. Davis and S. Harrell. Berkeley: University of California Press, 1993.

Haughton, Dominique, et al. *Ho gia dinh Viet Nam: Nhin qua phan tich dinh luong* [Vietnamese family: The general view of the analysis]. Hanoi: Nha Xuat Ban Chinh Tri Quoc Gia, 1999.

———, eds. *Health and Wealth in Vietnam: An Analysis of Household Living Standards*. Singapore: Institute of Southeast Asian Studies, 1999.

Hickey, Gerald. *Village in Vietnam*. New Haven: Yale University Press, 1964.

———. *Free in the Forest: Ethnohistory of the Vietnamese Central Highlands, 1954–1976*. New Haven: Yale University Press, 1982.

———. "Village through Time and War". In *Vietnam: Essays on History, Culture, and Society*. New York: Asia Society, 1985.

Hiebert, Murray. *Chasing the Tigers: A Portrait of the New Vietnam*. New York: Kodansha International, 1996.

Hirschman, Charles and Vu Manh Loi. "Family and Household Structure in Vietnam: Some Glimpses from a Recent Survey". *Pacific Affairs* 69, no. 2 (1996): 229–49.

Ho Le and Nguyen Lieu. "Sinh hoat van hoa o Dong Bang Song Cuu Long va nhung van de dang dat ra" [Cultural activities in the Mekong Delta and some controversial issues]. In *Mot so van de khoa hoc ve Dong Bang Song Cuu Long* [Some scientific issues in the Mekong Delta], edited by T.H. Mai. Hanoi: Nha Xuat Ban Khoa Hoc Xa Hoi, 1982.

Hong Ha. "Gia ding trong cong cuoc Doi Moi hien nay" [Family in today's Doi Moi project]. In *Gia dinh va van de giao duc gia dinh: De tai KX-07-09* [Family and problems of family education: Topic KX-07-09], edited by Trung tam Nghien cuu Khoa hoc ve Gia dinh va Phu nu. Hanoi: Nha Xuat Ban Khoa Hoc Xa Hoi, 1994.

Hoshall, Earle C. *Higher Education in Vietnam: 1967–1971*. Saigon: USAID, 1971.

Hunter, William Andrew, and Liem Thanh Nguyen. *Educational System in South Vietnam and of Southeast Asians in Comparison with Educational Systems in the United States*. Ames: Research Institute for Studies in Education, College of Education, Iowa State University, 1977.

Huynh Minh. *Can Tho xua va nay* [Can Tho past and present]. Can Tho: Tac Gia Xuat Ban, 1966.

Huynh Quoc Thang. "Van hoa dan toc trong le hoi dan gian o nam bo" [National cultures in folk ceremonies in South Vietnam]. In *Nam Bo Xua Va Nay* [The South in the Past and Present], edited by Tap Chi Xua Va Nay. Ho Chi Minh City: Nha Xuat Ban Thanh Pho Ho Chi Minh, 1999.

Ikels, Chalotte. "Settling Accounts: The Intergenerational Contract in an Age of Reform". In *Chinese Families in the Post-Mao Era,* edited by D. Davis and S. Harrell. Berkeley: University of California Press, 1993.

———. *The Return of the God of Wealth: The Transition to a Market Economy in Urban China*. Stanford: Stanford University Press, 1996.

Ireson, W. Randall. "Peasant Farmers and Community Norms: Agricultural Labor Exchange in Laos". *Peasant Studies* 19, no. 2 (1992): 67–92.

Jamieson, Neil. "Toward a Paradigm for Paradox: Observations on the Study of Social Organization in Southeast Asia". *Journal of Southeast Asian Studies* 15 (1984): 320–29.

———. "The Traditional Village in Vietnam". *The Vietnam Forum* 7 (1986*a*): 89–126.

———. "The Traditional Family in Vietnam". *The Vietnam Forum* 8 (1986*b*): 91–150.

———. *Understanding Vietnam*. Berkeley: University of California Press, 1993.

Johnson, Graham. "Family Strategies and Economic Transformation in Rural China: Some Evidence from the Pearl River Delta". In *Chinese Families in the Post-Mao Era,* edited by D. Davis and S. Harrell. Berkeley: University of California Press, 1993.

Jones, Gavin. "The Role of Education in Asian Economic Growth: Past and Future". In *Development and Challenge: Southeast Asia in the New Millennium,* edited by Wong Tai-Chee and Mohan Singh. Singapore: Times Academic Press, 1999.

Kaufman, Joan and Gita Sen. "Population, Health, and Gender in Vietnam: Social Policies under the Economic Reforms". In *The Challenge of Reform in Indochina*, edited by B. Ljunggren. Cambridge: Harvard Institute for International Development, 1993.

Kelly, Gail Paradise. *The Professionalization of Teachers and the Distribution of Classroom Knowledge: Perspectives from Colonial Vietnam*. Buffalo: State University of New York, 1980.

———. *Franco-Vietnamese Schools, 1918–1938: Regional Development and Implications for National Integration*. Madison: Center of Southeast Asian Studies, University of Wisconsin-Madison, 1982.

Kerblay, Basile. "Chayanov and the Theory of Peasantry as a Specific Type Economy". In *Peasants and Peasant Societies,* edited by T. Shanin. Harmondsworth: Penguin, 1971.

Kerkvliet, Benedict. *Dilemmas of Development: Vietnam Update 1994*. Canberra: Department of Political Social Change, Research School of Pacific and Asian Studies, Australian National University, 1995.

———, ed. *The Power of Everyday Politics: How Vietnamese Peasants Transformed National Policy*. Ithaca: Cornell University Press, 2005.

Keyes, Charles. *Golden Peninsula: Culture and Adaptation in Mainland Southeast Asia*. Honolulu: University of Hawaii Press, 1995.

Kim, On-Jook Leeq. "Casual Interpretation of the Effect of Mother's Education and Employment Status on Parental Decision-Making Role Patterns in the Korean Family". *Journal of Comparative Family Studies* 8, no. 1 (1977): 117–31.

Kleinen, John. *Facing the Future, Reviving the Past: A Study of Social Change in a Northern Vietnamese Village*. Singapore: Institute of Southeast Asian Studies, 1999.

Koentjaraningrat. "Changing Cultural Value Orientation of Javanese Peasants". In *Village-Level Modernization in Southeast Asia*, edited by G.B. Hainsworth. Vancouver: University of British Columbia Press, 1982.

Kondo, Dorinne. *Crafting Selves: Power, Gender, and Discourses of Identity in a Japanese Workplace*. Chicago: The University of Chicago Press, 1990.

Korson, Henry. "Modernization and Social Change — The Family in Pakistan". In *Family in Asia*, edited by M.S. Das and P. Bardis. London: George Allen and Unwin, 1978.

Kung, L. *Factory Women in Taiwan*. Ann Abor: University of Michigan Press, 1983.

Kwiatkowski, Lynn. "Domestic Violence and 'Happy Family' in Northern Vietnam. *Anthropology NOW* 3, no. 3 (2011): 20–28.

Lavergne, Daly C. and Abul H.K. Sassani. *Education in Viet Nam*. Washington, D.C.: United States Department of Health, Education, and Welfare, Office of Education, Division of International Education, 1955.

Le Kha Phieu. *Vietnam Entering the 21st Century: Selected Speeches and Writings of the General Secretary of the Central Committee of the Communist Party of Vietnam*. Hanoi: The Gioi Publishers, 2001.

Le Ngoc Lan. "Gia dinh va van de viec thuc hien cac chuc nang cua gia dinh hien nay" [Family and the issue regarding effects of family function today]. In *Gia dinh va van de giao duc gia dinh: De tai KX-07-09* [Family and problems of family education: Topic KX-07-09], edited by Trung tam Nghien cuu Khoa hoc ve Gia dinh va Phu nu. Hanoi: Nha xuat Ban Khoa Hoc Xa Hoi, 1994.

Le Ngoc Van. *Gia dinh Viet Nam voi chuc nang xa hoi hoa* [Vietnamese family with function of socialization]. Hanoi: Nha Xuat Ban Giao Duc, 1996.

Le Thi. "Gia dinh Viet Nam, cac trach nhiem, cac nguon luc trong su Doi Moi cua dat nuoc" [Vietnamese family, its responsibility and its power in the country's Doi Moi]. In *Gia dinh Viet Nam, cac trach nhiem, cac nguon luc trong su Doi Moi cua dat nuoc* [Vietnamese family, its responsibility and its power in the country's *Doi Moi*], edited by Trung tam Khoa hoc Xa hoi va Nhan van Quoc gia. Hanoi: Nha xuat ban Khoa hoc Xa hoi, 1995.

———. "Women, Marriage, Family and Gender Equality". In *Vietnam's Women in Transition*, edited by K. Barry. New York: St. Martin's Press, 1996.

———. *The Role of the Family in the Formation of Vietnamese Personality*. Hanoi: The Gioi Publishers, 1999.

Le Thi Ngoc Thanh. "Phu nu voi viec phat trien" [Women and development]. In *Hoi thao chuyen de: Phu nu & su phat trien* [Discussion theme: Women and development]. Can Tho: Can Tho University, 1995.

Le Xuan Sinh. "The Effects of Aquaculture on Farm Household Economy: A Case Study of Omon District, Can Tho Province, Vietnam". MA thesis, Thailand, 1995.

Le Xuan Sinh, Nguyen Thanh Toan, and Tran Thanh Be. *Socio-Economic Conditions of the Household Settings in Vodai Melaleuca Forest, Camau Province in the Mekong River Delta*. Global Environmental Consultants Ltd., 1997.

Leshkowich, Ann Marie. "Tightly Woven Threads: Gender, Kinship, and 'Secret Agency' among Cloth and Clothing Traders in Ho Chi Minh City's Ben Thanh Market". Ph.D. dissertation, Harvard University, 2000.

———. "Making Class and Gender: (Market) Socialist Enframing of Trader in Ho Chi Minh City". *American Anthropologist* 113, no. 2 (2011): 277–90.

———. "Rendering Infant Abandonment Technical and Moral: Expertise, Neoliberal Logics, and Class Differentiation in Ho Chi Minh City". *Positions* 20, no. 2 (2012): 497–526.

Levi-Strauss, Claude. *The Elementary Structure of Kinship*. Boston: Beacon Press, 1969.

Liljestrom, Rita and Tuong Lai, eds. *Sociological Studies on the Vietnamese Family*. Hanoi: Social Sciences Publishing House, 1991.

Limanonda, Brassorn. "Families in Thailand: Beliefs and Realities". *Journal of Comparative Family Studies* 26, no. 1 (1995): 67–82.

Luong Hong Quang. *Van hoa cong dong lang: Vung Dong Bang Song Cuu Long thap ky 80–90* [Village culture in the Mekong Delta in the decades 80–90]. Hanoi: Nha Xuat Ban Van Hoa — Thong Tin, 1997.

Luong, Hy Van. "Vietnamese Kinship: Structural Principles and the Socialist Transformation in Northern Vietnam". *Journal of Asian Studies* 48 (1989): 741–56.

———. *Revolution in the Village: Tradition and Transformation in North Vietnam, 1925–1988.* Honolulu: University of Hawaii Press, 1992.

———. "Economic Reform and the Intensification of Rituals in Two North Vietnamese Villages: 1980–90". In *The Challenge of Reform in Indochina,* edited by B. Ljunggren. Cambridge: Harvard Institute for International Development, 1993*a*.

———. "The Political Economy of Vietnamese Reforms: A Microscopic Perspective from Two Ceramics Manufacturing Centers". In *Reinventing Vietnamese Socialism:* Doi Moi *in Comparative Perspectives,* edited by W. Turley and M. Selden. Boulder: Westview Press, 1993*b*.

———. "The Marxist State and the Dialogic Re-structuration of Culture in Rural Vietnam". In *Indochina: Social and Cultural Change,* edited by D. Elliott. Claremont, CA: Keck Center for International and Strategic Studies, Claremont McKenna College, 1994.

Luong, Hy Van and Diep Dinh Hoa. "Culture and Capitalism in the Pottery Enterprises of Bien How, South Vietnam (1878–1975)". *Journal of Southeast Asian Studies* 22 (1991): 16–32.

Luong Thi Thuan. "Ket hop giua gia dinh: Cong dong trong viec cham soc va giao duc tre em" [Family cooperation: Taking care and educating children together]. *Tap chi Khoa hoc Xa hoi* 35, no. 1 (1998): 135–37.

Luro, Eliacin. *Le Pays d'Annam: Etude sur l'Organization Politique et Sociale des Annamites* [The country of Annam: A study on political and social organization of the Annamites]. Paris: E. Leroux, 1878.

Lutz, Catherine. *Language and the Politics of Emotion.* Cambridge: Cambridge University Press, 1990.

Mai, H.T., ed. *Mot so van de khoa hoc ve Dong Bang Song Cuu Long* [Some scientific problems of the Mekong Delta]. Hanoi: Nha Xuat Ban Khoa Hoc Xa Hoi, 1982.

Malarney, Shaun. "State Stigma, Family Prestige, and the Development of Entrepreneurship in the Red River Delta". PhD dissertation, University of Michigan, 1994.

———. *Culture, Ritual and Revolution in Vietnam.* Honolulu: University of Hawaii Press, 2002.

Marr, David. *Vietnamese Tradition on Trial, 1920–1945.* Berkeley: University of California Press, 1981.

———. *Vietnam Strives to Catch Up.* New York: Asia Society, 1995.

Marr, David and Christine White, eds. *Postwar Vietnam: Dilemmas in Socialist Development.* Ithaca: Cornell Southeast Asia Program, 1988.

Maybury-Lewis, David. "Conclusion: Kinship, Ideology and Culture". In *Dialectical Societies: The Ge and Bororo of Central Brazil,* edited by D. Maybury-Lewis. Cambridge, Mass: Harvard University Press, 1979.

———. "Social Theory and Social Practice: Binary Systems in Central Brazil". In *The Attractions of Opposites*, edited by D. Maybury-Lewis and U. Almagor. Ann Abor: University of Michigan Press, 1989.

McDonald, Peter. "Families in Developing Countries: Idealized Morality and Theories of Family Change". In *Tradition and Change in the Asian Family*, edited by L.-J. Cho and M. Yada. Honolulu: East-West Center, 1994.

Medick, Hans and David Sabean, eds. *Interest and Emotion: Essays on the Study of Family and Kinship*. Cambridge: Cambridge University Press, 1984.

Mills, Mary Beth. "Contesting the Margins of Modernity: Women, Migration, and Consumption in Thailand". *American Ethnologist* 24, no. 1 (1997): 37–61.

Miyazawa, Chiharu. "Betonamu hokubu sonraku kouzou no rekishiteki henka (1907–1997)" [Historical Changes of Village Structure in Nothern Vietnam (1907–1997)]. PhD dissertation, University of Tokyo, 1998.

———. "Betonamu hokubu no fukei shinzoku shudan no ichijirei: Jukyouteki kihan to jittai" [A Case Study of a Patrilineal Kin Group in Northern Vietnam: Confucian Norm and Reality]. *Betonamu no shakai to bunka* [Vietnamese society and culture] 1 (1999): 7–33.

Moise, Edwin. "The Moral Economy Dispute". *Belletin of Concerned Asian Scholars* 14 (1982): 72–76.

Ngo, Vinh Long. *Before the Revolution: The Vietnamese Peasants under the French.* Cambridge Mass: MIT Press, 1973.

———. "Some Aspects of Cooperativization in the Mekong Delta". In *Postwar Vietnam: Dilemmas of Socialist Development*, edited by D. Marr and C. White. Ithaca: Cornell Southeast Asia Program, 1988.

———. "Reform and Rural Development: Impact on Class Sectoral, and Regional Inequalities". In *Reinventing Vietnamese Socialism:* Doi Moi *in Comparative Perspective* edited by W. Turley and M. Selden. Boulder: Westview Press, 1993.

Nguyen Dinh Dau. "Dong Bang Song Me Kong 300 nam qua" [The Mekon Delta since 300 years ago]. In *Nam bo Xua va Nay* [The south in the past and present], edited by Tap chi Xua va Nay. Ho Chi Minh City: Nha xuat ban Thanh Pho Ho Chi Minh, 1999.

Nguyen Duy Quy and David Sloper. "Socio-Economic Background of Vietnam since 1986: Impact on Education and Higher Education". In *Higher Education in Vietnam*, edited by D. Sloper and Le Thac Can. New York: St. Martin Press, 1995.

Nguyen Ha. "Viet Nam Encourages Two-child Families". *Viet Nam News*, 30 July 2014.

Nguyen Hoang Ngoc. "Economic Renovation in Southern Vietnam: Challenges — Responses — Prospects". In Doi Moi: *Vietnam's Renovation Policy and*

Performance, edited by D. Frobes, T.H. Hull, D.G. Marr, and B. Brogan. Political and Social Change Monograph. Canberra: Department of Political and Social Change, Research School of Pacific Studies, Australian National University, 1991.

Nguyen Khanh. "Gia dinh Viet Nam hien nay: Nhung van de dat ra" [Vietnamese family today: Some problems to be solved]. In *Gia dinh Viet Nam, cac trach nhiem, can nhuon luc trong cu Doi Moi dat nuoc* [Vietnamese family, its responsibility and its power in the country's *Doi Moi*], edited by Trung tam Khoa hoc Xa hoi va Nhan van Quoc gia. Hanoi: Nha Xuat Ban Khoa Hoc Xa Hoi, 1995.

Nguyen Quang Kinh. "The Eradication of Illiteracy (EOI) and Universalization of Primary Education (UPE) in Vietnam". In *Education in Vietnam 1945–1991*, edited by P.M. Hac. Hanoi: Ministry of Education and Training of the Socialist Republic of Vietnam, 1991.

Nguyen The Anh. *Kinh te va xa hoi Viet-Nam duoi cac vua trieu* [Vietnamese economy and society in each *dinasgy*]. Saigon: Trinh Bay, 1968.

Nguyen The Long. *Gia dinh va dan toc* [Family and custom]. Hanoi: Nha Xuat Ban Lao Dong, 1998.

Nguyen Thi Hang. *Van de xoa doi giam ngheo o nong thon nuoc ta hien nay* [Problem of eliminating hunger and reducing poverty in the rural areas in our nation today]. Hanoi: Nha Xuat Ban Chinh Tri Quoc Gia, 1997.

Nguyen Thi Khoa. "Giao duc con trong gia dinh o nong thon hien nay" [Education of children in the family in the rural areas today]. In *Gia dinh va van de giao duc gia dinh: De tai KX-07-09*, edited by T.t.N.c.K.h.v.G.d.v.P. nu. Hanoi: Nha Xuat Ban Khoa Hoc Xa Hoi, 1994.

Nguyen Tuan Anh. "Kinship as Social Capital: Economic Social and Cultural Dimensions of Changing Kinship Relations in Northern Vietnamese Village". PhD dissertation, Vrige Universiteit Amsterdam, 2010.

Nong Quoc Chan. "Mot so van de van hoa trong qua tring tien hanh ba cuoc cach mang o vung Dong Bang Song Cuu Long" [Some cultural issues in the process of carrying out three revolutions in the Mekong Delta]. In *Mot so van de khoa hoc ve Dong Bang Song Cuu Long* edited by T.H. Mai. Hanoi: Nha Xuat Ban Khoa Hoc Xa Hoi, 1982.

Ong, Aihwa. *Spirits of Resistance and Capitalist Discipline: Factory Women in Malaysi*a. Albany: SUNY Press, 1987.

Owada-Shibuya, Setsuko. "Supporting Parents in Uncertainty: Filial Piety in the Rural Mekong Delta". In *Confucianism in Vietnam*. Ho Chi Minh City: Vietnam National University — Hochiminh City Publishing House, 2003.

Parker, Barbara. "Moral Economy, Political Economy, and the Culture of Entrepreneurship in Highland Nepal". *Ethnology* 27, no. 2 (1988): 181–94.

Pasquier, Pierre. *L'Annam d'Autrefois: Essai sur la Constitution de l'Annam avant l'Intervention Francais* [Annam in other days: A paper on the constitution of Annam before French intervention]. Paris: A. Challamel, 1907.

Peletz, Michael G. "Moral and Political Economies in Rural Southeast Asia". *Comparative Studies in Society and History* 25, no. 4 (1983): 731–39.

Pelzer, Kristin. "Socio-Cultural Dimensions of Revolution in Vietnam: *Doi Moi* as Dialogue and Transformation in Gender Relations". In *Reinventing Vietnamese Socialism:* Doi Moi *in Comparative Perspective,* edited by W. Turley and M. Seldan. Boulder: Westview Press, 1993.

Peterson, Jean Treloggen. "Return to Parental Investment in Children in Benguet Province, Philippines". *Journal of Comparative Family Studies* 22, no. 3 (1991): 313–28.

Pham Bich San. "Muu sinh, gia dinh va boi canh bien doi kinh te — Xa hoi o nong thon Viet Nam" [Household finance, family and situation of economic change in rural Vietnam]. In *Nhung nghien cuu xa hoi hoc ve gia dinh Viet Nam,* edited by Tuong Lai. Hanoi: Nha Xuat Ban Khoa Hoc Xa Hoi, 1996.

Pham Minh Hac. "Educational Reforms". In *Education in Vietnam 1945–1991,* edited by P.M. Hac. Hanoi: Ministry of Education and Training of the Socialist Republic of Vietnam, 1991.

———. *Vietnam's Education: The Current Position and Future Prospects.* Hanoi: The Gioi Publishers, 1998.

Pham Truong Khang and Hoang Le Minh. *Tu dien van hoa gia dinh* [Dictionary of family culture]. Hanoi: Nha Xuat Ban Van Hoa — Thong Tin, 2009.

Pham Van Bich. *The Changes of the Vietnamese Family in the Red River Delta.* Department of Sociology, University of Gothenburg, 1997.

———. *The Vietnamese Family in Change*. Richmond: Curzon, 1999.

Pham Xuan Nam. *Phat Trien Nong Thon* [Rural development]. Hanoi: Khoa Hoc Xa Hoi, 1997.

Phinney, Harriet. "Asking for a Child: The Refashioning of Reproductive Space in Post-War Northern Vietnam". *The Asia Pacific Journal of Anthropology* 6, no. 3 (2005): 215–30.

———. "'Rice Is Essential but Tiresome; You Should Get Some Noodles': Doi Moi and the Political Economy of Men's Extramarital Sexual Relations and Marital HIV Risk in Hanoi, Vietnam". *American Journal of Public Health* 98, no. 4 (2008): 650–60.

Piker, Steven. "Sources of Stability and Instability in Rural Thai Society". *Journal of Asian Studies* 27, no. 4 (1968): 777–90.

Popkin, Samuel. *Rational Peasant: The Political Economy of Rural Society in Vietnam*. Berkeley: University of California Press, 1979.

Potter, Sulamith H. *Family Life in a Northern Thai Village*. Berkeley: University of California Press, 1977.

Quan Truong. *Agricultural Collectivatization and Rural Development: A North-South Study, 1955–85*. Amsterdam: Universiteit te Amsterdam, 1987.

Robequain, Charles. *Le Thanh Hoa: Etude Geographique d'Une Province Annamite*. Paris, Bruxelles: G. Van Oest, 1929.

Rydstrom, Helle. *Embodying Morality: Growing up in Rural Northern Vietnam*. Honolulu: University of Hawaii Press, 2003.

Sakurai, Yumio. *Motto shiritai Betonamu* [Knowing Vietnam better]. Tokyo; Kobundo, 1995.

Sakurai, Yumio and Yoshiaki Ishizawa. *Tonanajia gendaishi: Vetonamu, Kambojia, Raosu* [Contemporary History of Southeast Asia: Vietnam, Cambodia, and Laos]. Tokyo: Yamakawa Shuppankai, 1997.

Salaff, Janet. *Working Daughters of Hong Kong: Filial Piety or Power in the Family?* New York: Columbia University Press, 1995.

Sansom, Robert L. *The Economics of Insurgency in the Mekong Delta of Vietnam*. Cambridge, MA: The M.I.T. Press, 1970.

Schlecker, Markus. "Life, Labor, and Merit: War Martyrdom as Support Encounters in Late Socialist Vietnam". In *Ethnographies of Social Support*, edited by M. Schlecker and F. Fleicher. New York: Palgrave Macmillan, 2013.

Scornet, Catherine. "State and the Family: Reproductive Policies and Practices". In *Reconfiguring Families in Contemporary Vietnam*, edited by M. Barberini and D. Belanger. Stanford: Stanford University Press, 2009.

Scott, James. *The Moral Economy of the Peasant: Rebellion and Subsistence in Southeast Asia*. New Haven: Yale University Press, 1976.

———. "Afterword to 'Moral Economies', State Spaces, and Categorical Violence". *American Anthropology* 107, no. 3 (2005): 395–402.

Shiraishi, Masaya. *Betonamu: Kakumei to kenkoku no hazama* [Vietnam: Between Revolution and Nation Building]. Tokyu: University of Tokyo Press, 1993.

Siriboon, Siriwan and John Knodel. "Thai Elderly Who Do Not Reside with Their Children". *Journal of Cross-Cultural Gerontology* 9, no. 1 (1994): 21–38.

Smith, Harold E. "The Thai Rural Family". In *The Family in Asia*, edited by M.S. Das and P.D. Bardis. London: George Allen & Unwin, 1979.

Son Nam. *Ca tinh cua mien Nam* [Characteristics of the South]. Saigon: Dong-phe, 1974.

———. *Dong Bang Song Cuu Long: Net sinh hoat xua* [The Mekon Delta: activities in the past]. Ho Chi Minh City: Nha Xuat Ban Thanh Pho Ho Chi Minh, 1985.

———. *Lich su khan hoang mien Nam: Khoa cu* [History of development in the South: examination]. Ho Chi Minh: Ban Nghe Tanh Pho Ho Chi Minh, 1994.

———. "Truyen thong gia dinh Nam bo" [Tradition of the Southern Family]. In *Nam bo xua va nay*, edited by Tap chi Xua va Nay. Ho Chi Minh City: Nha xuat ban Thanh Pho Ho Chi Minh, 1999.

Spragens, John Jr., ed. *Education in Vietnam* [introductory matter and translation of articles by John Sprangens]. Kawasaki: Looking Back, 1971.

Steedly, Mary Margaret. *Hanging Without a Rope: Narrative Experience in Colonial and Postcolonial Karoland*. Princeton: Princeton University Press, 1993.

Steinberg, David, ed. *In Search of Southeast Asia*. Honolulu: University of Hawaii Press, 1987.

Suenari, Michio. *Jinruigaku kara mita Betonamu shakai no kisoteki kenkyu* [Basic study of Vietnamese society from anthropological perspectives]. Tokyo: University of Tokyo, 1996.

Sun, Te-Hsing and Yin-Hsing Liu. "Changes in the Intergenerational Relations in the Chinese Family: Taiwan's Experiences". In *Tradition and Change in the Asian Family*, edited by L.-J. Cho and M. Yada. Honolulu: East-West Center, 1994.

Tai, Hue-Tam Ho. *Millenarianism and Peasant Politics in Vietnam*. Cambridge: Harvard University Press, 1983.

———. *Radicalism and the Origin of the Vietnamese Revolution*. Cambridge: Harvard University Press, 1992.

Tai, Van Ta. "The Status of Women in Traditional Vietnam: A Comparison of the Code of the Le Dynasty (1428–1788) with the Chinese Codes". *Journal of Asian History* 15, no. 2 (1981): 97–143.

Tap chi Xua va Nay. *Nam bo xua va nay* [The South in the past and now]. Ho Chi Minh City: Nha Xuat Ban Thanh Pho Ho Chi Minh, 1999.

Taussig, Michael. *The Devil and Commodity Fetishism in South America*. Chapel Hill: University of North Carolina Press, 1980.

Taylor, Philip. *Fragments of the South: Searching for Modernity in Vietnam's South*. Honolulu: University of Hawaii Press, 2001.

Thai Thi Ngoc Du. "Chuyen doi kinh te va doi song cua nu tri thuc tai Thanh Pho Ho Chi Minh" [Change in Economy and Life of Intellectural Women in Ho Chi Minh City]. In *Hoi Thao Chuyen De: Phu Nu & Su Phat Trien* [Discussion theme: Women and development]. Can Tho: Can Tho University, 1995.

———. "Divorce and Its Impacts on Women and Families in Ho Chi Minh City". In *Vietnam's Women in Transition*, edited by K. Barry. New York: St. Martin's Press, 1996.

Thuboi, Yoshiaki. *Vetonamu* [Vietnam]. Tokyo: Kawade Shobo Shinsha, 1995.

To Duy Hop. "Nong thon Viet Nam trong tien trinh Doi Moi: Thanh tuu van de, chinh luoc phat trien" [Rural Vietnam in the process of Doi Moi: Achievement, problems, and policy of development]. In *Nong thon trong buoc qua do sang king te thi truong* [Rural areas in the shift to market economy], edited by Trung Tam Khoa Hoc Xa Hoi Va Nhan Van Quoc Gia and Thong Tin Khoa Hoc Xa Hoi. Hanoi: Nha Xuat Ban Khoa Hoc Xa Hoi, 1999.

Tran Anh Tuan. "May van de ve nghien cuu khoa hoc xa hoi vung Dong Bang Song Cuu Long trong che do cu 1954–1975" [Some issues on socio-scientific research on the Mekong Delta in the old regime 1954–75]. In *Mot so van de khoa hoc ve Dong Bang Song Cuu Long*, edited by T.H. Mai. Hanoi: Nha Xuat Ban Khoa Hoc Xa Hoi, 1982.

Tran Dinh Huou. "Gia dinh va giao duc gia dinh" [Family and family education]. In *Nhung nghien cuu xa hoi hoc ve gia dinh Viet Nam*, edited by Tuong Lai. Hanoi: Nha Xuat Ban Khoa Hoc Xa Hoi, 1996.

Tran Hoang Kim. *Kinh te Viet Nam: Chang duong 1945–1995 va trien vong den nam 2020* [Vietnamese Economy: The Situation in 1945–1990 and Its Perspective by the Year 2020]. Hanoi: Statistical Publishing House, 1995.

Tran Thi Van Anh and Nguyen Manh Huan. "Changing Rural Institutions and Social Relations". In *Vietnam's Rural Transformation*, edited by B.J.T. Kerkvliet and D.J. Porter. Boulder: Westview Press, 1995.

Tran Tuan Lo. "Vai tro nguoi cha trong gia dinh" [Role of Father in the Family]. *Tap Chi Khoa Hoc Xa Hoi* 35, no. 1 (1998): 142–45.

Truitt, Allison. *Dreaming of Money in Ho Chi Minh City*. Critical Dialogues in Southeast Asian Studies. Seattle: University of Washington Press, 2013.

Trung Dinh Dang. "Post-1975 Land Reform in Southern Vietnam: How Local Actions and Responses Affected National Land Policy". *Journal of Vietnamese Studies* 5 (2010): 72–105.

Trung Tam Khoa Hoc Xa Hoi Va Nhan Van Quoc Gia. *Gia dinh Viet Nam, cac trach nhiem, cac nguon luc trong su Doi Moi cua dat nuoc* [Vietnamese family: Its responsibility and its power in the country's Doi Moi]. Hanoi: Nha Xuat Ban Khoa Hoc Xa Hoi, 1995.

Trung Tam Khoa Hoc Xa Hoi Va Nhan Van Quoc Gia and Thong Tin Khoa Hoc Xa Hoi. *Nong thon trong buoc qua do sang king te thi truong* [Rural areas in the process of shifting to free market economy]. Hanoi: Nha Xuat Ban Khoa Hoc Xa Hoi, 1999.

Truong Si Anh et al. "Living Arrangements, Patrilineality, and Sources of Support among Elderly Vietnamese". *Asia Pacific Population Journal* 12, no. 4 (1997): 69–88.

Truong Thi Kim Chuyen, Thai Thi Ngoc Dung, and Bach Hong Viet. "Yeu to anh huong den di hoc cap II" [Issues that Affect Going to Secondary School]. In *Ho gia dinh Vietnam: nhin qua phan thich dinh luong*, edited by Dominique Haughton, Truong Thi Kim Chuyen et al. Hanoi: Chinh Tri Quoc Gia, 1999.

Truong Thi Nga. "Gioi va net dep cua nguoi phu nu trong lich su phat trien cua xa hoi Viet Nam" [Gender and Elegance of Vietnamese Women in Historical Social Development of Vietnam]. In *Hoi thao chuyen de phu nu & su phat trien*. Can Tho: Can Tho City, 1995.

Tsuboi, Yoshiaki. *Vetonamu: Yutakasa e no yoake* [Vietnam: The dawn of prosperity]. Tokyo: Iwanami Shoten, 1994.

Tuong Lai, ed. *Nhung nghien cuu xa hoi hoc ve gia dinh Viet Nam* [Some Sociological Study on Vietnamese Family]. Hanoi: Nha Xuat Ban Khoa Hoc Xa Hoi, 1996.

Vietnam Living Standards Survey 1992–1993. Hanoi: State Planning Committee — General Statistical Office, 1994.

Vietnam Statistical Yearbook 2001. Hanoi: General Statistical Office, 2001.

Vo Nhan Tri. "Party Policies and Economic Performance: The Second and Third Five-year Plans Examined". In *Postwar Vietnam: Dilemmas in Socialist Development*, edited by D.G. Marr and C.P. White. Ithaca: Southeast Asia Program, Cornell University, 1988.

Vo Thi Cuc. *Van hoa gia dinh voi viec hinh thanh va phat trien nhan cach tre em* [Family culture and effects on personality development of children]. Hanoi: Nha Xuat Ban Dai Hoc Quoc Gia Hanoi, 1997.

Vo Tuan Huy "Nhung khia canh cua su bien doi dia dinh" [Some aspects of family changes]. In *Nhung nghien cuu xa hoi hoc ve gia dinh Viet Nam*, edited by Tuong Lai. Hanoi: Nha Xuat Ban Khoa Hoc Xa Hoi, 1996.

Vu Tam Ich. *A Historical Survey of Educational Developments in Vietnam*. Lexington, Kentucky: College of Education, University of Kentucky, 1959.

Watson, James L. "McDonald's in Hong Kong: Consumerism, Dietary Change, and the Rise of a Children's Culture". In *Golden Arches East: McDonald's in East Asia*, edited by J.L. Watson. Stanford: Stanford University Press, 1997.

Werner, Jayne. *Gender, Household and State in Post-Revolutionary Vietnam*. London, New York: Routledge, 2009.

Werner, Jayne and Daniele Belanger, eds. *Gender, Household and State: Doi Moi in Viet Nam*. Ithaca: Southeast Asia Program, Cornell University, 2006.

West-East-South Program. *Eco-Technological and Socio-Economic Analysis of Fish Farming Systems in the Freshwater Area of the Mekong Delta: 1996–7*. Can Tho: Can Tho University, 1997.

White, Christine P. "Alternative Approaches to the Socialist Transformations of Agriculture in Postwar Vietnam". In *Postwar Vietnam: Dilemmas in Socialist Development*, edited by D.G. Marr and C.P. White. Ithaca: Southeast Asia Program, Cornell University, 1988.

Whitmore, John. "Social Organization and Confucian Thought in Vietnam". *Journal of Southeast Asian Studies* 15 (1984): 296–306.

Williams, Alexander. *Community and Revolution in Modern Vietnam*. Boston: Houghton Mifflin, 1976.

Williams, Michael. *Vietnam at the Crossroads*. New York: The Royal Institute of International Affairs, 1992.

Wolf, Diane. *Factory Daughters: Gender, Household Dynamics, and Rural Industrialization in Java*. Berkeley: University of California Press, 1992.

Wolf, Margery. *Women and Family in Rural Taiwan*. Stanford: Stanford University Press, 1972.

———. *Revolution Postponed: Women in Contemporary China*. Stanford: Stanford University Press, 1985.

Woodside, Alexander. *Vietnam and the Chinese Model: A Comparative Study of Nguyen and Ching Civil Government in the First Half of the Nineteenth Century*. Cambridge, Mass: Harvard University Press, 1971.

———. "Vietnamese History: Confucianism, Colonialism, and the Struggle for Independence". In *Vietnam: Essays on History, Culture, and Society*. New York: Asia Society, 1985.

———. *Vietnam and the Chinese Model*. Cambridge: Council on East Asian Studies, Harvard University, 1988.

World Bank Report. *Vietnam Public Sector Management and Private Sector Incentives: An Economic Report*, 1994.

Yamazaki, Ryoichi and Duong Van Ni. "Modification of Farmers' Differentiation Process and Role of Farmers' Organizations: A Case Study in Hoa An Village, Mekong Delta of Vietnam". *JIRCAS Journal* 7 (1998): 117–32.

Yan, Yunxiang. "The Triumph of Conjugality: Structural Transformation of Family Relations in a Chinese Village". *Ethnology* 36, no. 3 (1997): 191–212.

———. "The Politics of Consumerism in Chinese Society". In *China Briefing 2000: The Continuing Transformation*, edited by T. White. Armonk, NY: Sharpe, 2000.

———. *The Individuation of Chinese Society*. London School of Economics Monographs on Social Anthropology. New York: Berg, 2009.

Yanagisako, Sylvia and Janet Collier. "Toward a Unified Analysis of Gender and Kinship". In *Gender and Kinship: Essays Toward a Unified Analysis*, edited by J. Collier and S. Yanagisako. Stanford: Stanford University Press, 1987.

Yu, Insun. *Law and Society in Seventeenth and Eighteenth Century Vietnam*. Seoul: Asiatic Research Center, Korea University, 1990.

INDEX

ABOUT THE AUTHOR

Setsuko Shibuya is Professor of Anthropology at Seisa University and Visiting Researcher at Showa Women's University in Japan. She has been studying the society and culture in the rural Mekong Delta in Vietnam since the 1990s, with a particular focus on the effects of social changes on everyday life of the rural residents.

www.ingramcontent.com/pod-product-compliance
Lightning Source LLC
Chambersburg PA
CBHW072100020426
42334CB00017B/1573